Succeed in Cambridge English

Advanced

10

CAE

Practice Tests

NEW 2015 format

Andrew Betsis
Lawrence Mamas

GlobalELT
English Language Teaching Books

Advanced 2015 Revised Format

Paper	Time	Task Types	Test Focus
Paper 1 Reading & Use of English	• 1 hour 30 min • 34 questions • length of texts: about 550–850 per part • word count 3,000–3,500	**Part 1** - multiple-choice cloze (eight gaps) **Part 2** - open cloze (eight gaps) **Part 3** - word formation (eight gaps) **Part 4** - key word transformations (six questions) **Part 5** - text followed by six 4-option multiple-choice questions **Part 6** - four short texts, followed by four cross-text multiple-matching questions **Part 7** - gapped text task – paragraphs removed **Part 8** - multiple matching - a text or several short texts, preceded by 10 multiple-matching questions	**Part 1** - lexical/lexico-grammatical, vocabulary, collocations, fixed phrases, idioms etc. **Part 2** - grammatical/lexico-grammatical, grammar with some focus on vocabulary **Part 3** - lexical/lexico-grammatical, focus on vocabulary, compounding **Part 4** - grammatical/lexico-grammatical, grammar, vocabulary & collocations **Part 5** - detail, opinion, tone, purpose, main idea, implication, attitude, text organisation features (exemplification, comparison, reference) **Part 6** - Understanding of opinion and attitude; comparing and contrasting of opinions and attitudes across texts. **Part 7** - text structure, cohesion and coherence **Part 8** - Detail, opinion, attitude, specific information.
Paper 2 Writing	• 1 hour 30 min • 2 parts	**Part 1** - compulsory task: essay with a discursive focus (220-260 words) **Part 2** - Q.2-4 choice of one task from the following: • letter • proposal • report • review (220-260 words)	**Part 1** – focus on evaluating, expressing opinions, hypothesising, persuading **Part 2** – varying focuses according to task; including giving opinions, persuading, justifying, giving advice, comparing
Paper 3 Listening	• Approximately 40 minutes • 30 questions	**Part 1** - multiple choice; three short unrelated extracts; exchanges between interacting speakers; two questions per text **Part 2** - sentence completion task with eight items; a monologue (could be introduced by a presenter) **Part 3** - 6 multiple choice questions; a conversation between interacting speakers **Part 4** - multiple matching task - five short themed monologues. Two linked tasks, requiring selection from list of eight options - 10 multiple-matching questions. All texts will be heard twice.	**Part 1** - feeling, attitude, opinion, purpose, function, agreement, course of action, general gist, detail, etc. **Part 2** - specific information, stated opinion **Part 3** - attitude and opinion **Part 4** - gist, attitude, main points, interpreting context
Paper 4 Speaking	• 15 minutes (for pairs) • 4 parts	**Part 1** - conversation between the interlocutor and each candidate (spoken questions) **Part 2** - individual one-minute 'long turn' for each candidate with brief response from second candidate; each candidate is given three visual stimuli, with questions **Part 3** - two-way conversation between the candidates (written stimuli with spoken instructions) **Part 4** - discussion on topics related to Part 3 (spoken questions)	**Part 1** - general interactional and social language **Part 2** - organising a larger unit of discourse; comparing, describing, expressing opinions and speculating **Part 3** - sustaining an interaction; exchanging ideas, expressing and justifying opinions, agreeing and / or disagreeing, suggesting, speculating, evaluating, reaching a decision through negotiation, etc. **Part 4** - expressing and justifying opinions, agreeing and / or disagreeing

CONTENTS

Published by GLOBAL ELT LTD
Brighton, East Sussex, UK
www.globalelt.co.uk

- Succeed in Cambridge English: Advanced - 2015 Format - 10 Practice Tests - Student's Book - ISBN: 9781781641521
- Succeed in Cambridge English: Advanced - 2015 Format - 10 Practice Tests - Teacher's Book - ISBN: 9781781641538

The authors and publishers wish to acknowledge the following use of material:
Salla, P., 'Recognizing Stress' © buzzle.com.
Lam, S., 'A feast of urban festivals' © The Independent UK (May 20th, 2004).
Wroe, N., 'The Power of Now' © Guardian News and Media Limited (October 14th, 2006).
Nuttall, P., 'Smoking: the office partition' © iVillage Limited 2000-2010, ivillage.co.uk.
Davis, H., 'Up, up and away' © Guardian News and Media Limited (October 14th, 2006).
Harrison, M., 'The A380 superjumbo: Europe's white elephant' © The Independent UK (Nov 22nd, 2006).
Vihear, P., '10 Journeys for the 21st Century' © Wanderlust 2010 (Dec 2006).
Chesshyre, T., 'Italy's Secret Getaway' © Times Newspapers Limited (Nov 24th 2006).
Morris, N., ''Supernannies' will try to improve behaviour of out-of-control children' © The Independent UK (Nov 22nd, 2006)
Pickrell, J., 'Introduction: Endangered Species' © Reed Business Information Ltd. (September 4th, 2006)
Pickard, P., 'Victoria's Secret' © Wanderlust 2010 (Dec 2006).
Hunt-Grubbe, C., 'A Life in the Day: Rachel Hogan' © Times Newspapers Limited (November 19th, 2006).
Milmo, C., 'World faces hottest year ever, as El Niño combines with global warming' © The Independent UK (January 1st, 2007)
Extract from *Girl from the South* by Joanna Trollope. Copyright © Joanna Trollope, reprinted with permission of Rbooks from the Random House Book Group.
Dawson, T., 'Bread and Tulips'© bbc.co.uk (September 13th, 2005).
Davies, C., "Teenage girls 'too embarrassed' to keep fit" © Telegraph Media Group Limited (October 7th, 2004).
Author Unknown, "Teens 'inherit' Weight Worries", © Associated Newspapers Limited
Harding, L., 'Mobiles: exeunt after St Petersburg theatre installs jammers' © Guardian News and Media Limited (March 6th, 2007).
Tremlett, G., 'Spanish cars to use different type of juice' © Guardian News and Media Limited (March 6th, 2007).
Scheiber, D., 'Robots to the Rescue' © St. Petersburg Times (March 2nd, 2003)
Crace, J., Screen Writing' © Guardian News and Media Limited (March 6th, 2007)
Kennedy, D., 'Jets that could fly to Australia in two hours' © Times Newspapers Limited (March 29th, 2004)
Giles, T., 'The future at your fingertips' © Telegraph Media group Limited (February 24th, 2007)
Extract from *Death in Malta* by Rosanne Dingli. Copyright © Rosanne Dingli, reprinted with permission of BeWrite Books
Rowan, D., 'Parking Hell: The parking industry investigated' © Times Newspapers Limited (February 11th, 2006).
Papamichael, S., Pride and Prejudice DVD © bbc.co.uk
Papamichael, S., Mr Bean's Holiday DVD © bbc.co.uk
Papamichael, S., Fast Food Nation DVD © bbc.co.uk
Papamichael, S., Shooter DVD © bbc.co.uk
Papamichael, S., The Namesake DVD © bbc.co.uk
Papamichael, S., Amazing Grace DVD © bbc.co.uk
Extract from *Chasm City* by Alastair Reynolds. Copyright Alastair Reynolds, reprinted with permission of Victor Gollancz Ltd.
Lemonick, M., 'What makes us different', © Time Inc. (October 1st, 2006).

TEST 1

Paper 4: SPEAKING
Time: 15 minutes per pair of candidates

Candidates take the Speaking test in pairs (occasionally, where there is an uneven number of candidates, three students may be required to take the test together). There are two examiners (an assessor and an interlocutor) and one of them (the assessor) does not take part in the interaction but assesses your performance according to four analytical scales. The other examiner (the interlocutor) conducts the test and tells you what you have to do. The interlocutor also gives you a global mark for your performance in the test as a whole.

Part 1 *2 minutes (5 minutes for groups of three)*

In Part 1 of the Speaking test, you may be asked to talk about your interests, general experiences, studies or career, and plans for the future. The examiner will first ask you for some general information about yourself, and then widen the scope of the conversation to include subjects like leisure activities, studies, travel, holiday experiences and daily life. Respond directly to the examiner's questions, avoid very short answers, and listen when your partner is speaking. You are not required to interact with your partner in this part, but you may do so if you wish.

Interlocutor: Good morning/afternoon/evening. My name is .... and this is my colleague ....
And your names are? Can I have your mark sheets, please? Thank you. —
First of all, we'd like to know something about you.

Select one or two questions and ask candidates in turn, as appropriate.
- Where are you from?
- What do you do?
- How long have you been studying English?
- What do you enjoy most about learning English?

Select one or more questions from any of the following categories, as appropriate.

Family and Friends
- How important do you think family is? ... (Why?)
- How much time do you spend with your family and what do you enjoy doing with them?
- What qualities does a close friend need to possess?
- With whom would you discuss a difficult personal situation, a family member or a close friend? ...(Why?)

Art
- What would you say your relationship with the arts is?
- Which kind of art are you most interested in? ... (Why?)
- When was the last time you visited a museum, gallery or an exhibition? What were your impressions on this visit?
- Who is your favourite artist? ... (Why?)

Travel
- Who do you prefer to travel with? ... (Why?)
- Are you more fond of long or short distance travel?
- What has been your most exciting travel experience thus far?
- Name some things that you would never leave behind you when you travel.

Sports
- Do you prefer team sports or individual sports?
- What qualities do you need to possess in order to do well in a team sport?
- What do you think about extreme sports?
- What are the most popular sports in your country?

Celebrities
- What are some of the advantages and disadvantages of being famous?
- Who is your favourite celebrity? ... (Why?)
- What would you be willing to sacrifice in order to be famous?
- Why do you think more and more young people nowadays long for fame and money?

Part 2 – Long turn *4 minutes (6 minutes for groups of three)*

In this part of the test you each have to speak for 1 minute without interruption. The examiner will give you a set of pictures and ask you to talk about them. You may be asked to describe, compare or contrast the pictures, and to make a further comment on them. Your partner will get a different set of pictures, but you should pay attention during your partner's turn because the examiner will ask you to comment for about 30 seconds after your partner has finished speaking.

1: Isolated places

Interlocutor: In this part of the test, I' m going to give each of you three pictures. I'd like you to talk about two of them on your own for about a minute, and also to answer a question briefly about your partner's pictures.

(Candidate A), it's your turn first. Here are your pictures. They show **people in isolated places.**

Look at page 6, Part 2, Task 1.

I'd like you to compare two of the pictures, and say **how the people might be feeling and why they might be in these situations.** All right?

Candidate A: - (1 minute) Contestar ....
Interlocutor: Thank you.

Candidate B, which of these places looks the most isolated? ... (Why?)
Candidate B: - (approx. 30 seconds) ....
Interlocutor: Thank you.

2: People taking a break

Interlocutor: Now, **(Candidate B)**, here are your pictures. They show people **taking a break.**
I'd like you to compare two of the pictures, and say **how the people might be feeling and how demanding their activities might be.** All right?

Look at page 6, Part 2, Task 2.

Candidate B: - (1 minute) ....
Interlocutor: Thank you.

(Candidate A), who needs a break most? ... (Why?)
Candidate A: - (approx. 30 seconds) ....
Interlocutor: Thank you.

Part 3 - Collaborative task *4 minutes (6 minutes for groups of three)*

This part tests your ability to take part in a discussion with the other candidate and reach a decision.

Interlocutor: Now, I'd like you to talk about something together for about two minutes. *(3 minutes for groups of three)*

Here are some things that people consider when deciding what career path they will pursue in life and a question for you to discuss. First you have some time to look at the task.

Look at page 7, Part 3. (You have 15 seconds to look at the task).

Now, talk to each other about **what people might have to consider when deciding on a career path.**

Candidates A & B: - (2 minutes or 3 minutes for groups of three)

Interlocutor: Thank you. Now you have about a minute (2 minutes for groups of three) to decide **which would be the best career path for you**.

Candidates A & B: - (1 minute or 2 minutes for groups of three)

Interlocutor: Thank you.

Part 2 – Long turn

1: Isolated places

- How might the people be feeling?
- Why might they be in these situations?

Part 2 – Long turn

2: People taking a break

- How might the people be feeling?
- How demanding might their activities be?

Part 3 - Collaborative task

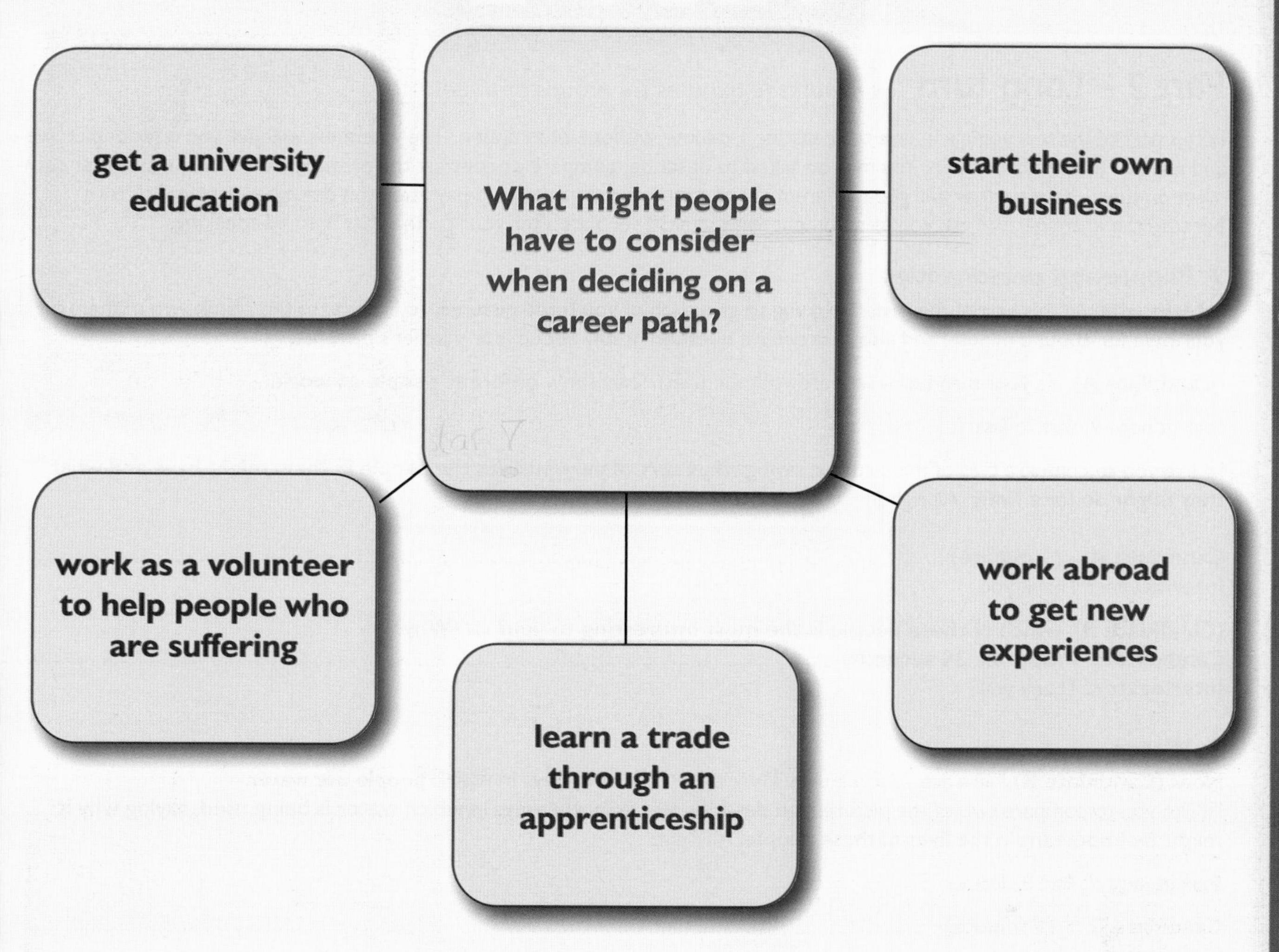

Part 4 – Discussion *5 minutes (8 minutes for groups of three)*

Interlocutor:

- In what ways can training change people's attitudes in the workplace?
- Some people think that school does not train young people adequately for the world of work today. Do you agree?
- Which is more important to teach people: a sense of team spirit or individual initiative? Why?
- How difficult is it for young people to find jobs nowadays in your country? Why?
- What can be done to create jobs for young people?

Thank you. That is the end of the test.

- What do you think?
- Do you agree?
- What about you?

TEST 2

Part 2 – Long turn *4 minutes (6 minutes for groups of three)*

In this part of the test you each have to speak for 1 minute without interruption. The examiner will give you a set of pictures and ask you to talk about them. You may be asked to describe, compare or contrast the pictures, and to make a further comment on them. Your partner will get a different set of pictures, but you should pay attention during your partner's turn because the examiner will ask you to comment for about 30 seconds after your partner has finished speaking.

1: People and personalities

Interlocutor: In this part of the test, I' m going to give each of you three pictures. I'd like you to talk about two of them on your own for about a minute, and also to answer a question briefly about your partner's pictures.

(Candidate A), it's your turn first. Here are your pictures. They show **different people at work.**

Look at page 9, Part 2, Task 1.

I'd like you to compare two of the pictures, saying **what sort of personalities the people in them might have and what they might do for a living.** All right?

Candidate A: - (1 minute) ....
Interlocutor: Thank you.

(Candidate B), which of these people is the most interesting to you? ... (Why?)
Candidate B: - (approx. 30 seconds) ....
Interlocutor: Thank you.

2: Water

Now, **(Candidate B)**, here are your pictures.They show **different ways in which people use water.**
I'd like you to compare two of the pictures and **describe the different ways in which water is being used, saying why it might be important in the lives of these people.** All right?

Look at page 9, Part 2, Task 2.

Candidate B: - (1 minute) ....
Interlocutor: Thank you.

(Candidate A), in which picture do you think the water is most important? ... (Why?)
Candidate A: - (approx. 30 seconds) ....
Interlocutor: Thank you.

Part 3 - Collaborative task *4 minutes (6 minutes for groups of three)*

This part tests your ability to take part in a discussion with the other candidate and reach a decision.

Interlocutor: Now, I'd like you to talk about something together for about two minutes. *(3 minutes for groups of three)*

Here are some ways in which companies market and sell their services and/or products to their customers and a question for you to discuss. First you have some time to look at the task.

Look at page 10, Part 3. (You have 15 seconds to look at the task).

Now, talk to each other about **what companies might have to consider when marketing and selling their products to consumers.**

Candidates A & B: - (2 minutes or 3 minutes for groups of three)

Interlocutor: Thank you. Now you have about a minute (2 minutes for groups of three) to decide **which would be the least expensive way to market and sell their products to consumers.**

Candidates A & B: - (1 minute or 2 minutes for groups of three)

Interlocutor: Thank you.

Part 2 – Long turn

1: People and personalities

- What sort of personalities might they have?
- What might they do for a living?

Part 2 – Long turn

2: Water

- What are the different ways in which water is being used?
- Why might water be important in the lives of these people?

Speaking Section

Part 3 - Collaborative task

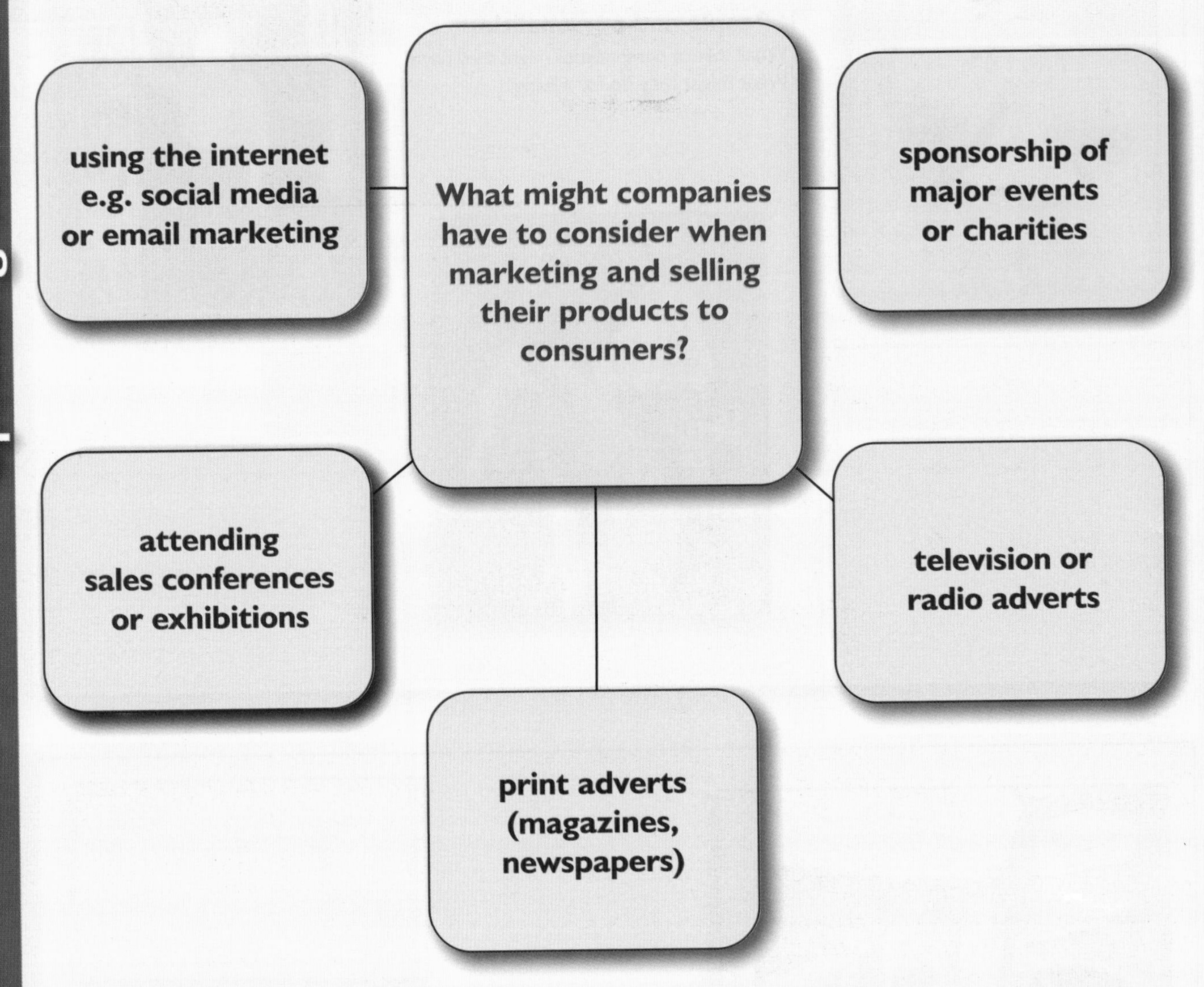

Part 4 – Discussion *5 minutes (8 minutes for groups of three)*

- What do you think?
- Do you agree?
- What about you?

Interlocutor:

- In what other ways can a company keep its customers happy?
- The best form of publicity for a product was once thought to be "word of mouth". How true is this nowadays?
- Advertising campaigns persuade us to buy unnecessary things. To what extent do you agree?
- What future is there for small companies in today's world?
- How important is it for companies to be aware of environmental issues?

Thank you. That is the end of the test.

Part 2 – Long turn *4 minutes (6 minutes for groups of three)*

In this part of the test you each have to speak for 1 minute without interruption. The examiner will give you a set of pictures and ask you to talk about them. You may be asked to describe, compare or contrast the pictures, and to make a further comment on them. Your partner will get a different set of pictures, but you should pay attention during your partner's turn because the examiner will ask you to comment for about 30 seconds after your partner has finished speaking.

1: Sharing

Interlocutor: In this part of the test, I' m going to give each of you three pictures. I'd like you to talk about two of them on your own for about a minute, and also to answer a question briefly about your partner's pictures.

(Candidate A), it's your turn first. Here are your pictures. They show **people sharing different experiences.**

Look at page 12, Part 2, Task 1.

I'd like you to compare two of the pictures, saying **what moments or experiences are being shared and how the people might feel about each other.** All right?

Candidate A: - (1 minute) ....
Interlocutor: Thank you.

(Candidate B), which picture appeals to you most as an example of sharing? ... (Why?)
Candidate B: - (approx. 30 seconds) ....
Interlocutor: Thank you.

2: Up in the air

Now, **(Candidate B)**, here are your pictures.They show **people who are up in the air for various reasons.**
I'd like you to compare two of the pictures saying **what the people are doing and how you think they might be feeling.** All right?

Look at page 12, Part 2, Task 2.

(Candidate B - 1 minute) Thank you.
(Candidate A), which of these situations looks the most dangerous? ... (Why?)
Candidate A: - (approx. 30 seconds) ....
Interlocutor: Thank you.

Part 3 - Collaborative task *4 minutes (6 minutes for groups of three)*

This part tests your ability to take part in a discussion with the other candidate and reach a decision.

Interlocutor: Now, I'd like you to talk about something together for about two minutes. *(3 minutes for groups of three)*

Here are some ways that people make extra money and a question for you to discuss. First you have some time to look at the task.

Look at page 13, Part 3. (You have 15 seconds to look at the task).

Now, talk to each other about **what options one might consider when looking to increase his or her income.**

Candidates A & B: - (2 minutes or 3 minutes for groups of three)

Interlocutor: Thank you. Now you have about a minute (2 minutes for groups of three) to decide **which option would be the most suitable for a student and why.**

Candidates A & B: - (1 minute or 2 minutes for groups of three)

Interlocutor: Thank you.

Part 2 – Long turn

1: Sharing

- What moments or experiences are being shared?
- How might the people feel about each other?

Part 2 – Long turn

2: Up in the air

- What are the people doing?
- How might they be feeling?

Part 3 - Collaborative task

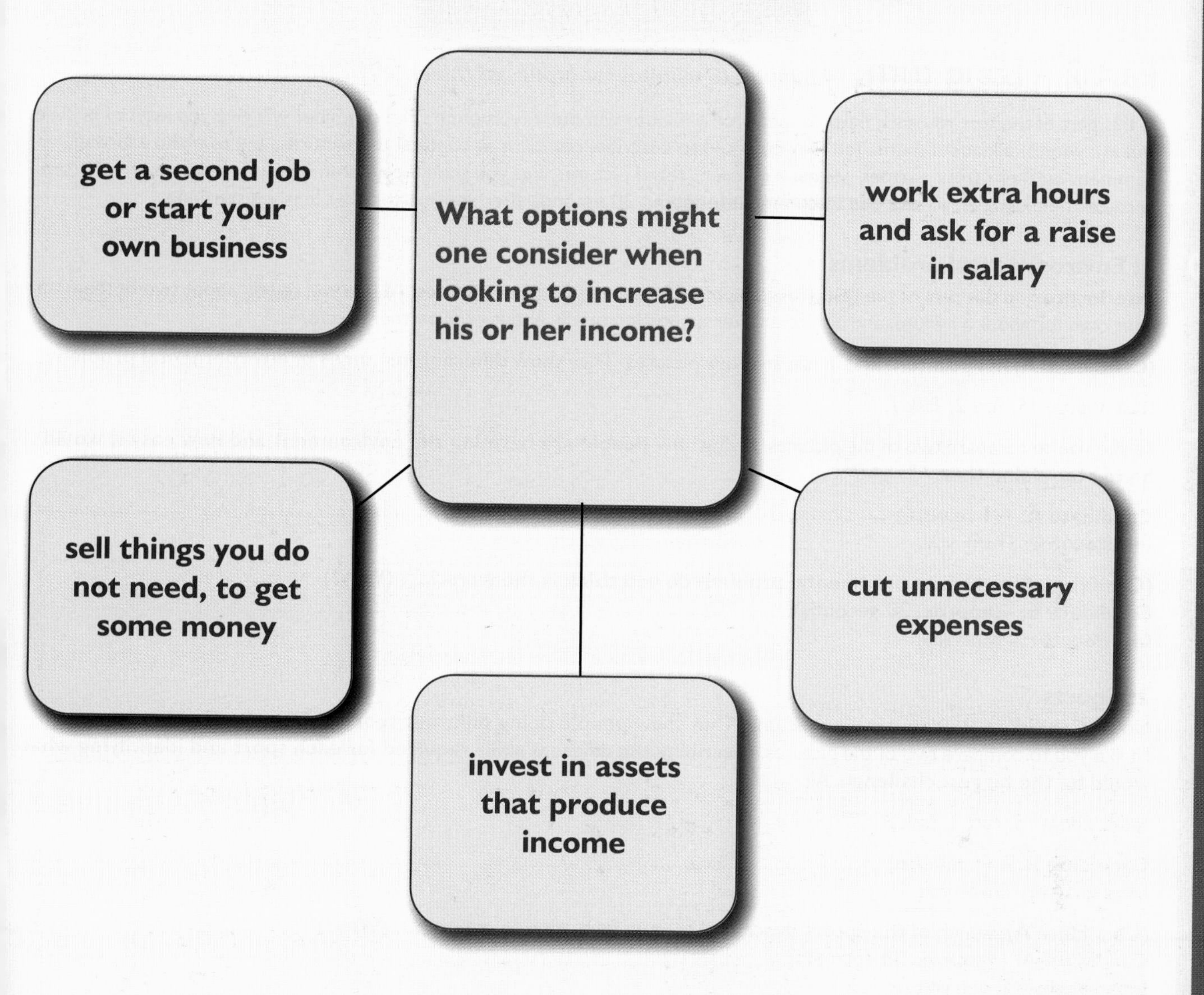

Part 4 – Discussion *5 minutes (8 minutes for groups of three)*

Interlocutor:

- Are we slaves to consumerism?
- How do we avoid credit card debt?
- How important is it to save money?
- Some people earn much more money than others. Is this fair? Why (not)?
- Some people say money can't buy happiness. To what extent do you agree with this?

> - What do you think?
> - Do you agree?
> - What about you?

Thank you. That is the end of the test.

Speaking Section

TEST 4

Part 2 – Long turn *4 minutes (6 minutes for groups of three)*

In this part of the test you each have to speak for 1 minute without interruption. The examiner will give you a set of pictures and ask you to talk about them. You may be asked to describe, compare or contrast the pictures, and to make a further comment on them. Your partner will get a different set of pictures, but you should pay attention during your partner's turn because the examiner will ask you to comment for about 30 seconds after your partner has finished speaking.

1: Environmental problems

Interlocutor: In this part of the test, I' m going to give each of you three pictures. I'd like you to talk about two of them on your own for about a minute, and also to answer a question briefly about your partner's pictures.

(Candidate A), it's your turn first. Here are your pictures. They show **different instances of environmental problems.**

Look at page 15, Part 2, Task 1.

I'd like you to compare two of the pictures, saying h**ow people are harming the environment and how easy it would be to stop doing that**. All right?

Candidate A: - (1 minute) ....
Interlocutor: Thank you.

(Candidate B), which environmental problem do you think is the worst? ... (Why?)
Candidate B: - (approx. 30 seconds) ....
Interlocutor: Thank you.

2: Sports

Now, **(Candidate B)**, here are your pictures.They show **people doing different sports.**
I'd like you to compare two of the pictures, **describing the different skills required for each sport and identifying what would be the biggest challenge**. All right?

Look at page 15, Part 2, Task 2.

Candidate B: - (1 minute) ....
Interlocutor: Thank you.

(Candidate A), which of the sports described is your favourite to watch? ... (Why?)
Candidate A: - (approx. 30 seconds) ....
Interlocutor: Thank you.

Part 3 - Collaborative task *4 minutes (6 minutes for groups of three)*

This part tests your ability to take part in a discussion with the other candidate and reach a decision.

Interlocutor: Now, I'd like you to talk about something together for about two minutes. *(3 minutes for groups of three)*

Here are some ways that people spend their holidays and a question for you to discuss. First you have some time to look at the task.

Look at page 16, Part 3. (You have 15 seconds to look at the task).

Now, talk to each other about **what people might have to consider when choosing one of the holiday options provided**.

Candidates A & B: - (2 minutes or 3 minutes for groups of three)

Interlocutor: Thank you. Now you have about a minute (2 minutes for groups of three) to decide **which holiday option you would recommend to somebody who is stressed and needs a break.**

Candidates A & B: - (1 minute or 2 minutes for groups of three)

Interlocutor: Thank you.

Part 2 – Long turn

1: Environmental problems

- In what ways are people polluting the environment
- How easy would it be to stop doing that?

Part 2 – Long turn

2: Sports

- What are the different skills required for each sport?
- What would be the biggest challenge?

Speaking Section

Part 3 - Collaborative task

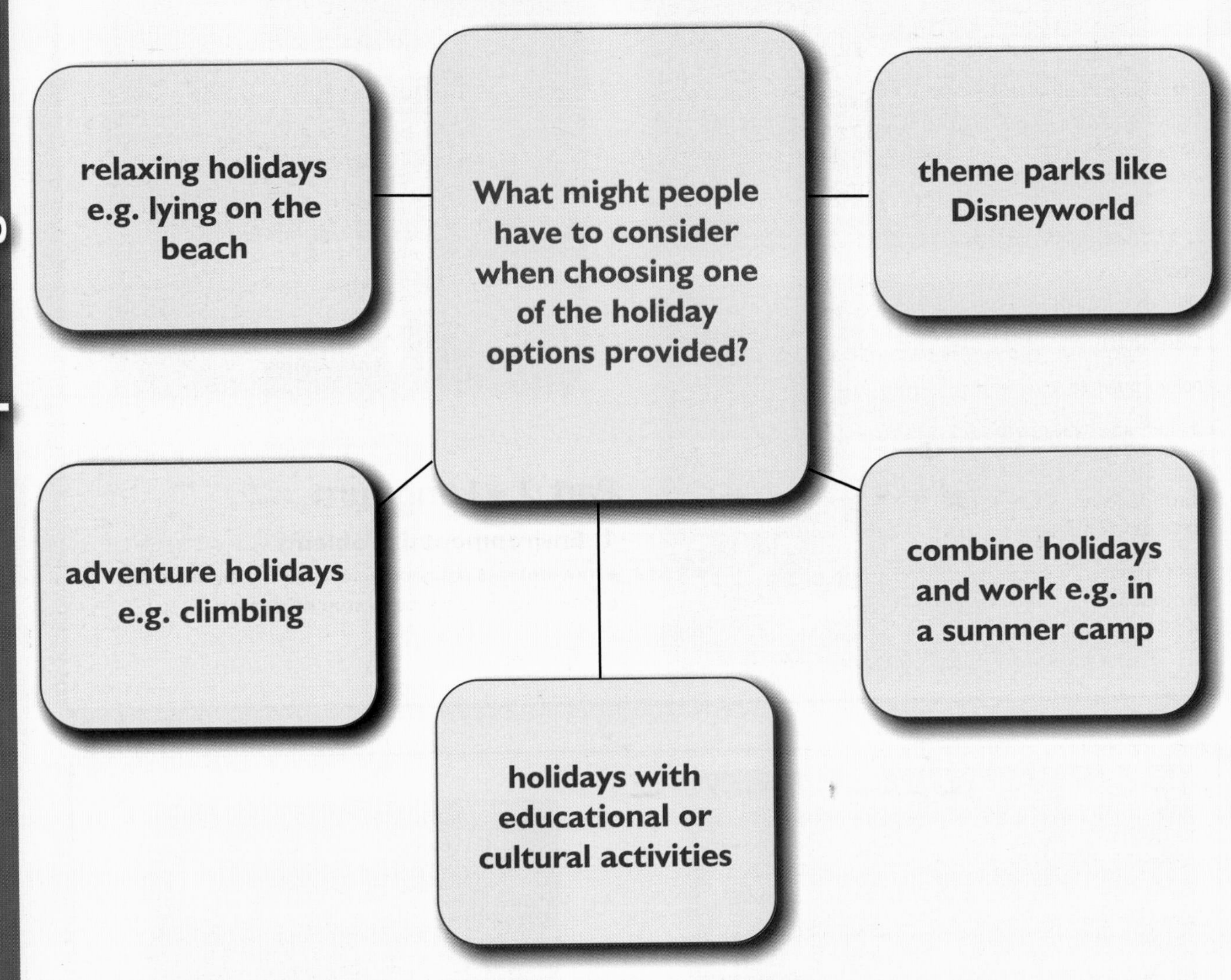

- What do you think?
- Do you agree?
- What about you?

Part 4 – Discussion *5 minutes (8 minutes for groups of three)*

Interlocutor:

- How good an idea would it be to build a new tourism development in your area? Where do you think the best place to build it would be?
- What environmental considerations should one think about when building holiday developments like this?
- Do people overestimate the importance of holidays?
- Are there any places where you think it is inappropriate to build theme parks and specially designed holiday resorts?
- What are the advantages of going abroad on holiday?

Thank you. That is the end of the test.

TEST 5

Part 2 – Long turn *4 minutes (6 minutes for groups of three)*

In this part of the test you each have to speak for 1 minute without interruption. The examiner will give you a set of pictures and ask you to talk about them. You may be asked to describe, compare or contrast the pictures, and to make a further comment on them. Your partner will get a different set of pictures, but you should pay attention during your partner's turn because the examiner will ask you to comment for about 30 seconds after your partner has finished speaking.

1: Unusual situations

Interlocutor: In this part of the test, I' m going to give each of you three pictures. I'd like you to talk about two of them on your own for about a minute, and also to answer a question briefly about your partner's pictures.

(Candidate A), it's your turn first. Here are your pictures. They show **strange or unusual situations.**

Look at page 18, Part 2, Task 1.

I'd like you to compare two of the pictures, saying **what is strange or unusual about them and which picture you think is the most unusual**. All right?

Candidate A: - (1 minute) ....
Interlocutor: Thank you.

(Candidate B), what point might the photographer have wanted to make? ... (Why?)
Candidate B: - (approx. 30 seconds) ....
Interlocutor: Thank you.

2: Emotional states

Now, **(Candidate B)**, here are your pictures. They show **people in different emotional states**. I'd like you to compare two of the pictures and say **what emotional states they show and what might have caused these emotional states**. All right?

Look at page 18, Part 2, Task 2.

Candidate B: - (1 minute) ....
Interlocutor: Thank you.

(Candidate A), which of these emotional states is the most difficult to deal with? ... (Why?)
Candidate A: - (approx. 30 seconds) ....
Interlocutor: Thank you.

Part 3 - Collaborative task *4 minutes (6 minutes for groups of three)*

This part tests your ability to take part in a discussion with the other candidate and reach a decision.

Interlocutor: Now, I'd like you to talk about something together for about two minutes. *(3 minutes for groups of three)*

Here are some of the technological devices that people have made part of their daily lives and a question for you to discuss. First you have some time to look at the task.

Look at page 19, Part 3. (You have 15 seconds to look at the task).

Now, talk to each other about which **are the best new technological devices available to consumers**.

Candidates A & B: - (2 minutes or 3 minutes for groups of three)

Interlocutor: Thank you. Now you have about a minute (2 minutes for groups of three) to decide **which device you consider to be the most useful for people who work in an office.**

Candidates A & B: - (1 minute or 2 minutes for groups of three)

Interlocutor: Thank you.

Part 2 – Long turn

1: Unusual situations

- What is strange or unusual about the pictures?
- Which picture is the most unusual?

Part 2 – Long turn

2: Emotional states

- What emotional states do they show?
- What might have caused each of these emotional states?

Part 3 - Collaborative task

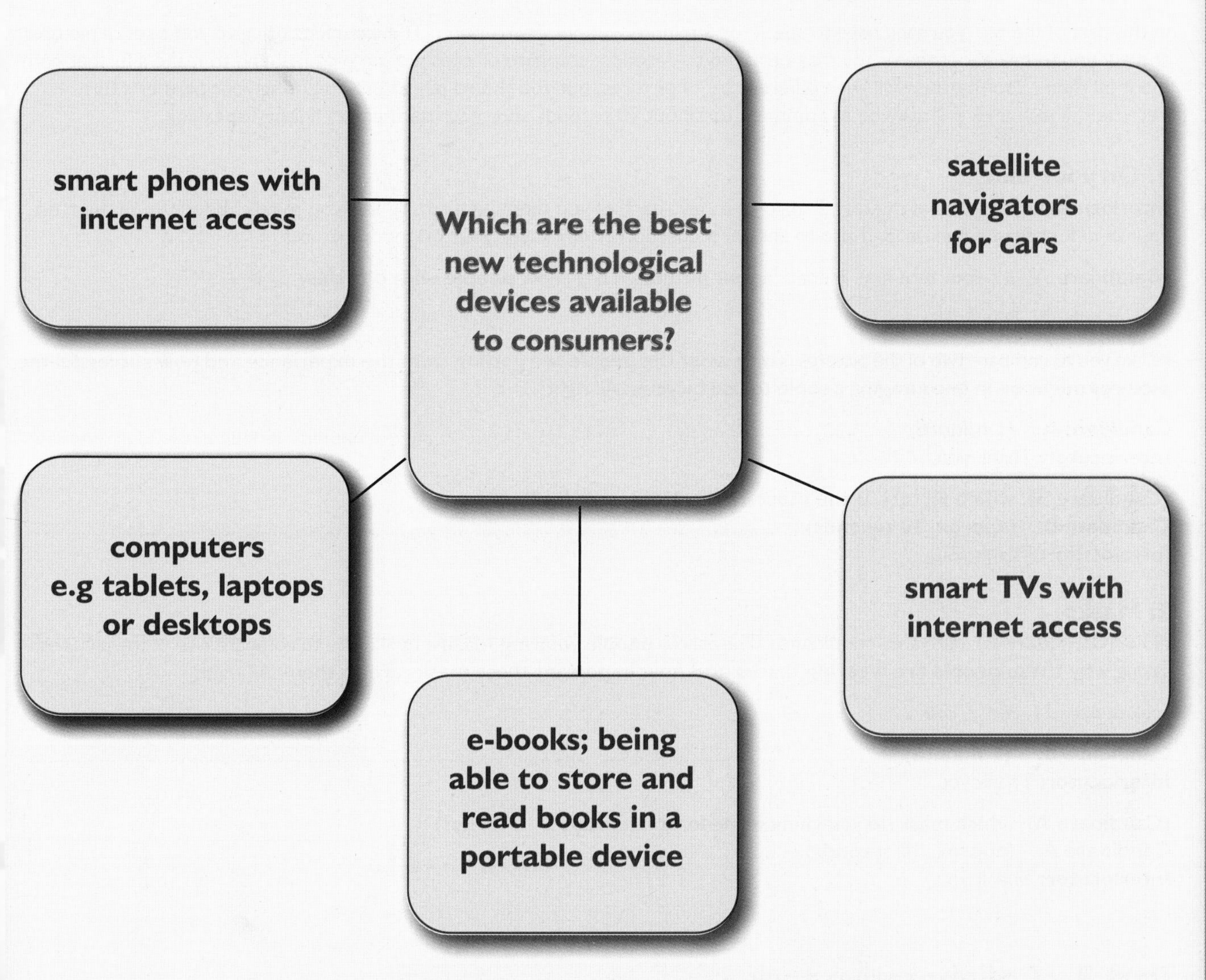

Part 4 – Discussion *5 minutes (8 minutes for groups of three)*

Interlocutor:

- Are all these new gadgets really necessary?
- Are you fascinated by new gadgets like iPods?
- Are technological advances always for the best?
- Can you imagine your life without a mobile phone?
- How can we use technology in education?

- What do you think?
- Do you agree?
- What about you?

Thank you. That is the end of the test.

TEST 6

Part 2 – Long turn *4 minutes (6 minutes for groups of three)*

In this part of the test you each have to speak for 1 minute without interruption. The examiner will give you a set of pictures and ask you to talk about them. You may be asked to describe, compare or contrast the pictures, and to make a further comment on them. Your partner will get a different set of pictures, but you should pay attention during your partner's turn because the examiner will ask you to comment for about 30 seconds after your partner has finished speaking.

1: On your bike

Interlocutor: In this part of the test, I' m going to give each of you three pictures. I'd like you to talk about two of them on your own for about a minute, and also to answer a question briefly about your partner's pictures.

(Candidate A), it's your turn first. Here are your pictures. They show **people with bicycles**.

Look at page 21, Part 2, Task 1.

I'd like you to compare two of the pictures, saying **what the people are getting from the experience and how successful the pictures might be in encouraging people to use bicycles**. All right?

Candidate A: - (1 minute) ....
Interlocutor: Thank you.

(Candidate B), which picture is the most interesting? ... (Why?)
Candidate B: - (approx. 30 seconds) ....
Interlocutor: Thank you.

2: Masks

Now, **(Candidate B)**, here are your pictures. They show **people wearing masks**. I'd like you to compare two of the pictures, saying **why these people are wearing masks and how important these masks are to them**. All right?

Look at page 21, Part 2, Task 2.

Candidate B: - (1 minute) ....
Interlocutor: Thank you.

(Candidate A), which mask do you think is the least necessary? ... (Why?)
Candidate A: - (approx. 30 seconds) ....
Interlocutor: Thank you.

Part 3 - Collaborative task *4 minutes (6 minutes for groups of three)*

This part tests your ability to take part in a discussion with the other candidate and reach a decision.

Interlocutor: Now, I'd like you to talk about something together for about two minutes. *(3 minutes for groups of three)*

Here are some industries or fields that have been greatly affected by advances in technology and a question for you to discuss. First you have some time to look at the task.

Look at page 22, Part 3. (You have 15 seconds to look at the task).

Now, talk to each other about **how these fields have benefited from advances in technology.**

Candidates A & B: - (2 minutes or 3 minutes for groups of three)

Interlocutor: Thank you. Now you have about a minute (2 minutes for groups of three) to decide **which field has been affected by advances in technology in a negative way.**

Candidates A & B: - (1 minute or 2 minutes for groups of three)

Interlocutor: Thank you.

Part 2 – Long turn

1: On your bike

- What are the people getting from the experience?
- How successful might these photos be in encouraging people to use bicycles?

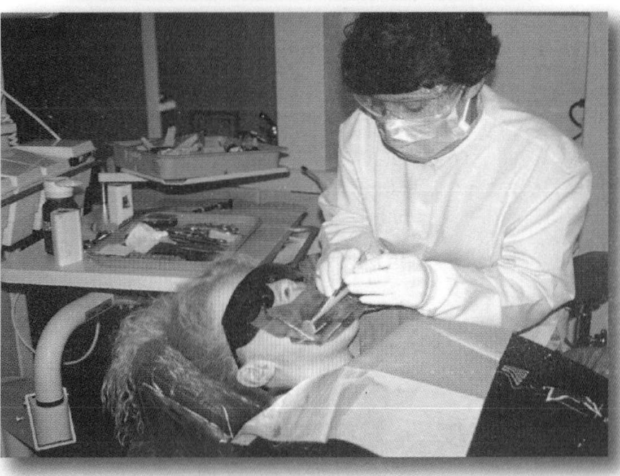

Part 2 – Long turn

2: Masks

- Why are these people wearing masks?
- How important are the masks to the people wearing them?

Part 3 - Collaborative task

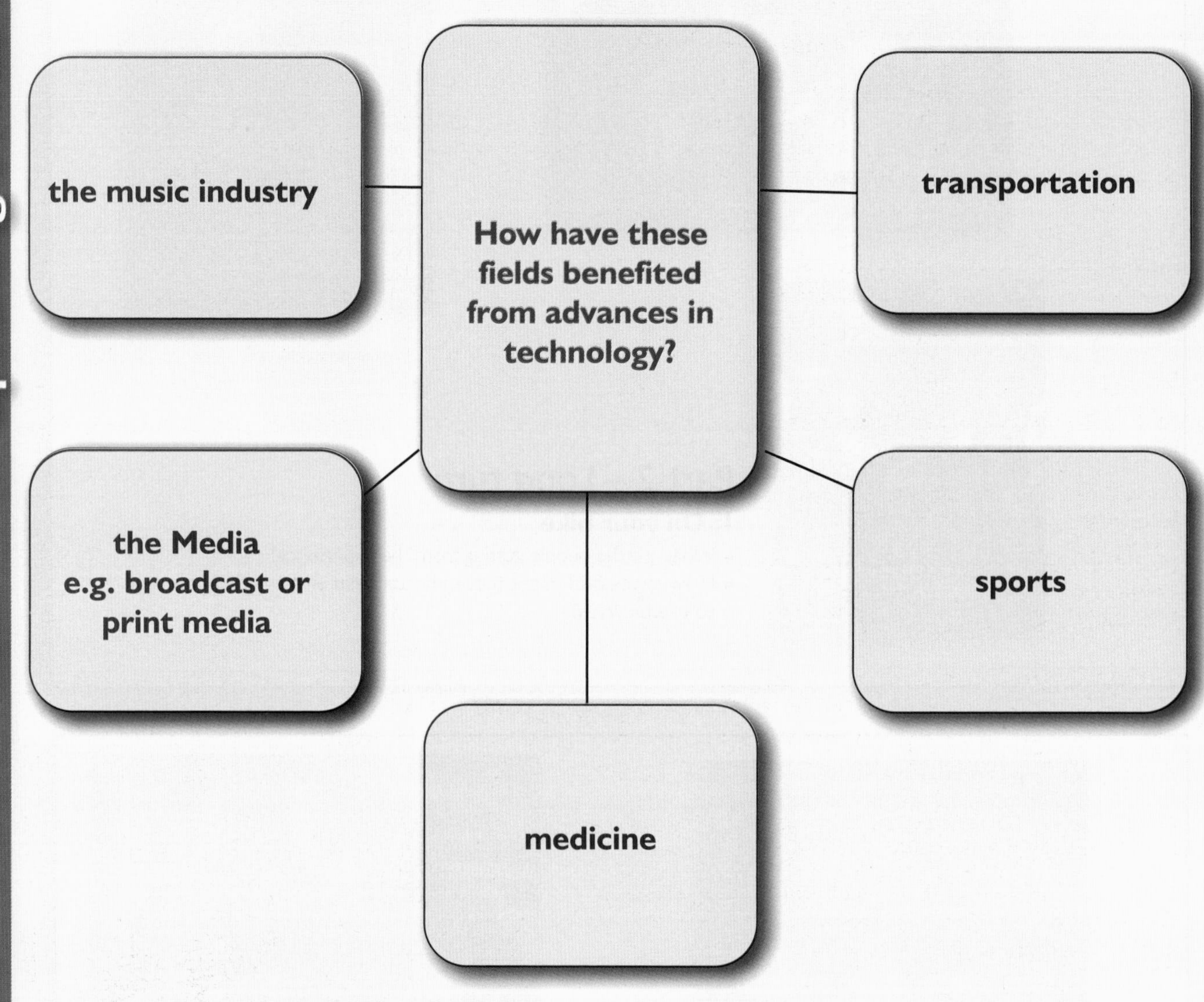

Part 4 – Discussion *5 minutes (8 minutes for groups of three)*

Interlocutor:

- How has technology made our lives more dangerous?
- New technology often leads to unemployment. What should governments do about this?
- Do you believe that one day technology will provide solutions to all our problems? Why (not)?
- What effect has modern technology had on the lives of young children?
- Some people say life was better and simpler fifty years ago. To what extent would you agree with them?

- What do you think?
- Do you agree?
- What about you?

Thank you. That is the end of the test.

TEST 7

Part 2 – Long turn *4 minutes (6 minutes for groups of three)*

In this part of the test you each have to speak for 1 minute without interruption. The examiner will give you a set of pictures and ask you to talk about them. You may be asked to describe, compare or contrast the pictures, and to make a further comment on them. Your partner will get a different set of pictures, but you should pay attention during your partner's turn because the examiner will ask you to comment for about 30 seconds after your partner has finished speaking.

1: Speaking on the phone

Interlocutor: In this part of the test, I' m going to give each of you three pictures. I'd like you to talk about two of them on your own for about a minute, and also to answer a question briefly about your partner's pictures.

(Candidate A), it's your turn first. Here are your pictures. They show **people speaking on the phone**.

Look at page 24, Part 2, Task 1.

I'd like you to compare two of the pictures, and say **why the telephone is important for each of the people and how they might be feeling**. All right?

Candidate A: - (1 minute) ....
Interlocutor: Thank you.

(Candidate B), which picture shows somebody talking about work on the phone? ... (Why?)
Candidate B: - (approx. 30 seconds) ....
Interlocutor: Thank you.

2: People outdoors

Now, **(Candidate B)**, here are your pictures. They show **people who are outdoors**. I'd like you to compare two of the pictures and say **what the people might be doing, and how they might be feeling?** All right?

Look at page 24, Part 2, Task 2.

Candidate B: - (1 minute) ....
Interlocutor: Thank you.

(Candidate A), which of the people are enjoying themselves most? ... (Why?)
Candidate A: - (approx. 30 seconds) ....
Interlocutor: Thank you.

Part 3 - Collaborative task *4 minutes (6 minutes for groups of three)*

This part tests your ability to take part in a discussion with the other candidate and reach a decision.

Interlocutor: Now, I'd like you to talk about something together for about two minutes. *(3 minutes for groups of three)*

Here are some careers that people study for in school and a question for you to discuss. First you have some time to look at the task.

Look at page 25, Part 3. (You have 15 seconds to look at the task).

Now, talk to each other about **which are some of the benefits and drawbacks of each profession**..

Candidates A & B: - (2 minutes or 3 minutes for groups of three)

Interlocutor: Thank you. Now you have about a minute (2 minutes for groups of three) to discuss **which profession has a bigger impact on people's lives**.

Candidates A & B: - (1 minute or 2 minutes for groups of three)

Interlocutor: Thank you.

Part 2 – Long turn

1: Speaking on the phone

- Why is the telephone important for each of these people?
- How might the people be feeling?

Part 2 – Long turn

2: People outdoors

- What are the people doing outdoors?
- How might they be feeling?

Part 3 - Collaborative task

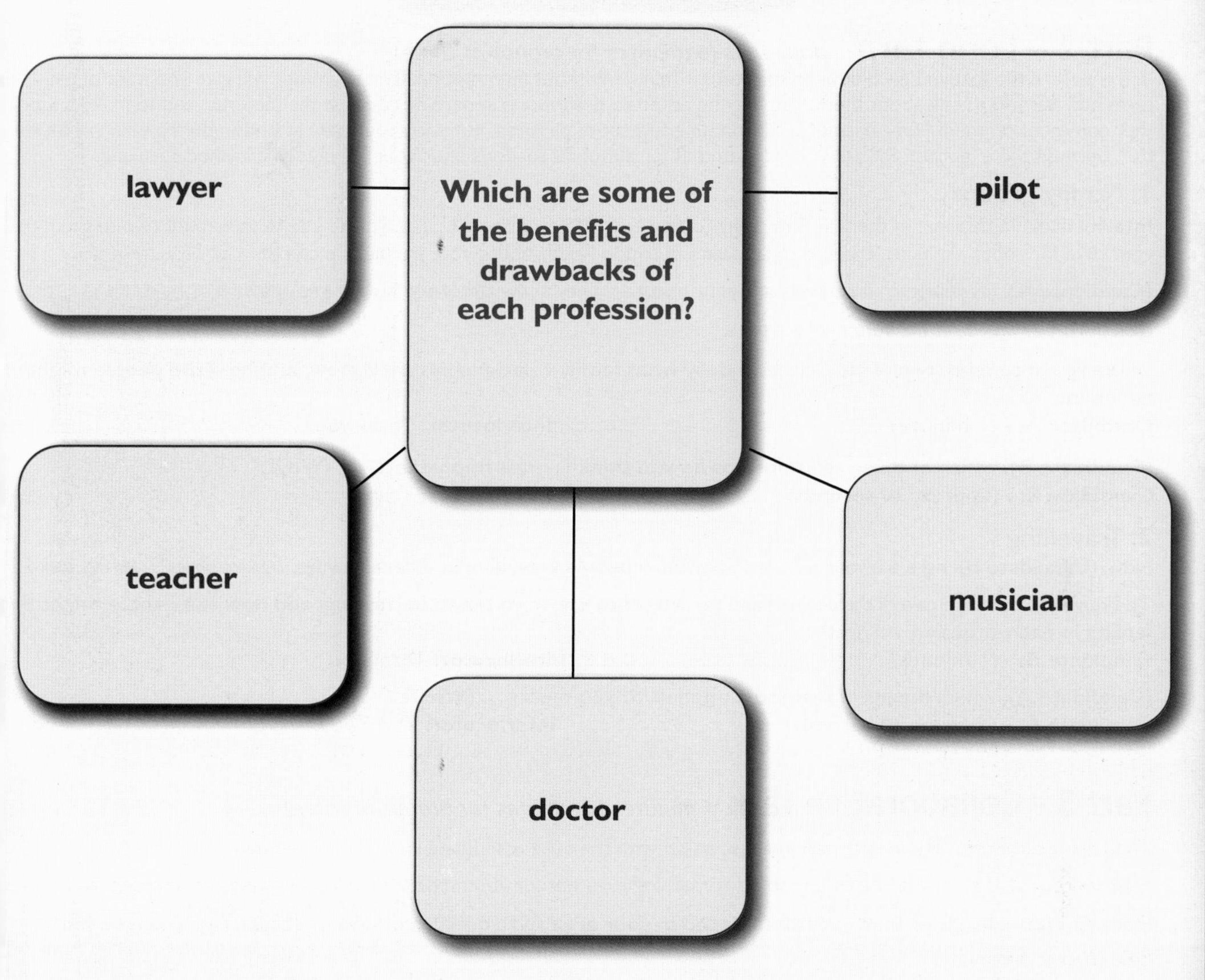

Part 4 – Discussion *5 minutes (8 minutes for groups of three)*

- What do you think?
- Do you agree?
- What about you?

Interlocutor:

- What are the most important characteristics of a job that make it a good job?
- Is it better to be a lawyer or a construction worker? (Why? / Why not?)
- When people retire from their jobs they are often quite unhappy at first. Why do you think this is?
- In times of recession, many people lose their jobs, but others do not. What are some jobs that we will always need people to do, however bad the economy is? (Why?)

Thank you. That is the end of the test.

TEST 8

Part 2 – Long turn *4 minutes (6 minutes for groups of three)*

In this part of the test you each have to speak for 1 minute without interruption. The examiner will give you a set of pictures and ask you to talk about them. You may be asked to describe, compare or contrast the pictures, and to make a further comment on them. Your partner will get a different set of pictures, but you should pay attention during your partner's turn because the examiner will ask you to comment for about 30 seconds after your partner has finished speaking.

1: Family groups

Interlocutor: In this part of the test, I' m going to give each of you three pictures. I'd like you to talk about two of them on your own for about a minute, and also to answer a question briefly about your partner's pictures.

(Candidate A), it's your turn first. Here are your pictures. They show **different family groups.**

Look at Part 2, Task 1, at the bottom of the page.

I'd like you to compare two of the pictures and say **what family relationships they show, and how the people might be feeling**. All right?
Candidate A: - (1 minute) .... **Interlocutor:** Thank you.

(Candidate B), which of these relationships do you think is most important?? ... (Why?)
Candidate B: - (approx. 30 seconds) .... **Interlocutor:** Thank you.

2: Travelling

Now, **(Candidate B)**, here are your pictures. They show **people travelling in different ways**. *Look at page 27, Part 2, Task 2.*

I'd like you to compare two of the pictures and say **why they chose to travel in this way and how the people might be feeling in each situation**. All right?
Candidate B: - (1 minute) .... **Interlocutor:** Thank you.

(Candidate A), which means of transport appeals to you most? ... (Why?)
Candidate A: - (approx. 30 seconds) .... **Interlocutor:** Thank you.

Part 3 - Collaborative task *4 minutes (6 minutes for groups of three)*

This part tests your ability to take part in a discussion with the other candidate and reach a decision. .

Interlocutor: Now, I'd like you to talk about something together for about two minutes. *(3 minutes for groups of three)*

Here are some facilities that might be needed in your area and a question for you to discuss. First you have some time to look at the task.
Look at page 27, Part 3. (You have 15 seconds to look at the task).

Now, talk to each other about **what the local council might have to consider when deciding which facility is needed most.**

Candidates A & B: - (2 minutes or 3 minutes for groups of three)
Interlocutor: Thank you. Now you have about a minute (2 minutes for groups of three) to decide **which facility would be more beneficial for a village**.

Candidates A & B: - (1 minute or 2 minutes for groups of three)
Interlocutor: Thank you.

Part 2 – Long turn

1: Family groups

- What family relationships are the pictures showing?
- How are the people feeling?

Part 2 – Long turn

2: Travelling

- Why did they choose to travel in this way?
- How might the people be feeling in each situation?

Part 3 - Collaborative task

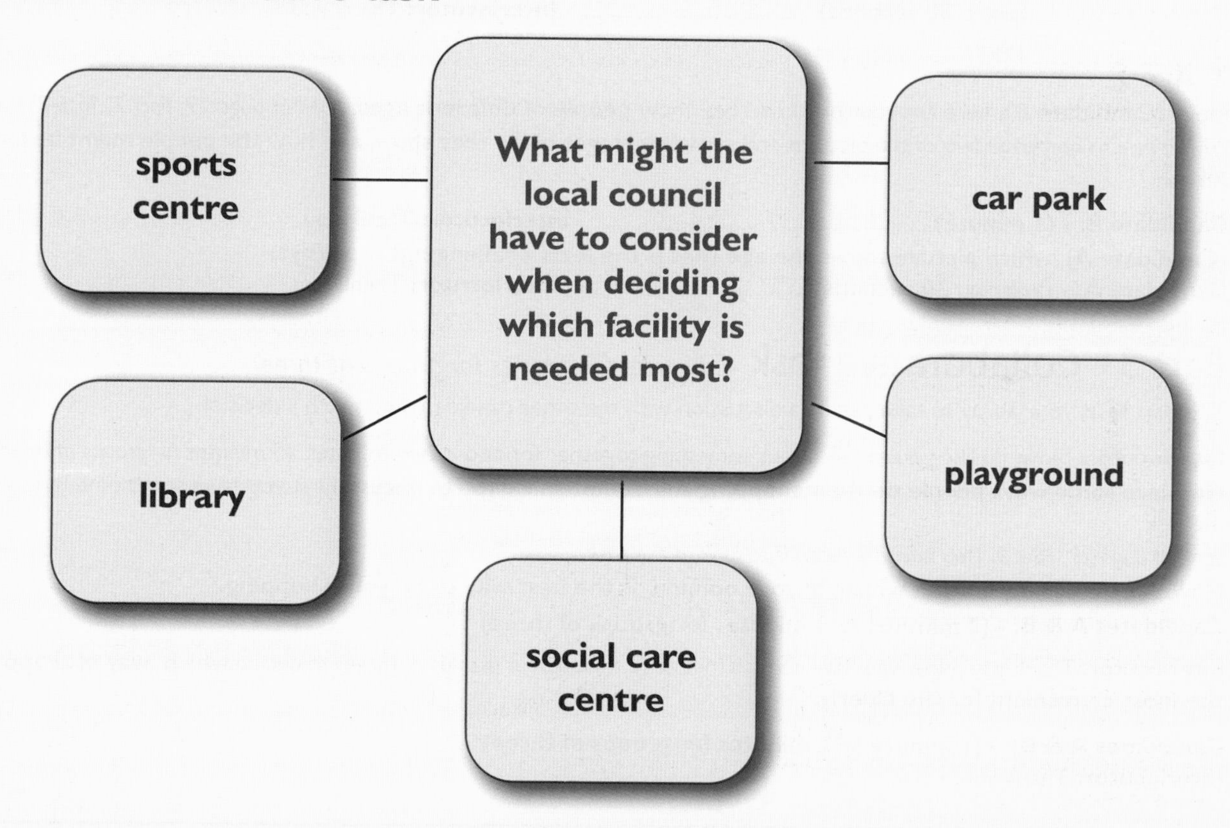

Part 4 – Discussion *5 minutes (8 minutes for groups of three)*

- What do you think?
- Do you agree?
- What about you?

Interlocutor:

- What services should local authorities provide to people in their communities?
- Can the people of an area influence the decisions of local authorities?
- Should most decisions be taken by central governments or by local authorities?
- In what ways can local communities help people who are unemployed and have no money?

Thank you. That is the end of the test.

Speaking Section

TEST 9

Part 2 – Long turn *4 minutes (6 minutes for groups of three)*

In this part of the test you each have to speak for 1 minute without interruption. The examiner will give you a set of pictures and ask you to talk about them. You may be asked to describe, compare or contrast the pictures, and to make a further comment on them. Your partner will get a different set of pictures, but you should pay attention during your partner's turn because the examiner will ask you to comment for about 30 seconds after your partner has finished speaking.

1: Dress styles

Interlocutor: In this part of the test, I' m going to give each of you three pictures. I'd like you to talk about two of them on your own for about a minute, and also to answer a question briefly about your partner's pictures.

(Candidate A), it's your turn first. Here are your pictures. They show **different styles of dress**.
Look at Part 2, Task 1, at the bottom of the page.
I'd like you to compare two of the pictures and say **what different styles of dress they show and to whom each one might appeal**. All right?
Candidate A: - (1 minute) .... **Interlocutor:** Thank you.

(Candidate B), which of these styles of dress is the most popular in your country? ... (Why?)
Candidate B: - (approx. 30 seconds) .... **Interlocutor:** Thank you.

2: Age

Now, **(Candidate B)**, here are your pictures.They show **people of different ages.** *Look at page 29, Part 2, Task 2*
I'd like you to compare two of the pictures and say **what stages of life they show, and how the people might be feeling**. All right?
Candidate B: - (1 minute) .... **Interlocutor:** Thank you.
(Candidate A), **which picture shows the age that is the least challenging? ... (Why?)**
Candidate A: - (approx. 30 seconds) .... **Interlocutor:** Thank you.

Part 3 - Collaborative task *4 minutes (6 minutes for groups of three)*

This part tests your ability to take part in a discussion with the other candidate and reach a decision.

Interlocutor: Now, I'd like you to talk about something together for about two minutes. *(3 minutes for groups of three)* **Here are some ways people do their shopping** and a question for you to discuss. First you have some time to look at the task.
Look at page 29, Part 3. (You have 15 seconds to look at the task).
Now, talk to each other about **which, in your opinion, is the best way to do your shopping.**
Candidates A & B: - (2 minutes or 3 minutes for groups of three)

Interlocutor: Thank you. Now you have about a minute (2 minutes for groups of three) to decide **which way of shopping is the most convenient for the elderly.**

Candidates A & B: - (1 minute or 2 minutes for groups of three)
Interlocutor: Thank you.

Part 2 – Long turn

1: Dress styles

- What different styles of dress do they show?
- To whom might each style appeal?

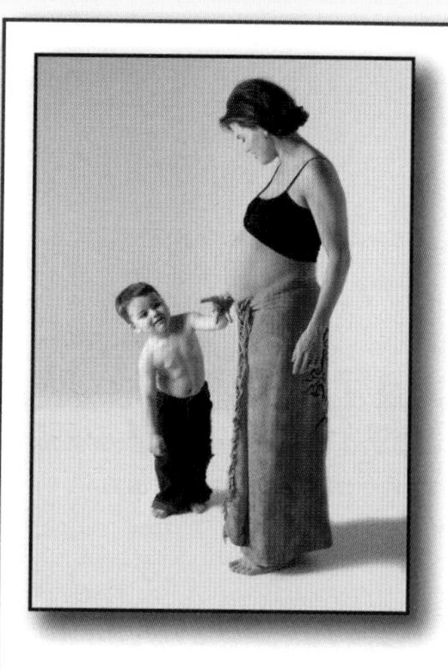

Part 2 – Long turn

2: Age

- What different stages of life do the pictures show?
- How might the people be feeling?

Part 3 - Collaborative task

Which, in your opinion, is the best way to do your shopping?

- **shop online; use the internet and pay by credit card**
- **flea markets or bazaars, where items are sold at low prices**
- **shopping malls; big shopping centres with many shops**
- **second-hand shops where used items are sold at low prices**
- **high-street shops in the city centre**

Part 4 – Discussion *5 minutes (8 minutes for groups of three)*

Interlocutor:

- Is it possible to have too many possessions? What is your opinion?
- Why would people buy things that they cannot afford?
- Often, people make assumptions about others based on the clothes they are wearing. How do you feel about this?
- Shopping is therapeutic. Do you agree?
- What are the risks involved when using credit cards?

- What do you think?
- Do you agree?
- What about you?

Thank you. That is the end of the test.

TEST 10

Part 2 – Long turn *4 minutes (6 minutes for groups of three)*

In this part of the test you each have to speak for 1 minute without interruption. The examiner will give you a set of pictures and ask you to talk about them. You may be asked to describe, compare or contrast the pictures, and to make a further comment on them. Your partner will get a different set of pictures, but you should pay attention during your partner's turn because the examiner will ask you to comment for about 30 seconds after your partner has finished speaking.

1: Crowds

Interlocutor: In this part of the test, I' m going to give each of you three pictures. I'd like you to talk about two of them on your own for about a minute, and also to answer a question briefly about your partner's pictures.

(Candidate A), it's your turn first. Here are your pictures. They show **different situations where crowds occur.**

Look at page 31, Part 2, Task 1.

I'd like you to compare two of the pictures and say **in what situations the crowds might occur, and how the people might be feeling**. All right?

Candidate A: - (1 minute) ....
Interlocutor: Thank you.

(Candidate B), which picture shows the most unsafe situation? ... (Why?)
Candidate B: - (approx. 30 seconds) ....
Interlocutor: Thank you.

2: People and animals

Now, **(Candidate B)**, here are your pictures. They show **people interacting with animals**. I'd like you to compare two of the pictures and say **how the people are connected with the animals, and why the animals are important to them**. All right?

Look at page 31, Part 2, Task 2.

Candidate B: - (1 minute) ....
Interlocutor: Thank you.

(Candidate A), which picture is the least appealing to you? ... (Why?)
Candidate A: - (approx. 30 seconds) ....
Interlocutor: Thank you.

Part 3 - Collaborative task *4 minutes (6 minutes for groups of three)*

This part tests your ability to take part in a discussion with the other candidate and reach a decision.

Interlocutor: Now, I'd like you to talk about something together for about two minutes. *(3 minutes for groups of three)*

Here are some ways to reduce pollution levels in big cities and a question for you to discuss. First you have some time to look at the task.

Look at page 32, Part 3. (You have 15 seconds to look at the task).

Now, talk to each other about **how these methods can reduce pollution levels in big cities.**

Candidates A & B: - (2 minutes or 3 minutes for groups of three)

Interlocutor: Thank you. Now you have about a minute (2 minutes for groups of three) to decide **which method can be used without investing huge amounts of money.**

Candidates A & B: - (1 minute or 2 minutes for groups of three)

Interlocutor: Thank you.

Part 2 – Long turn

1: Crowds

- In what situations might these crowds occur?
- How might the people be feeling?

Part 2 – Long turn

2: People and animals

- How are the people connected with the animals in the pictures?
- Why are the animals important to them?

Part 3 - Collaborative task

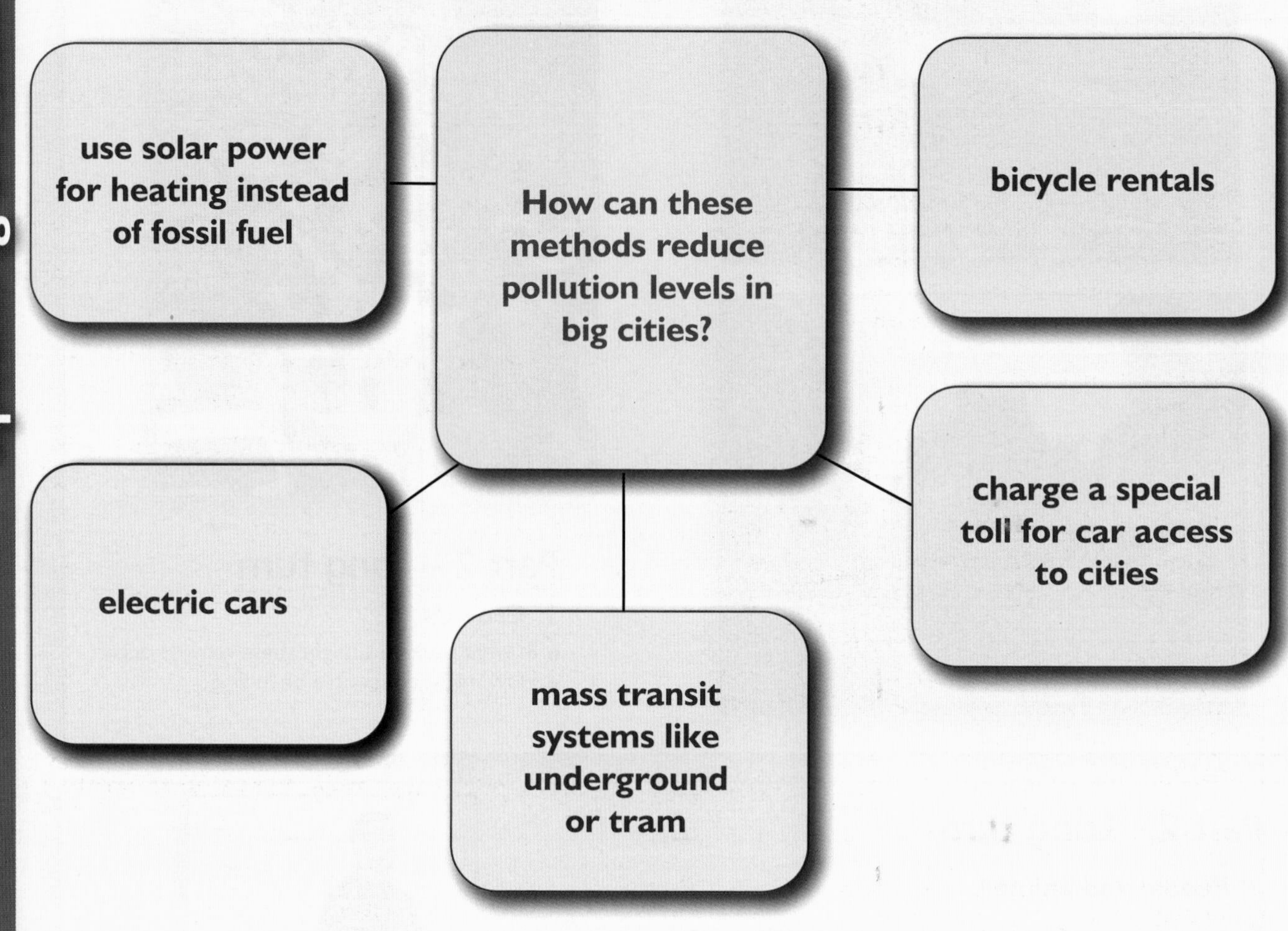

Part 4 – Discussion *5 minutes (8 minutes for groups of three)*

Interlocutor:

- Some people say that we will run out of petrol before too long. What do you think about this?
- How has the availability of affordable long distance flights changed the world?
- What can be done to a city to make it a better place for pedestrians?
- How do you think we will get around in a hundred years' time?

Thank you. That is the end of the test.

- What do you think?
- Do you agree?
- What about you?

Cambridge English: Advanced EXAM GUIDE

Cambridge English: Advanced (CAE)
Introduction

About Cambridge English Language Assessment

Cambridge English: Advanced (CAE) is created by Cambridge English Language Assessment, part of the University of Cambridge. In excess of 8 million Cambridge Assessment exams are taken yearly in over 160 countries around the world. Cambridge English Language Assessment features the world's leading range of qualifications for learners and teachers of English. Over 4 million people take their exams each year throughout the world.

Key features of Cambridge English exams

The tests:

- simulate authentic tasks and situations so that preparing for the exam gives learners practical language skills.
- accurately and consistently assess all four language skills – reading, writing, listening and speaking – as well as knowledge of language structure and its use.
- encourage positive learning experiences and seek to achieve a positive impact on teaching wherever possible.
- are as fair as possible to all candidates, regardless of their national, ethnic and linguistic background, gender or disability.

Cambridge English: Advanced (CAE)
An Overview

The test is developed under an extensive programme of research and evaluation, and by continuous analysis of the marking and grading of all Cambridge English exams. Of particular value are the rigorous procedures employed in the creation and pretesting of question papers.

The standard for the test is centred on quality management designed around five essential principles:
Validity – the exam provides a genuine evaluation of real-life English
Reliability – the exam functions evenly and fairly
Impact – the assessment has a positive effect on teaching and learning
Practicality – the evaluation meets the needs of learners within available resources
Quality – the exam is planned, delivered and checked to provide excellence in all of these criteria

The exam is a high-level qualification that is officially recognised by universities, employers and governments around the world. Regular updating has allowed the examination to keep pace with changes in language teaching and testing while ensuring the exam remains reliable, relevant and user friendly for candidates.
Candidates can choose to take the exam as either a paper-based or a computer-based exam.

Who takes the exam?

Cambridge English: Advanced (CAE) targets learners who endeavour to:

- work in an English-speaking environment.
- study at an upper-intermediate level, such as foundation or pathway courses.
- live in an English-speaking country.

Who accepts the exam?

- The test is recognised by thousands of industrial, administrative and service-based employers as a qualification in upper-intermediate English. Overall, Cambridge English exams are recognised by 13,500 institutions and employers.
- It is also accepted by a wide range of educational institutions for study purposes.
- The exam has been accredited by Ofqual, the statutory regulatory authority for external qualifications in England and its counterparts in Wales and Northern Ireland.
- The UK Border Agency accepts the test as meeting the language requirements for Tier 1, 2, 4 and spouse or partner visa applications.

Cambridge English: Advanced (CAE)
What level is the exam?

The test is targeted at Level C1 on the CEFR scale. Level C1 is required in demanding academic and professional settings.

What can candidates do at Level C1?
The Association of Language Testers in Europe (ALTE) has carried out research to determine what language learners can typically do at each CEFR level. It has described these abilities in a series of Can Do Statements using examples taken from real-life situations.

Reading and Writing
- **can** read quickly enough to complete an academic course
- **can** take accurate notes in meetings or compose a piece of communication effectively
- **can** comprehend complex opinions or arguments published in various media sources

Listening and Speaking
- **can** contribute effectively in meetings and comparable settings with a good degree of fluency while negotiating abstract expressions
- **can** maintain conversations for extended periods of time with a range of expressions across various formal and informal subject matters
- **can** follow questions by probing for more detail as well as express disagreement or criticism without offence

Cambridge English: Advanced (CAE)
Exam Components

There are four papers: Reading and Use of English, Writing, Listening and Speaking. The Reading and Use of English paper carries 40% of the marks, while Writing, Listening and Speaking each carry 20% of the marks.
A detailed description of each test and sample papers is contained in the book, but the overall focus of each test is as follows:

Reading and Use of English: 1 hour 30 minutes
Candidates are required to comprehend texts from publications such as fiction and non-fiction books, journals, newspapers and magazines.
Writing: 1 hour 30 minutes
Candidates must demonstrate that they can produce two different pieces of writing: a compulsory task in Part 1 and one from a choice of three in Part 2.
Listening: 40 minutes (approximately)
Candidates must show they can understand the meaning of a range of spoken material, including lectures, radio broadcasts, speeches and talks.
Speaking: 15 minutes
Candidates perform the Speaking test with another candidate or in a group of three and are evaluated on their ability to execute different types of interaction: with the examiner, with the other candidate and by themselves.
Each of these four test components provides a unique contribution to a profile of overall communicative language ability that defines what a candidate can do at this level.

International English
English is used in a variety of global contexts. To reflect this, candidates' responses to tasks in the exam are acceptable in all forms and accents of English, provided they do not impede overall communication. Materials used feature a range of accents and texts from English-speaking countries, including the UK, North America and Australia. US and other versions of spelling are accepted if used consistently.

Marks and results
Cambridge English: Advanced provides a comprehensive assessment. All candidates receive a Statement of Results. Candidates whose performance achieves between CEFR Levels B2 and C2 will also receive a certificate.
Statement of Results
- a display of the candidate's performance in each skill with a scale of ***Exceptional – Good – Borderline – Weak***
- a standardised score out of 100 that enables the candidates to view exactly how they performed.

Paper 1 - Reading and Use of English

General description
Content: The paper contains eight parts. For Parts 1 to 4, the test contains texts with accompanying grammar and vocabulary tasks and separate items with a grammar and vocabulary focus. For Parts 5 to 8, the test contains a range of texts and accompanying reading comprehension tasks.
Time Allotted: 1 hour 30 minutes
Number of Parts: 8
Number of Questions: 56
Task Types: Multiple-choice cloze, open cloze, word formation, key word transformation, multiple choice, cross-text multiple matching, gapped text, multiple matching.
Word Count: 3,000–3,500
Scoring: Parts 1–3: each correct answer receives 1 mark; Part 4: each correct answer receives up to 2 marks; Parts 5–7: each correct answer receives 2 marks; Part 8: each correct answer receives 1 mark.

Part 1 - Task: Multiple-choice cloze

The main focus is on vocabulary, including idioms, collocations, complementation, phrasal verbs and semantic precision. A text containing eight gaps followed by eight 4-option multiple-choice items.
Number of Questions: 8

Part 2 - Task: Open cloze

The main focus is on awareness and control of grammar with some vocabulary. A text containing eight gaps.
Number of Questions: 8

Part 3 - Task: Word formation

The main focus is on vocabulary, namely the use of affixation, internal changes and compounding in word formation. A text containing eight gaps. Each gap corresponds to a word. The stems of the missing words are given beside the text and must be altered to form the missing word.
Number of Questions: 8

Part 4 - Task: Key word transformation

The focus is on grammar, vocabulary and collocation. Six separate items, each with a lead-in sentence and a gapped second sentence to be completed in three to six words, one of which is given as a 'key' word.
Number of Questions: 6

Tips for Paper 1 - Reading & Use of English

Parts 1 - 4

1. The passages in Parts 1, 2 and 3 all have titles. Look at each title closely for it will indicate the main idea of the text.
2. Read each text in this section carefully prior to answering any questions so that you fully understand what each passage explores.
3. For Parts 2 and 4, there may be more than one possible answer for each question. However, you should only provide one answer for each question. Should you give two responses and one of them is incorrect, you will not receive a mark.
4. Each part of the exam features detailed instructions and completed examples. Study these examples closely to understand what type of answers you are expected to provide.
5. Read broadly to develop your vocabulary and your familiarity with various styles and structures. This will prepare you to marshal a variety of lexical items and grammatical structures.
6. Make use of dictionaries, thesauri and grammar resources in your preparation for the exam. Note, though, that resource books like dictionaries are not permitted during the exam.
7. Develop a system for accumulating a broader vocabulary. Make use of flashcards, for example, to practice and expand your word power.
8. Remember to not dedicate too much time to any single part of the test. Try to save a few minutes at the conclusion of each test to review your answers.
9. Be careful with spelling mistakes, as they detract from your overall score.
10. Write with clear penmanship so that the markers will be able to grade your responses efficiently.

Part 5 - Task: Multiple choice

Detail, opinion, attitude, tone, purpose, main idea, specific information, implication. A text followed by 4-option multiple-choice questions.
Number of Questions: 6

Part 6 - Task: Cross-text-multiple matching

Understanding of opinion and attitude: comparing and contrasting opinions and attitudes across texts. Four short texts, followed by multiple matching questions. Candidates must read across texts to match a prompt to elements in the text.
Number of Questions: 4

Part 7 - Task: Gapped text

Cohesion, coherence, text structure and global meaning. A text from which paragraphs have been removed and placed in scrambled sequence after the text. Candidates are asked to decide from where in the text the paragraphs have been removed.
Number of Questions: 6

Part 8 - Task: Multiple matching

Detail, opinion, attitude, specific information. A text or several short texts, preceded by multiple-matching questions. Candidates must match a prompt to elements in the passage.
Number of Questions: 10

Tips for Paper 1 - Reading & Use of English

Parts 5 - 8

1 Again, read broadly in both classes and in your spare time. This will build your skill with a variety of texts. In addition, focus on the pre-reading questions to refine your prediction capabilities.
2 Consider developing written or oral reviews of the materials you read in and out of class. Choose from shorts stories, novels, magazine articles, non-fiction books, etc. to build your skills.
3 Familiarise yourself with the format of the Reading part of the test. Practice with sample exams. This will prepare you for what to expect in each part of the paper.
4 As you read, it's not important that you understand every single word. Refine your ability to deduce the meaning of unknown words based on the context. Don't make the mistake of fretting over a single word here and there, instead of striving to develop an overall understanding of what you read.
5 The instructions, title and sub-title of each text provide insight as to what to expect from each passage. Make use of visuals that are included; they are featured with the intent of helping you understand content that you may not be completely familiar with in the passage. These may take the form of a photo or graphic of a city or animal.
6 Note the instructions on the first page of the question paper and for each section of the exam. Practice the technique of marking your answer on the separate answer sheet to ensure you are able to do this efficiently.
7 Learn to manage your time while taking the test. Parts 5, 6 and 7 are given two marks per question, while Part 8 is allocated 1 mark per question. Remember, the test require you to process large amounts of reading in timed manner and thus you must use your time wisely.

The Eight Sections of the Reading and Use of English Paper

Paper 1 - Reading and Use of English - Part 1: Multiple Choice Cloze

The main focus is on vocabulary, including idioms, collocations, complementation, fixed phrases, semantic precision and phrasal verbs. Part 1 features a text in which there are eight gaps. Each gap represents a missing word or phrase. The text is followed by eight sets of four words or phrases, each set corresponding to a gap. You must choose which of the four options in the set completes the expression correctly.

Tips for Reading and Use of English - Part 1

1 When building your vocabulary power for the paper, note the collocation, the differentiating sets of similar words and complementation (e.g. whether words are followed by a certain preposition, by a gerund or an infinitive etc.)
2 Look closely at each of the options before choosing an answer. Some of the options may seem correct, but only one choice will be semantically and grammatically correct in that particular context.

Paper 1 - Reading and Use of English - Part 2: Open Cloze

The main focus is on awareness and control of grammar with some focus on vocabulary.
Part 2 consists of a text in which there are eight gaps. You are asked to draw on your knowledge of the structure of the language and understanding of the text to fill the gaps. In this part, as there are no sets of words from which to choose the answers, you have to think of a word that will fill the gap appropriately.

Tips for Reading and Use of English - Part 2

1 Engage in tasks that help you develop your grammatical accuracy, especially those that focus on verb forms and the use of auxiliary and modal verbs, pronouns, prepositions, conjunctions, modifiers and determiners.
2 Remember only one word is required for each question. Answers that have more than one word will not earn the mark.
3 Some gaps in this section can be answered by referring just to the immediate phrase or sentence, but other items will require understanding of the paragraph or whole text.

Paper 1 - Reading and Use of English - Part 3: Word Formation

The main focus is on vocabulary, in particular the use of affixation, compounding in word formation and internal changes.
Part 3 consists of a text with 8 gaps. At the end of some of the lines, and separate from the text, there is a stem word in capital letters. You are required to form an appropriate word from given stem words to fill each gap.
The point of this section is primarily lexical, though an understanding of structure is also required. It evaluates your knowledge of the use of prefixes, suffixes, internal changes and compounds in forming words. You may be asked to demonstrate understanding of the text beyond sentence level.

Tips for Reading and Use of English - Part 3

1 Preparation tasks that promote familiarity with the principles of word formation, including use of prefixes, suffixes, internal changes, will be helpful.
2 Remember you need to fully comprehend the context of each gap in the text to decide which part of speech (noun, verb, adjective or adverb) is needed.
3 Sometimes you may need to provide a negative prefix. Traditionally there is usually at least one world requiring a prefix in each Part 3 task, so remember to look for these.

Paper 1 - Reading and Use of English - Part 4: Key Word Transformations

The focus is on grammar, vocabulary and collocation.
Part 4 features six questions. Each item contains three parts: a lead-in sentence, a key word and a second sentence of which only the beginning and end are given. You have to fill the gap in the second sentence so that the completed sentence is similar in meaning to the lead-in sentence. The gap must be filled with between three and six words, one of which is the key word. You must not change the key word in any manner.
In this part of the exam you are asked to focus on a range of both lexical and grammatical structures. The ability to express a message in different ways demonstrates flexibility and resource in the use of language.
The mark scheme splits the answers into two parts and you receive one mark for each part which is correct.

Tips for Reading and Use of English - Part 4

1 Practice transformation tasks which increase awareness of expressions with parallel or synonymous meanings and develop flexibility in the use of language.
2 Remember that the key word MUST be used in each answer and that the key word may NOT be changed in any way.
3 Also your answer must NOT exceed six words. Contractions do count as two words.

Paper 1 - Reading and Use of English - Part 5: Multiple Choice

This part focuses on the comprehension of a long text, including detail, opinion, purpose, main idea, tone, attitude, implication and also text organisation features such as exemplification, reference and comparison.
Part 5 features one long text stemming from a variety of sources which may include fiction. The text is accompanied by six four-option multiple-choice questions that are presented in the same order as the information in the text so that candidates can follow the development of the passage.

This task evaluates understanding including opinions and attitudes expressed; the ability to differentiate between, for instance, seemingly similar viewpoints, reasons or outcomes. You should be able to deduce meaning from the context and interpret the text for inference and style. You also should be able to comprehend the text organisation features, such as referencing, comparison and exemplification.

Tips for Reading and Use of English - Part 5

1. Familiarise yourself with a variety of sources, registers, topics and lexical fields. In your preparation practise reading a text quickly for an initial overall impression, then followed by a close reading of the text to prevent any misunderstanding.
2. Read the question and underline the part of the text which answers the question. Examine the options and decide which is the closest to answering the question. Often candidates mistakenly only briefly refer to the text when answering a question and just choose an answer which sounds plausible or supports their own ideas.
3. Check the questions that take the form of incomplete sentences carefully; the whole sentence must reflect what is written in the text and not merely the phrase in the four options provided.
4. Read materials that express opinions, attitudes and feelings such as interviews with famous people that explore how they became successful or short stories that relate how characters interpret the circumstances they endure. Engage also in activities that focus on recognising and evaluating attitudes and opinions. This will enhance your skills in inferring the implicit meaning of a passage.
5. Have practice in text organisation features. You may encounter a question, for example, that evaluates your ability to distinguish between a main idea and an example or one which requires you to draw connections between an abstract argument and a concrete illustration. Items may test your skill at comparing and contrasting both literally and metaphorically.

Paper 1 - Reading and Use of English - Part 6: Cross Textual Multiple-Matching

In this part, there is an emphasis on identifying opinions and attitudes expressed across texts.
You must read through texts to match a prompt to elements in the texts. The prompts ask you to read across the four passages to comprehend the opinions and attitudes expressed to identify agreement and disagreement between the writers. The items only provide information on the subject of the opinion, not the opinion itself: this is for you to identify. You will most likely encounter two patterns of questions where you will need to select an opinion expressed in one of the texts and then choose which other text shares or contradicts this opinion or you may be required to identify the passage that differs from the other three in terms of an expressed opinion.

Tips for Reading and Use of English - Part 6

1. Familiarise yourself with reading samples that express various viewpoints on a related theme, such as different reviews of the same book or some experts giving their opinion on a subject.
2. The texts will feature a sophisticated reading level without assuming in-depth subject-specific knowledge, so develop your skills in using complex vocabulary and the structures, such as verbal phrases commonly found in academic and other high level reading materials.
3. Read the texts to gather the general attitude of each writer on the subject being discussed. Underlining the part or parts of a text that express an opinion or attitude and then determining whether this is negative or positive is helpful.
4. Look at each question and underline the key words. If a question asks you for 'a similar or different opinion to' for example, writer B, on a subject, underline what aspect of B's opinion is being evaluated and then find and underline that opinion in option B. The task will then involve looking at all the other writers and identifying the similar or different opinion.

Paper I - Reading and Use of English - Part 7: Gapped Text

This part emphasises the understanding of how texts are structured and the ability to follow text development.
Part 7 features one long gapped text from which six paragraphs of equal length have been taken out and placed in scrambled order following the text, coupled with a seventh paragraph that does not fit in any of the gaps. Traditionally the text is taken from non-fiction sources like journalism. The section of the exam evaluates your comprehension of text structure, cohesion, coherence and global meaning.
You must decide where in the text each paragraph has been removed. Each paragraph may be used only one time and there is one paragraph that you do not need.
Read the gapped text first to obtain an overall understanding of the structure and the meaning of the text, making note of the information and ideas before and after each gap as well as throughout the whole of the gapped text. Then, decide which paragraphs fit the gaps, remembering that each letter may only be used once and that there is one paragraph that you won't need.

Tips for Reading and Use of English - Part 7

1. Read the text as a whole and not to focus on each gap individually. Gathering an idea of the structure and the development of the them of the text are both important prerequisites to performing the task. Often candidates select the wrong answer by choosing an option that fits the text before the gap, but neglect to check that the text after the gap continues smoothly.
2. At times you may need to choose between two paragraphs as possible answers and will need to practice making decisions about which is the most logical paragraph to complete the gap. Practice recognising a variety of linguistic devices that mark the logical and cohesive construction of a text, such as words and phrases that indicate time, cause and effect, contrasting arguments use of pronouns, paraphrasing of vocabulary, repetition and the use of verb tenses.
3. Be aware of the risks of approaching the gapped-text task as an exercise requiring you to identify extracts from the text and sections in the text containing the same words including names and dates. The task aims to evaluate your understanding of the development of ideas, opinions and events rather than the recognition of individual words.

Paper I - Reading and Use of English - Part 8: Multiple Matching

This part of the exam emphasises locating specific information, attitude and opinion in a text or a group of short texts.
Part 8 includes one or two sets of questions followed by a single page of text: the passage may be continuous, divided into sections or consist of a group of short texts. There are a total of ten questions and four to six options.
You are required to match the questions with the relevant information from the text. To execute this, you need to understand detail, attitude or opinion in the question, and locate a section of the text where that idea is expressed, discounting ideas in other sections that may seem similar but that do not reflect the entirety of the question. Some of the options may be correct for more than one question and there may be more than one correct answer to some items. The instructions will mention this explicitly, if this is the case.
In addition to the use of the letters, A-F, the range of potential responses may be presented in the form of a list of names, people, titles of books or films as well as types of professions.

Tips for Reading and Use of English - Part 8

1. Practice skimming and scanning texts to prepare for the multiple-matching task. Practise examining texts for particular information required without reading every word in the text. Also practise reading under timed conditions.
2. Note that the questions for the multiple-matching task are printed before the text so that you know what to look for in the text.
3. Notice the particular wording of questions as these are intended to lead the reader to specific information and to disregard unnecessary information. You may find it helpful to underline key words in the questions, as this helps you to find the information in the text which contains the answers.
4. Sometimes a question may consist of two parts: such as an author's surprise at being confronted by a difficult matter. You may find evidence of a hard situation in a section of the passage but fail to understand that it may be the incorrect section as no surprise is expressed in that part. It is essential that you comprehend that you need to find a paraphrased form of the whole question, not just one part.
5. Resist selecting a response solely on the basis of matching a word in the question with a word in the text, as a close reading of a particular part of the passage is essential to ensure an accurate match in terms of meaning.
6. Read a broad range of articles and reviews in media where different people explore trends in work, books, films, etc. Come up with your own questions as an exercise to enhance your skills. This help you gather a better understanding of how the exam is constructed providing you with insight in identifying what clues you need to take into account when completing this section of the exam.

Paper 2 - Writing

General description
Format: The paper contains two parts.
Timing: 1 hour 30 minutes
Parts: 2
Task: Candidates are required to complete two tasks:
1) a compulsory task in **Part 1** and **2) one task from a choice of three** in **Part 2**.
A range from the following: article; email/letter; essay; report; review.
Scoring: Each question on this paper carries equal weight.

Structure & Tasks

Part 1 - Writing a discursive essay

Candidates are asked to write an essay based on two points given in the input text. They will be asked to explain which of the two points is more important and to give reasons to support their argument. The essay title will be on a subject of general interest not requiring any specialised knowledge.
Word Requirement: 220–260 words

Part 2 - Writing paper

Writing one from a number of possible text types based on a contextualised writing task.
Candidates have a choice of task. In questions 2–4, the tasks provide candidates with a clear context, topic, purpose and target reader for their writing. The output text types are: • ***article*** • ***email/letter*** • ***report*** • ***review.***
Word Requirement: 220–260 words

Task types in the Writing paper:

The different task types endeavour to establish frameworks for candidates to develop their ideas on a topic with a purpose for writing and a target reader in mind.

A PROPOSAL is written for a group of contemporaries like club members or colleagues. Candidates will be expected to make suggestions backed by facts to persuade their readers.

AN EMAIL/A LETTER is written to respond to a situation outlined in the question reflecting the appropriate register and tone for the specified target reader. Candidates are asked to develop correspondence to, for example, an English-speaking friend or colleague, a potential employer, a college principal or a magazine editor.

AN ESSAY is always written for a teacher. It should address the prompt provided in terms of addressing both content points and providing a new viewpoint of the writer's own. The essay should be well developed with an introduction, appropriate conclusion as well as written in an appropriate register and tone.

A REPORT is usually developed for a superior (e.g. a teacher) or a peer group (e.g. members of an English club). The question identifies the subject of the composition and the areas to be covered. Candidates must provide some factual information and make recommendations, but there is space for them to incorporate their own ideas and experiences.

A REVIEW is written traditionally for an English-language magazine, newspaper or website. The main purpose is to describe and express a personal opinion about something which the writer has experienced (e.g. a film, a holiday, a product, a website etc.) and to give the reader a clear impression of what the item discussed is like. Description and explanation are key functions for this task and a review will normally include a recommendation to the reader.

For all task types, questions are constructed to enable candidates to display their English language proficiency at CEFR C1 level; candidates should take special care to read every part of each question, and not to omit any required development of the topic.

Guidelines on length

Guidelines on length are provided for each task; essays that are too short may not have an adequate range of language and may not provide all the information that is required, while responses which are too long may contain extraneous content and have a negative effect on the reader. These may affect candidates' marks on the relevant subscales.
Candidates are expected to employ a consistent form of English in areas, such as spelling and not, for example, switch from using a British spelling of a word to an American spelling of the same word.

Writing Part 1: Essay

A composition in the Writing section is traditionally composed for an academic tutor and may be developed as a follow-up to a class activity, like attending a seminar or watching a documentary film. The main purpose of this task is to highlight relevant salient issues on the stated topic as well as to support an argument with subsidiary points and reasons. Your essay should be organised well, including an introduction, supporting paragraphs and a compelling conclusion. The composition should capture the reader's attention and express sophisticated ideas using a range of stylistic structures and vocabulary.

Task Format

There will be no choice of tasks in this Part. The task will introduce a topic that is to be written as a response to an academic activity like a panel discussion or listening to a radio show. A set of notes on the subject matter will be provided, expressed as three bullet points plus three short opinions related to the bullet points.

Task Type and Focus

You are asked to compose an essay drawing on two of the bullet points. You will be asked to explain which of the two points is more important and to express reasons for your viewpoint. The objective of this exercise is to enable you to identify the most relevant issues on a topic and to support the argument with supporting ideas. Your essay should include a well-organised introduction, supporting paragraphs and an appropriate conclusion.
The writing task is constructed to permit you to demonstrate your ability to write at this elevated level. You should read every part of the task carefully, not to omit any required development of the topic.

Tips for Writing Part 1

1 Read the entire task before beginning to plan your response. You will need to familiarise yourself with reading the input, understanding the instructions in full and then deciding on how to organise and construct your response.
2 Select two bullet points and develop your essay around them. Avoid trying to discuss more than two of the points, for this would lead the composition to being less developed than needed.
3 You may use the opinions expressed in the task to develop your answer, but be sure to use your own words as much as possible. No credit will be given for text that has been copied directly from the prompt.

Writing Part 2: Letter, Proposal, Report or Review

A **letter** is composed to respond to a situation provided in the task. Expect to be required to write letters to the editor of a publication, the director of a company, to a friend or to a university administrator. Letters will not be restricted to a narrative element but will also require candidates to execute other objectives, such as to resolve a misunderstanding or advocate for a course of action.
A **proposal** may be composed for a group of contemporaries at work or to a person in a position of authority, like a professor. You will be asked to express suggestions that are supported by facts, employing persuasive language.
A **report** may be composed for a superior or a peer group. The content of the document is somewhat factual, stemming from the prompt, though you will have the room to inject your own ideas and experience. You will be required to do more than simply describe a situation, including evaluating how a particular objective may be achieved or to suggest an alternative course of action.
A **review** may concern a book, film or work of art as well as a product or service. A review in the Writing exam does not simply require a general description of the item reviewed, instead calls for an evaluation of its appropriateness for its intended audience. The target audience is specified in the task and thus candidates should be encouraged to use this information when choosing ideas and language to incorporate into their response.

Task Format

This part of the exam includes three tasks from which candidates must choose. Each item in the section features a context, a purpose for writing and the target audience. Attention to detail is key for every component of the question to generate an effective response. Be careful to choose language that is appropriate for the task.

Tips for Writing Part 2

1 It is imperative that you become familiar with the various task types that the exam requires. All of the task types do not appear on each exam, thus it is important to be prepared to write in any of the styles.
2 Develop your skills in deciding which type of task you will complete. Evaluate the required functions, grammatical structures, vocabulary and register required by each task. Then, you may select the task that you believe you can complete at the highest level.
3 Be cognisant of your audience when crafting your essay. Consider whether the person is someone you know, a stranger or someone in a position of authority etc. It is vital to develop a balanced approach whereby you equally weigh the functions required by the task and the relationship with the target audience.

Paper 2 - Writing

Tips for Writing

1 Candidates write best when they select tasks and topics aligned with their interests and background. In preparation for the exam, expose yourself to a wide variety of tasks and topics. You will benefit from guidance on the particular features of each task as well as the appropriate style and tone for your readers.
2 Read each question closely, highlight the most important facets and develop a response that addresses all of the points required by the task. This will facilitate your ability to develop well-structured and balanced compositions.
3 Be sure to not simply reproduce an essay you may have written in preparation for the test. It is unlikely that at previous response will satisfy the exact requirements of the exam.
4 Practise developing ideas fully to illustrate a variety of vocabulary and grammatical structures to express more complex ideas where appropriate.
5 Make effective use of linking words and phrases to polish the flow of your ideas. In addition, to enhance the logic and ease of your composition use a variety of cohesive devices and organisational patterns.
6 Employ a range of complex language structures where suitable. The examiner will give you credit for attempting for sophisticated modes of expression, even if you make some mistakes, as long as it does not preclude the comprehension of the overall idea you are trying to convey.
7 The time permitted allows for a brief period of planning and then the composition of your essay. It does not account for time to compose fair copies or to count words. Each item on the Writing section carries with it equal marks. So practise using your time carefully on each question.
8 Write legibly so that your answers can be marked fairly, though the quality of your penmanship will not be assessed. It is immaterial whether your handwriting is joined up or not, nor whether you write in upper or lower case characters.
9 Be sure to compose your answers on the lined pages in the separate Answer Sheets for Writing. There is no need to make a "fair copy" of a response and copying what has been written previously is a poor use of time. Should you need to make a revision to what you have written, simply cross out the relevant words. The examiners, subsequently, will ignore these words. This will not have a detrimental effect on your overall score.
10 Practice writing the compositions within the word limit so that you are well versed in what is required. It is wasteful to spend time counting words and this often leads to poor alterations that erode the overall quality of your essay.
11 Check your work for spelling, grammar and errors in punctuation. These mistakes are not penalised specifically but these mistakes can preclude communication and/or have an adverse effect on the reader.
12 American and other variations of the English spelling and usage are acceptable.
13 Practice writing your essays without a dictionary, for they are not permitted in the examination room.

PAPER 3 - Listening

General description
Content: The paper contains four parts. Each part contains a recorded text or texts and corresponding comprehension tasks. Each part is heard twice.
Time Allotted: Approximately 40 minutes
Number of Parts: 4
Number of Questions: 30
Task Types: Multiple choice, sentence completion and multiple matching.
Text Types: *Monologues*: lectures, talks, speeches, anecdotes, radio broadcasts, etc.
Interacting speakers: interviews, radio broadcasts, discussions, conversations, etc.
Scoring: Each correct answer receives 1 mark.

Part 1: Multiple choice

Task Type: The focus is on identifying speaker feeling, attitude, opinion, purpose, agreement between speakers, gist and detail.
Format: Three short, unrelated extracts of approximately 30 seconds each, from a series of either monologues or exchanges between interacting speakers. There are two multiple choice question per extract, each with three options.
Number of Questions: 6

Part 2: Sentence completion

Task Type: The focus is on identifying detail, specific information and stated opinion.
Format: A monologue lasting approximately 3 minutes. Candidates are required to complete the sentences with information heard on the recording.
Number of Questions: 8

Part 3: Multiple choice

Task Type: The focus is on identifying opinion, attitude, detail, gist, main idea and specific information.
Format: An interview or an exchange between two speakers lasting 3–4 minutes. There are six 4-option multiple-choice questions.
Number of Questions: 6

Part 4: Multiple matching

Task: The focus is on identifying attitude, opinion, gist, purpose, feeling, main points and detail.
Format: Five short, related monologues of approximately 30 seconds each. There are two tasks with five questions each, which require the selection of the correct option from a list of eight.
Number of Questions: 10

Paper 3 - Listening

Tips for Listening

1 The instructions for each task are provided on the question paper and are also heard on the audio recording, including details about the speakers, the topic and the context of the passage. Before you listen to each passage, you will have time to scan through and reflect on the questions. The length of the preparation time is provided on the tape. Candidates should use this time to familiarise themselves with the task and start to develop predictions about what they are likely to encounter on the recording.
2 A variety of voices, accents and styles of delivery will he hard in each Listening exam to underscore various contexts expressed in the audio.
3 Embark upon daily learning practices where you listen to English language audio on the Internet or television, for example. Expose yourself to a range of English styles, including speakers of various ages and backgrounds as well as different contexts like lectures, radio programmes, sporting events etc.
4 In longer texts, remember that the questions are asked in the same order as the information in the recording reflecting the structure of the text. Identify discourse markers, interview questions and other textual features that construct the text and are often reflected in the organization of the passage.
5 Write you answers clearly in CAPITAL LETTERS in the sentence-completion tasks.
6 Be sure to provide responses to all of the questions, as you will not lose any points for incorrect answers and you may actually score more than you believe.

The Four Parts of the Listening Paper

Listening Part 1: Multiple Choice

This part of the exam evaluates you ability to listen to short dialogues and demonstrate comprehension of detail, gist, function, course of action as well as the speakers' feelings, attitudes and opinions.

Part 1 includes three unrelated short texts. They are approximately 1 minute in length and feature two or more speakers. The content is taken from a variety of real-life contexts and, therefore, expect a range of topics, voice and style of delivery.

There are two 3-option multiple-choice questions on each text.

Tips for Listening Part 1

1 Listen to the entire text once before selecting your response and never assume you have heard the right answer. The two questions have a different focus and thus the information relevant to the answers may originate from different parts of the audio recording.

2 Avoid selecting a response simply because it features words and phrases heard on the recording. Read through each question before listening to the audio and reflect upon what you are being asked to gather, including the purpose of the talk, the gist of the argument or the speaker's viewpoint on the matter.

3 Most of the questions will require you to draw inferences from what you hear. As a result, mark one answer to each question at the end of the first listening, even if you're uncertain if it is correct. Use the second listening to confirm whether your choice is correct.

Listening Part 2: Sentence Completion

This section of the exam evaluates your ability to follow the main points of a passage and obtain relevant information and opinions. This part features a monologue of roughly three minutes in the form of a talk, lecture or broadcast. The content is aimed at a general audience and is presented in accessible style.

A series of eight independent clauses expresses the main ideas from the passage whereby you will be asked to demonstrate your comprehension by completing gaps in these sentences. There is one blank per sentence, which is completed by a single word or short phrase from the listening text. The task centers on the retrieval of specific information and opinions expressed from the text. The questions follow the order of information conveyed in the text.

Correct spelling, whether it be British or US English, is required at this level.

Tips for Listening Part 2

1 The task information and the set of notes on the page provide you with a good idea of what you are about to hear, thus make good use of your preparation time. Review the information in the instructions and visualise the speaker and the situation, trying to predict what kind of information will be expressed and the type of language used.

2 Read through the set of sentences and think about what type of information is missing. Most questions focus on strong pieces of information like proper names and will be single words of very short noun groups where no more than three words are required.

3 Endeavour to write long answers without writing information that is already on the page. It is not advisable to simply para phrase the information you hear on the audio sample.

4 For the sentence completion tasks, use the actual words you hear on the audio without concerning yourself too much with the grammar. Check to be sure you have heard the correct form of the word. If you do not hear clearly whether a word is singular or plural, look at the rest of the sentence to see what is required.

Listening Part 3: Multiple Choice

This section of the exam evaluates your ability to understand longer interviews and discussions as well as demonstrate your aptitude at comprehending the speakers' attitudes and opinions.
Part 3 includes interviews and discussions involving two or more speakers. The text is approximately 3-4 minutes long and typically takes the form of a broadcast discussion or interview for a general audience.
A set of six four-option multiple choice questions examine the attitude and viewpoints of the speakers. These questions focus on gist understanding, purpose or function and follow the order of the information presented in the text.

Tips for Listening Part 3

1 As this is the longest part of the Listening exam, give yourself plenty of time to comprehend the more expansive interviews and discussions. Keep track of the line of development in these texts and recognise when the conversation has transitioned from one point to another.
2 For the multiple-choice tasks, focus on the question stems instead of the options in your preparation time, so that you can listen for the answer in the text and then match it to the closest option.
3 This section of the test employs language that paraphrases and expresses ideas from the text. As these often focus on the viewpoints and outlooks of the speakers, you need to have a strong command of the meaning and use of the type of language used to communicate these ideas concisely. Make note especially of reporting verbs like admits or resents; adjectives and adverbs that express feelings, such as disappointed or unexpected as well as words used to convey opinions like denies or suggests.

Listening Part 4: Multiple Matching

This section tests your skill at identifying the gist of several short texts as well as recognizing the attitude, viewpoint and main points.
Part 4 consists of a series of five short monologues on a subject matter. The passage is 3-4 minutes in length with each monologue lasting approximately 30 seconds. The monologues represent spontaneous speech, delivered in an informal spoken style by speakers with a variety of backgrounds and voices. There are two parallel multiple-matching tasks, each with a different focus. In each case, the correct answer must be selected from the eight options.
The set of monologues is heard twice, but candidates may approach the tasks in either order. Each focuses on a different element of gist understanding like interpreting context, viewpoints, attitudes, speaker purpose or identifying main points.

Tips for Listening Part 4

1 Remember the five speakers will be linked thematically. You will hear the set of passages once and then the entire series is repeated.
2 Reflect on the themes of the text as well as the ideas and attitudes you expect to hear in connection with the topic in question.
3 Be certain to listen for gist meaning rather than detail in these passages. Though you may not be able to understand every single word, you should be able to fathom the speaker's main idea, attitude or opinion.
4 Answer both tasks and note that you will only hear the series of monologues twice. It is up to your judgment as to how you approach the tasks, but you may find it useful to attempt one item on each listening or by approaching both tasks at the same time answering the most accessible questions on the first listening and the more difficult questions when the audio repeats.

Paper 4 - Speaking

General description
Content: The Speaking test contains four parts.
Time Allotted: 15 minutes
Number of Parts: 4
Interaction Pattern: The exam features a paired format consisting of two examiners and two candidates. This offers you the opportunity to demonstrate in a controlled by amicable setting your spoken language skills. One of the examiners, the interlocutor, conducts the test and provides a global assessment of your and the other candidate's performance. The other, the assessor does not take any part in the interaction but focuses solely on listening to, and making an assessment of, your and the other candidate's proficiency.
Task Types: Short exchanges with the interlocutor and with the other candidate; a 1-minute individual 'long turn'; a collaborative task involving the two candidates; a discussion.
Scoring: Candidates are assessed on their performance throughout.

Part 1

Task Type and Format: A conversation between the interlocutor and each candidate (spoken questions).
Focus: general interactional and social language
Timing: 2 minutes

Part 2

Type and Format: An individual 'long turn' by each candidate, with a response from the second candidate. In turn, the candidates are given a pair of photographs to talk about.
Focus: organising a larger unit of discourse, comparing, describing and expressing opinions
Timing: A 1-minute 'long turn' for each candidate, plus a 30-second response from the second candidate. The total time for Part 2 is 4 minutes.

Part 3

Task Type and Format: A two-way conversation between the candidates. The candidates are given spoken instructions with written stimuli, which are used in discussion and decision-making tasks.
Focus: sustaining an interaction, exchanging ideas, expressing and justifying opinions, agreeing and/or disagreeing, suggesting, speculating, evaluating, reaching a decision through negotiation, etc.
Timing: A 2-minute discussion followed by a 1-minute decision-making task. The total time for Part 3 is 4 minutes.

Part 4

Task Type and Format: A discussion on topics related to the collaborative task (spoken questions).
Focus: expressing and justifying opinions, agreeing and/or disagreeing and speculating
Timing: 5 minutes

Tips for Paper 4 - Speaking

1 It is imperative that you practice with someone in group or pair activities, thereby helping you to interface convincingly by starting conversations and responding suitably.
2 Listen closely to the interlocutor's questions and instructions and make use of the written prompts on the visuals page to remind yourself what you have to accomplish in the task.
3 React to the visuals you are given that accompany the tasks, while relating them to the test items rather than merely describing them.
4 Familiarise yourself with the examination format and be conscious of what is expected from you in each part. You should be prepared with the right kind of language for each section of the test, whereby you are providing personal information, exchanging opinions speculating, agreeing or disagreeing politely and/or negotiating.
5 Remember to speak clearly so that the interlocutor and examiner can hear you.
6 Refrain from pausing too long before you speak. A short pause is acceptable to organise your thoughts, though anything longer will impede your ability to express a sound response. Paraphrase if you cannot remember a word or phrase and try to extend your answers rather than give merely one-word responses.
7 Organise a "mock" test with someone who has a strong command of English to simulate the exam environment.
8 Feel free to ask the interlocutor to repeat the answers or questions if you need clarification.

Speaking Part 1: Interview

This section of the test evaluates your ability to employ social and interactional language.
Part 1 provides you with the opportunity to demonstrate your skill at using general social and interactional language and talk about yourself and your interests, career plans etc. The interlocutor asks you and the other candidate for basic information about yourself and then expands the scope of the discussion by asking questions about leisure activities, travel, holiday experiences etc. You are not asked to actively speak with the other candidate at this section of the exam. This merely serves as a warm-up to the more involved parts of the speaking exam to follow in the latter sections.

Tips for Speaking - Part 1

1 Respond promptly to the interlocutor with complete answers that are extemporaneous in nature. Avoid rehearsed speeches as they are easily spotted and may be inappropriate based on the context.
2 Learn to 'think on your feet' and provide answers to questions quickly even if you have little practice with a particular subject matter.
3 Make use of a range of tenses, structures and rich vocabulary during this part of the exam. This will foster a positive impression and provide you with the confidence to perform at a high level during the other parts of the exam.

Speaking Part 2: Long Turn

This section evaluates your ability to develop an extended response. Part 2 provides you with the opportunity to speak for one minute without interruption. Each candidate is presented with a set of pictures and asked to comment on each and react to them. A prompt is given to you in the form of a direct question written above the pictures. You are asked to compare and contrast, speculate and express viewpoints about two of the three pictures shown.
You will have the opportunity to demonstrate your ability to organise your thoughts and ideas. In addition, you will be asked to comment on your fellow candidate's response for approximately 30 seconds.

Note you will be asked to speculate or expound on the visual in some manner never merely to describe it. For example:
a. "This image shows two people having dinner together. They are sharing a bottle of wine and eating steak." does not feature a speculative element like
b. "These two men are dressed in suits and seem to be having some type of business dinner or meeting. Perhaps, they are discussing a new venture or deal. Perhaps, they are even celebrating a recent success or the signing of a new client or employee. They may be travelling on business and are having an evening out. One of the persons might be entertaining the other as part of a business courtesy."

Tips for Speaking - Part 2

1 Practise speaking for extended periods of time so that you become familiar with speaking for one minute uninterrupted. Sometimes candidates finish their long turn too soon, for they are unprepared for how long one minute takes.
2 Collect pictures from various forms of media and group them into sets and speculate on what might you be asked to talk about in a Part 2 task in the exam.
3 Avoid 'closure' cues such as "That's it." or "I'm done." Speak until the interlocutor says, "Thank you." With this approach, you will maximise the time available for each 1-minute long turn.
4 Spend time organising your ideas coherently. Become familiar with useful phrases that link ideas and compare images. Develop your own list of appropriate phrases during your preparation providing you with a broad range of language and structures to draw on when necessary.

Speaking Part 3: Collaborative Task

This section of the exam evaluates your ability to engage in a discussion and develop a negotiated decision.
You will be provided with oral instructions and written prompts to form the foundation for the two tasks. You are required to discuss some or even all of the prompts related to a question, expressing and justifying opinions as well as speculating. Then, you will be asked another question which you will be asked to engage your fellow candidate in working towards a decision through negotiation.
The first task will be introduced with the words: "Here are some... and a question about them". The document with the written prompts and the central question will then be placed in front of you and the other candidate. You will be given 15 seconds to read the question and the prompts, which will be made explicit with the words: "You now have some time to look at the task."
This part of the exam enables you to demonstrate your range with the language and your skill at soliciting opinions and ideas for your partner. You are expected to create an interactive dynamic with your fellow candidate initiating ideas and responding accordingly.
Following this component, you are then provided with another task whereby you must make a decision. You will be prompted with the following words: "Now you have a minute to decide...". The choice will be related to the prompts you have been discussing. You will be evaluated on your ability to employ language in the spirit of negotiation and collaboration, though you will not be penalised if you fail to reach a negotiated consensus with your colleague. In other words, there is no right or wrong answer to the task.

Tips for Speaking - Part 3

1. Employ conversation fillers like "Well" or "Let me see" to give yourself some more time to gather your thoughts. Of course, refrain from overusing these expressions as it will limit your range of language. Adopt a strategy of engaging your fellow candidate in the talk, though avoid relying on him or her too much.
2. Maintain a notebook of phrases that facilitate your ability to interject your thoughts politely or manners of soliciting a response from the other candidate. Develop a range of expressions to seem natural and to avoid repetition.
3. Avoid the tendency to rush through the prompts in the discussion. It is more effective to deal with several of them in depth rather than trying to explore all of them superficially.
4. Focus on formulating your own original thoughts on the visual stimuli provided. Merely agreeing or echoing what your fellow candidate says will not facilitate your ability to demonstrate your command of the language.
5. Simulate the exam environment with a friend or colleague to practise expressing your opinion, interjecting your thoughts and soliciting a response from another person. This will enable you to become more comfortable with the exam format.

Speaking Part 4: Discussion

This section of the exam evaluates your skill at engaging in a conversation based on the content raised in the collaborative task in Part 3. For Part 4, the interlocutor will moderate the discussion by asking questions that expand upon the topics explored in Part 3. The questions may well focus on more abstract issues as the discussion develops.
This component of the exam furnishes you with an opportunity to demonstrate your skill at exchanging ideas, supporting opinions, agreeing and disagreeing as well as show your ability to speak for subject matters with greater depth and nuance.

Tips for Speaking - Part 4

1. When practising Part 3, try to predict what types of questions you may encounter in Part 4. Try this with a friend or classmate and exchange feedback and ideas to enrich your depth of knowledge.
2. Note you are not being evaluated on your ideas, rather simply your ability to express them.
3. Remember to not interrupt your fellow candidate or trying to monopolise the discussion.
4. Train yourself to respond quickly to the questions you are asked by using expressions that enable you to play for time such as: "Well that's something I've never considered, though, I'd have to say...".
5. Refine your skills over time under simulated test conditions, especially in terms of time requirements. In addition, the impression you make at the end of the exam is equally important as the one you make at the beginning.

Cambridge English: Advanced - CAE

10 PRACTICE TESTS

Test 1

Part 1

For questions 1-8, read the text below and decide which answer (**A**,**B**,**C** or **D**) best fits each gap. There is an example at the beginning (0).

Example:

0 **A** make **B** take **C** do **D** have

0	A	B	C	D
		▬		

Long hours and health don't mix

Women are much healthier when they (0) .... it easy, (1) .... a new survey. Those who work long hours are more likely than men to indulge in unhealthy behaviour such as eating snacks, smoking and drinking caffeine. (Long hours have no such (2) .... on men.) One positive benefit of long hours for both sexes, however, is that alcohol (3) .... is reduced.

The study, funded by the Economic and Social Research Council, is part of a wider study by psychologists from the University of Leeds, into the effects of stress on eating. 'Stress causes people to (4) .... for unhealthy high-fat and high-sugar snacks in preference to healthier food choices,' says researcher Dr Daryl O'Connor of the University of Leeds. 'People under stress eat less than usual in their main meals, including their vegetable (5) ...., but shift their preference to high-fat, high-sugar snacks instead.

'Our (6)............ are disturbing in that they show stress produces harmful changes in diet and leads to unhealthy eating behaviour,' continues Dr O'Connor. 'An overwhelming (7) .... of evidence shows the importance of maintaining a balanced diet in (8) .... of reducing the risk of cancer and cardiovascular diseases - and that means eating a low-fat diet and five portions of fruit and vegetables a day.

	A	B	C	D
1	**A** betrays	**B** sustains	**C** reveals	**D** conceals
2	**A** contact	**B** clash	**C** conflict	**D** impact
3	**A** beverage	**B** consumption	**C** expenditure	**D** acceptance
4	**A** choose	**B** select	**C** design	**D** opt
5	**A** intake	**B** influx	**C** emission	**D** immersion
6	**A** instructions	**B** rulings	**C** findings	**D** institutions
7	**A** lump	**B** body	**C** sack	**D** packet
8	**A** moments	**B** sessions	**C** terms	**D** senses

Part 2

For questions 9-16, read the text below and think of the word which best fits each gap. Use only one word in each gap. There is an example at the beginning (0).
Write your answers in **CAPITAL LETTERS**.

Example:

0	EVER

The breath of life

Anyone who has (0) .... been to a yoga or meditation class will know the enormous benefits of something as simple and natural as breathing. Inhale slowly and steadily, and you can relax your entire body. Stop and focus on the flow of (9) .... breath you take in and out, and you can quieten and focus your mind. In (10) ...., positive breathing will help you feel calmer, bring down your blood pressure and increase your mental alertness and energy levels.

Yet, breathing is so instinctive that most of the time we're hardly even aware of it. Of course, that's (11) .... why it's easy to develop bad habits and why many of us don't do it as well as we (12) .... But with a little practice, (13) .... it right can bring instant health benefits. These include feeling more relaxed and being more mentally alert. You may also find that there's an improvement in (14) .... physical symptoms, such as bloating and stomach pains, dizziness, headaches, pins and needles and low energy.

Learning to breathe correctly can dramatically improve your wellbeing and quality of life. Most people think that poor breathing means that you don't get enough oxygen, but it's (15) .... the carbon dioxide you're missing out (16) ....

Part 3

For questions **17-24**, read the text below. Use the word given in capitals at the end of some of the lines to form a word that fits in the gap **in the same line.** There is an example at the beginning **(0)**.
Write your answers in **CAPITAL LETTERS**.

Example:

0	SIGNIFICANTLY

The cooling oceans

The upper layers of Earth's oceans have cooled **(0)** .... over the past two years, even though	**SIGNIFY**
the planet as a whole is warming up. While this may just be part of the natural **(17)** variety	**VARY**
of oceans, climatologists are still confounded by the massive unaccountable loss of heat.	
Scientists have been **(18)** increasing .... concerned by rising sea temperatures over	**INCREASE**
the last 50 years but these new **(19)** finded .... tell a different story.	**FIND**
Generally speaking, the **(20)** absorvation .... of heat by the oceans reduces atmospheric warming.	**ABSORB**
Now **(21)** measures .... taken by the National Oceanic and Atmospheric Administration have put	**MEASURE**
a wrinkle in the trend. The researchers used data from 3000 floating buoys which monitor	
the oceans **(22)**	**WORLD**
They found that the oceans dropped in temperature by an **(23)** .... 0.02 degrees	**BELIEVE**
centigrade between 2011 and 2013.	
Now, that may not seem like much, but trying to account for the missing energy is proving	
to be enormously **(24)** problem .... It is possible that volcanic eruptions are one main cause	**PROBLEM**
of the phenomenon, but no firm answers have yet been provided.	

Part 4

For questions **25-30**, complete the second sentence so that it has a similar meaning to the first sentence, using the word given. **Do not change the word given**. You must use between **three** and **six** words, including the word given. Here is an example **(0)**.

Example: 0 George should have worked harder if he wanted to pass the exam. **succeeded**
Had George worked harder, ... passing the exam.

Write the missing words **IN CAPITAL LETTERS.**

0	HE WOULD HAVE SUCCEEDED IN

25 Paul tends to play his music loudly when he's not feeling very happy. **habit**
Paul is .... his music loudly when he is not feeling very happy.

26 They could easily win the game. **chance**
They .... the game.

27 Of course I did not agree to lend them the money. **saying**
It .... not agree to lend them the money.

28 Did anything about his behaviour seem unusual to you? **strike**
Did anything about his behaviour .... unusual?

29 I can barely cook a meal for myself, so I certainly couldn't cook for eight people. **alone**
I would struggle .... for eight people.

30 The reporter said that the blast was so forceful that the car was blown right across the street. **such**
According to the reporter,.. the blast, that the car was blown right across the street.

Part 5

You are going to read a magazine article about identity theft. For questions 31-36, choose the answer **(A, B, C or D)** which you think fits best according to the text.

Identity fraud - the new hot crime

Identity theft - cases where thieves steal your personal data to rip through your bank or credit card accounts - is a fast-growing crime. Home office statistics estimate a £1.7bn loss over the past 12 months, which, in cash terms, is far ahead of mugging. In the US, where the crime is even more rampant, figures point to a staggering $50bn (about £28bn) a year.

The government believes that there are at least 100,000 identity theft victims every year. Others put the figure significantly higher, as some people may not even know their accounts have been raided: identity thieves often stop short of clearing out an account to keep their crime profile low. Identity theft flourishes today because many financial transactions are not face to face. Once criminals get hold of data such as your bank account number and address, they can go on a spending spree. Terrifyingly, they do not need all your details; just a few will do.

'It's easy,' says Glen Hastings, a reformed identity thief and author of Identity Theft, Inc. 'The only prerequisite is the ability to read and write. It certainly helps to be computer literate, but it's far from essential. I stole several hundred identities in my career.' Hastings' modus operandi was to discover individuals with excellent credit records, the very people banks adore. By impersonating these pillars of financial rectitude, he borrowed large amounts in their name - money that he never, of course, repaid. Even your home could be at risk. Last year, a schoolteacher, who was renting out his unmortgaged Brighton home while he was working in the Far East, was the victim of an audacious identity fraud. A new 'tenant' paid six months' rent in advance but was never to spend a night there, instead, assuming the teacher's identity using documents and items received through the post at the house. The fraudster managed to remortgage the property for £210,000, which he then took out of the country. It took the unfortunate schoolteacher months of trauma to get his house back. The mortgage company, meanwhile, has never seen a penny of its money back.

In the US, one identity victim had her details so closely associated with a $50,000 criminal spending spree that a warrant was put out in her name. The real criminal - who was also a drug dealer - never stopped using the victim's name, even when caught and imprisoned, which led to further problems.

Hastings states that he only stole from 'banks, casinos, credit card companies, airlines and big stores - never the little guy.' But we all pay for that, and in any case, most ID thieves are not so selective. And even if you get your money back - most banks and credit card companies treat victims sympathetically - you will still have weeks of worry when you may be unable to access your money and may have to prove that you did not spend £10,000 on internet poker.

As an actor, Carolyn Tomkinson is used to taking other people's identities. But when someone impersonated her and cleaned out her Nationwide account, she knew it wasn't play-acting. 'When I found out, I burst into tears,' she says. 'It was all my money gone overnight. Colleagues clubbed together and lent some cash, but it was awful - I felt stunned, upset and violated.' Carolyn had taken £20 from a cash machine the night before. Somehow - probably with concealed gadgetry to read her PIN and clone the card - thieves took £570 from other machines in London, showing a typical fraud pattern in the way they tested her daily limit, then hit her again just after midnight.

'I discovered it the next day when I wanted to take out a further £20. The machine said I had no further credit available. I then discovered what had happened from the mini-statement. I rang Nationwide, who said they would cancel my card and asked me to report it to the police. The building society was very sympathetic, but said it could take up to six weeks before I got my money back. In the event, it only took a week. 'I've always been very careful, but now I try to avoid ATMs by getting cashback at the supermarket checkout.'

Architectural librarian Claudia Mernick has been 'cloned' three times. The third attack was on her credit card. 'I'd been out buying food one lunchtime. Almost as soon as I got home, the credit card company called me to see how I could have used my card in two places that were far from each other, at the same time. It was an obvious fraud. I was really impressed with their speed. My credit card was cancelled and it took a week or so before I had a new one. But I would like to know what happened and how to avoid it. The thieves didn't cost me a lot of money but a lot of hassle.'

31. What is said about identity theft in the first two paragraphs?

A. It has caused many criminals to stop mugging people.
B. Compared to the US, there is not a serious problem in Britain.
C. It can be done so discreetly that the victim is unaware of the crime.
D. If an account is not emptied, the victim will probably never realise that they have lost money.

32. According to Glen Hastings

A. his computer skills made him exceptionally good as an identity thief.
B. banks are only willing to lend money to people who already have a lot of money.
C. he had always intended to repay the money he borrowed.
D. almost anyone is capable of identity theft.

33. What did the tenant who rented a house from a schoolteacher do?

A. He didn't pay the rent that he'd promised to pay in advance.
B. He used the house as security to borrow a large amount of money.
C. He sold the house to another individual and then fled the country.
D. He pretended to be the schoolteacher and spent all the money in his account.

34. What was the immediate effect of identity theft on Carolyn Tomkinson?

A. She was shocked.
B. She was angry.
C. She felt physically ill.
D. She pretended to be more upset than she actually was.

35. What was the situation with Carolyn Tomkinson?

A. Her cash card had been stolen.
B. The thieves had used her card too many times on the same day.
C. The building society managed to stop her card before the thieves could empty her account.
D. Her card had been copied.

36. Claudia Mernick's experience

A. shows that the finance company is usually to blame.
B. proves that vigilance by the credit card company is crucial when it comes to identity fraud.
C. illustrates that only the finance company can detect when a card is being used in a fraudulent way.
D. proves that finance companies solve identity fraud cases very quickly.

Part 6

You are going to read four reviews of an art exhibition. For questions 37-40, choose from reviews A-D. The reviews may be chosen more than once.

Matisse Retrospective

Four critics comment on an exhibition of the artist Henri Matisse

A

Midway through the museum's retrospective on Matisse, I bumped into the painter Alex Katz. He looked at me, agog, and said, "I thought I was going to faint when I saw these paintings." He gestured at two Matisse still life works from the mid 1940s. Already in a stunned state of my own, I followed his lead and gulped at the revolutionary pictorial power and radical colour radiating off these two power-houses, one dominated by a celestial red and an arrangement on a table. In the foreground, were either a dog and cat chasing each other, or a pair of animal-skin rugs. Then I looked at the painting next to it, which also showed Matisse's inherent ability to depict form and colour, with stupendous results. I saw the same still life depicted on the same table with the same vase, goblet, and fruit. But this version was totally different. Where the dog and cat were, there's an ultra flat still life within the still life. It's so categorically compressed that it looks less than two-dimensional; maybe, one-half-dimensional. I thought I, like Katz, might pass out.

B

The great French modernist painter Henri Matisse was not a joiner. In the early 20th century, he refused to join any of the popular art movements of the time. He communed with artists of the distant or not-so-distant past, from Giotto to Cezanne, and periodically brushed shoulders with Cubism and the work of his chief rival, Pablo Picasso, from Spain. But his main desire was, as he stated, to "push further and deeper into true painting". His evolution, a result of studied attempts to master his art, is the subject of the exhibition at the museum and one of the most thrillingly instructive shows about this painter, or painting in general, that you may ever see. As ravishing as it is succinct, it skims across this French master's long, productive career with a mere 49 paintings, but nearly all are stellar if not pivotal works.

C

The exhibition at the museum should dispel any doubts about how hard this father of modern art laboured to create the colourful and seemingly insouciant paintings and works on paper that have become so well-known and loved. As the wall texts in the show point out, "Painting did not, and never had, come easily to Matisse. Throughout his career, he constantly hesitated, questioned, repainted and re-evaluated his work." Today it seems clearer than ever that Matisse was, first and foremost, a supreme colourist. His use of pinks and purples, clarets, oranges and crimsons, is more surprising and electric, than any other European's of that generation. Even when you compare him to that other 20th-century giant Picasso, Matisse wins the colour wars hands down (even Picasso admitted it, once). Far from the intuitive, child-like genius that some have imagined him to be, Matisse was someone who turned himself into a major artist through years of prodigious effort. In that respect, he's no different from the vast majority of artists throughout history.

D

Ravishing colours, flowing lines, sinuous bodies: Henri Matisse made it all look effortless. But it wasn't. Throughout his career Matisse wrestled with the fundamentals of painting; he revisited the same subjects over and over, and he often used completed canvases as models for later ones. Extraordinary insights into his process of creation are laid bare in the eye-opening new exhibition at the museum. The nearly 50 paintings on display reveal how Matisse used older works to generate new ideas. Sometimes the differences are subtle, and sometimes the works are shockingly unalike. But Matisse was using repeated images to push his art further. Later in his career, Matisse hired a photographer to capture his work in the studio. He used photographs of his own paintings to judge whether he was making progress, or whether he'd gone off track. Ultimately, the show reveals Matisse as an artist who made the act of painting into something as important, and as inspiring, as his finished works.

Which reviewer

unlike the other three reviewers, makes no reference to Matisse's use of colour in his work?	37	
disagrees with the other three reviewers, in saying that Matisse's ability was innate?	38	
explores some of the techniques Matisse used in his artistic process?	39	
makes comparisons between Matisse and a Spanish artist like reviewer B?	40	

Part 7

You are going to read an extract from a magazine article. Choose from the paragraphs **A-G** the one which fits each gap (41-46). There is one extra paragraph which you do not need to use.

Bridge under troubled water

Sitting at the crossroads of Europe and Asia, the ancient city of Istanbul has seen thousands of years of trade, battles and invasions. Now it is the scene of one of the most audacious engineering projects in the world.

41 ____________

Istanbul is divided by the Bosporus strait that connects the Black Sea to the north of the city with the Sea of Marmara to the south. Part of the city lies in Europe, on the western side of the strait, while the rest is in Asia.

42 ____________

Recently, a mix of technical expertise, foreign investment and national pride finally came together to make the sultan's dream a reality. This time the plan is not so much to unite an empire as to deliver modern Turks from traffic hell.

43 ____________

The plan is first to improve the existing railways on both sides of the strait and then extend them to the coast via tunnels bored through the bedrock. The centre section, under the Bosporus, will be a 1.4-kilometre tube made up of several shorter sections that will be built on land, floated into position and sunk into place. End to end, the tunnel will be 12 kilometres long.

44 ____________

The result is what geologists refer to as a right-lateral strike-slip fault, similar in size and type to the San Andreas fault in California. The NAF runs for 1600 kilometres across northern Turkey, and the abutting plates move about 2 to 3 centimetres relative to each other every year.

45 ____________

Almost every quake along the NAF in the past 100 years seems to have set up a larger one, to the west. The process appears cyclic: quakes march along the fault in sequence until stress falls below a certain threshold, and then start again after a period of quiet.

In 1997, geologists studying the most recent cycle predicted that the next shock would hit near the port city of Izmit, 80 kilometres east of Istanbul. Sure enough, a major quake of magnitude 7.4 struck close to Izmit in August 1999, followed by another in Duzce in December, together killing over 18,000 people and causing $10 to $25 billion of damage.

46 ____________

Recent estimates by the US Geological Survey, the University of Tokyo and Istanbul Technical University estimate that the probability of a strong quake hitting Istanbul is up to 44 per cent in the next decade and as much as 77 per cent in the next 30 years. A major earthquake and accompanying tsunami are considered inevitable within a generation.

A Earthquakes along the NAF are common. In the past seven decades, Turkey has endured seven earthquakes of magnitude 7.0 or greater. While some earthquakes release the stress that has built up on a fault, seismologists have come to realise that others simply shift it along the fault, leaving it even more prone to slip.

B Two road bridges cross the strait and there are plans for a third, but ever since the Ottoman sultan Abdul Mecit suggested it in 1860, city leaders have dreamed of building a tunnel to link the two halves of the city.

C Seismologists agree that the most recent quakes on the NAF have shifted the stress steadily closer to Istanbul. Now the question isn't if a major earthquake will strike the city, but when.

D Today, crossing the Bosporus means either a 3-hour trip by rail and ferry, or braving grid lock in narrow, 2000-year-old streets and the two overcrowded road bridges. The Marmaray project, which takes its name from the Sea of Marmara and "ray", the Turkish word for rail, aims to ease the strain by replacing car traffic with an upgraded rail service that will whisk commuters between Europe and Asia.

E The crucial factor that lets the tunnels withstand quakes of this magnitude is the fact that both are "immersed tubes". In this design, engineers dig a channel into the seabed and float the fabricated sections into position above it before sinking them and covering them over. The Marmaray tunnel will use a similar approach.

F The Marmaray Rail Tube Tunnel, the first stage of which opened on October 29th, 2013, will not only be the deepest underwater tunnel ever constructed. It will also pass within 16 kilometres of one of the most active geological faults in the world. A major earthquake is not only expected, but also imminent. No wonder the Turkish government is calling it the project of the century.

G It might sound straightforward, but the project engineers face a major geological hurdle. Twenty kilometres south of Istanbul lies the North Anatolian Fault (NAF), where the Anatolian plate that underlies Turkey, Greece and the north Aegean is being squeezed to the south and south-west by the surrounding Arabian, Eurasia and African plates.

Part 8

You are going to read some reviews for festivals in the UK. For questions 47-56, choose from the reviews (**A-F**). The reviews may be chosen more than once.

In which review is the following mentioned?

A cheap way to learn how to do an activity.	47
An event opened by young people.	48
Art reflecting life.	49
Watching a film in the fresh air.	50
Watching professionals fighting.	51
The chance to make a long-term investment.	52
Someone who did quite well in a competition.	53
Spending time with contemporary literary celebrities.	54
Music in a religious building.	55
People pretending to be dolls.	56

UK Festivals

A Brighton

The Brighton festival runs from 1st-23rd May this year, and some 300,000 visitors are expected. More than 700 dance, theatre, music, art and literature events will take place throughout the city, ranging from outdoor events in the Lanes and by the seafront, to theatre and dance in the Dome auditorium. The festival kicks off on May Day in Sydney Street with the "Children's Classics" parade of 4,000 children; they'll be dressed as characters from the books of authors such as one-time Brighton resident Lewis Carroll. Other events include exhibitions and street performances. There will be a special exhibition of work by recent graduates of the University of Brighton Fine Art Department. All the work will be for sale so it's a good chance to pick up a potential masterpiece.

B Norfolk and Norwich

This year's offerings combine tradition with modern events such as a comedy evening. To help warm up for the festival, which runs from May 5th to the 23rd, a free street festival will take place on 24th April, with human mannequin window displays at Jarrod's department store, acrobatic skateboarders and life-size garden gnomes. There will also be a beer festival with over 100 real ales and wine tasting offering a selection of British wines. For those people who are more adventurous there will be the opportunity to have a ride in a hot air balloon, weather permitting. There will also be a book exhibition in the park and special storytelling afternoons for children by some of Britain's leading authors. Or your child can borrow a book and read for himself or herself.

C Preston

Promoting its status as one of England's newest cities, Preston's International City Festival takes place 11th-20th June. The festival will have an international flavour because this year the Preston Caribbean Festival will be incorporated into the proceedings with a lively carnival and Preston's Asian community will stage dance, art and music events. The festival will have a gastronomic theme, with demonstrations from some of Europe's top chefs and cookery workshops given by the city's Indian and Chinese communities. There will also be a "proms in the park", an open-air cinema in Avenham Park and a street theatre.

D Liverpool

The Mersey River Festival is the largest maritime event in England this year and will take place around Albert Dock and Pier Head on 18th-21st June. Visiting tall ships will be open to the public. Blue Badge guides will lead tours around Liverpool landmarks such as the Cunard building, and voices will unite for the International Sea Shanty festival.

Get into the festival spirit by trying out kayaking, water polo and a variety of other water sports for free at the Watersports Centre. If you sign up for a course of watersports lessons which start after the festival, you will receive a 50% discount. There will also be unarmed combat displays by the Royal Marines to raise money for charity, a river parade, an illuminated narrow boat parade through the docks, and an historic diving exhibition.

E City of London

This year's festival, 21st June - 13th July, celebrates the 10th anniversary of democratic elections in South Africa. Events include a performance by Ladysmith Black Mambazo at St Paul's Cathedral, a varied programme of South African music at the Spitz Club and a range of free dance events in Guildhall Yard. There will also be performances of Beethoven's string quartets by the Borodin Quartet at various concert halls, as well as many other classical offerings, dance, theatre and literary events.

There will also be an exhibition of art by local youths. The images all illustrate life in the city of London and provide some interesting insights into how London is viewed by its young inhabitants.

F Exeter

The summer festival in Devon's principal city takes place 2nd-18th July. Hot tickets are likely to be the audiences with Joan Bakewell and director Ken Russell at the Northcott Theatre and a concert given by Mercury music Prize 2000 nominee Nitin Sawhney.

Theatrical offerings include hit comedy *Art*, directed by Nigel Havers at Escot House, and a world premiere of the English Chamber Theatre's production of Chekov's *Leading Lady*.

The 4th of July will also resound to a Latin beat, with dance performances from the Jaleo Flamenco Dance Company taking place around Exeter Quay. The London Community Gospel Choir, the Brodsky Quartet and the New Berlin Chamber Orchestra will also perform during the festival.

WRITING - Part 1

You **must** answer this question. Write your answer in **220-260** words in an appropriate style.

1. You have listened to a radio discussion programme about which facilities are needed most in your area. You have made the notes below:

Which facilities are needed most in your area?
- car park
- sport centre
- history museum

Some opinions expressed in the discussion:
"Young people need sports facilities."
"Car parks are only for people who own a car!"
"Museums help to educate people."

Write an essay discussing **two** of the facilities in your notes. You should explain **which facility is needed most** in your area, **giving reasons** in support of your answer.

You may, if you wish, make use of the opinions expressed in the discussion, but you should use your own words as far as possible.

WRITING - Part 2

Write an answer to **one** of the questions **2-4** in this part. Write your answer in **220-260** words in an appropriate style.

2. You have just completed a cooking course. As part of the school's research and efforts to offer superior classes, they have asked you to write an evaluation of your experience as a student.

   Your report should discuss what you learned from the class and what you thought of the teachers and their instruction methods. Mention any ways you think the class could be improved and say whether you would or would not recommend the course to a friend or relative.

   Write your **report**.

3. You see this advert in a newspaper:

   Tour guides needed
   We need a hard-working team of people to work as tour guides throughout the summer period. A good knowledge of your local area is required, as well as the ability to get on well with people. If you are at least 18 years old, write to us and tell us about your character and interests. We would also like you to say what you think is one of the highlights of your area and why.

   Write a **letter** applying for the job advertised. You do not need to include postal addresses.

4. You are the arts review writer for a magazine. Your editor has asked you to review a film. Choose a film that you have seen. Describe the plot and the characters involved. Say who the film is suitable for and why. Mention any special effects or aspects of the film that stood out in some way.
   Would you recommend the film? Why, why not?

   Write your **review.**

LISTENING - Part 1

You will hear three different extracts. For questions 1-6, choose the answer (**A**, **B** or **C**) which fits best according to what you hear. There are two questions for each extract.

Extract One

You will hear two people talking about a play they saw at the theatre.

1 What do we learn about the writer of the play?

A He died.
B He is dying.
C He nearly died.

1	

2 What do the speakers agree on?

A The writer is quite predictable.
B The writer's style has changed direction.
C The play wasn't as funny as some of the writer's earlier plays.

2	

Extract Two

You will hear part of a radio interview with a trade and commerce researcher.

3 According to Pablo Jenson

A a variety of different shops tends to boost sales.
B traders that have something in common can boost each other's sales.
C butchers are the most successful traders.

3	

4 Jenson's theory

A advertised for similar retailers to open shops in one particular area.
B works better for bakers and butchers than for other kinds of retailers.
C seems to have been proved to be credible.

4	

Extract Three

You will hear a report about holiday homes in the Mediterranean.

5 The Costa de la Cruz

A is being spoiled by developers.
B is the cheapest area of Spain in which you can buy a holiday home.
C is close to Portugal.

5	

6 According to Chris Mercer

A there is a danger that the Costa de la Cruz will lose its appeal.
B the Costa de la Cruz can be developed without the area being damaged.
C the government has put a stop to the Costa de la Cruz being developed further.

6	

LISTENING - Part 2

You will hear a representative from British Waterways called John Sampson talking about a canal network in England. For questions **7-14**, complete the sentences.

The Grand Union Canal

The canals were built despite the fact that there was no **7** ______ and very little technology.

From 1790 to 1929, there were many canals that were **8** ______ with each other but which were not uniform in size.

The new union of canals provided a **9** ______ between major industrial cities.

There are plenty of **10** ______ for a variety of wildlife on and around the canals.

Walkers can go to the nearest waterway office to get information on **11** ______ so they can start and end at the same place.

Anglers can fish in the canals and **12** ______.

If you want to go fishing, you must buy a **13** ______.

The waterways authority request that people are **14** ______ towards other canal users.

LISTENING - Part 3

You will hear part of a radio interview with the comedian, Lenny Henry. For questions **15-20**, choose the answer (**A, B, C** or **D**), which fits best according to what you hear.

15 Why did Lenny decide to do a degree?

A He was self-conscious because he didn't have one.
B Other actors persuaded him that it was a good idea.
C He needed one to further his acting career.
D He was impressed by other actors who had been to university.

16 What effect has studying for a degree had on Lenny?

A It has developed his ability to think more clearly about his work in general.
B It has made him think more seriously about his career.
C It has given him the confidence to try for more challenging acting roles.
D It causes him a lot of stress when he has to write an essay.

17 According to Lenny, how does comedy affect the way people feel?

A It hinders their appreciation of the seriousness of a situation.
B It helps them deal with disturbing images.
C It makes people more sensitive.
D It enables them to laugh at heartbreaking stories.

18 What does Lenny say about the work of Comic Relief in Africa?

A People in Africa now have new ways of raising money for themselves.
B The task they are facing is too big for them to make a real difference.
C People aren't committed enough yet to the cause.
D It should be a steady process to help the local communities.

19 What does Lenny say about his visit to Debre Zeit?

A He enjoyed working as a care worker for a while.
B He was impressed by Fanti's bravery despite his illness.
C He was moved by the way the people there handled their situation.
D He was impressed by the way Fanti praised comic Relief.

20 What does Lenny say about writing comedy?

A He hopes that he will soon be a more self-confident writer.
B He finds it really easy since starting his degree.
C He doesn't think he'll ever have the confidence to write something on his own.
D He no longer likes working with other writers.

LISTENING - Part 4

You will hear five short extracts in which people are talking about animals.
While you listen you must complete both tasks.

TASK ONE

For questions 21-25, choose from the list A-H the person who is speaking.

A	a doctor		
B	a circus trainer	Speaker 1	21
C	a retired person		
D	a zoo keeper	Speaker 2	22
E	a pet shop owner	Speaker 3	23
F	a vet		
G	a blind person	Speaker 4	24
H	a patient	Speaker 5	25

TASK TWO

For questions **26-30**, choose from the list **A-H** what each speaker is expressing.

A	anger at how people can be so rude		
B	a need for experience and total competence when doing a job	Speaker 1	26
C	the value of making a difference to the world		
D	pride at their own courage	Speaker 2	27
E	the need to train young people with technological skills	Speaker 3	28
F	surprise at someone's reluctance to deal with a problem	Speaker 4	29
G	annoyance at other people being inconsiderate	Speaker 5	30
H	reluctance to be sociable		

Test 2

Part 1

For questions 1-8, read the text below and decide which answer (A,B,C or D) best fits each gap. There is an example at the beginning (0).

Example:

0 **A** data **B** information **C** perception **D** discussion

0	A	B	C	D
	▭	▭	■	▭

Is Work Bad for you?

Popular (0) .... is that working (1) .... are now so over-regulated the only people likely to be injured at work are bosses, strangled by (2) .... tape. But beware a hidden epidemic raging in British workplaces. In this post-industrial age, when most jobs are in light industry, information technology and the service sector, we expect working life to be relatively comfortable and at the very (3) .... safe. We don't expect to be maimed, laid off for life or to work ourselves into the ground.

(4) .... again. In the UK there are still 1.6 million workplace injuries every year as well as 2.2 million cases of ill health caused by work. Some of these injuries wouldn't have been out of place in Charles Dickens' England. Last year 350 people died as a result of building site accidents, a large increase on previous years.

But some of the worst dangers are the hidden ones. 400,000 cases of asthma are caused by working conditions, (5) .... to high levels of dust or traffic pollution, and asbestos still kills over 4,000 people a year. There are no (6) .... at present requiring owners to record the (7) .... of asbestos, meaning that builders and fire-fighters have no way of anticipating the problem. However, a non-profit organisation has taken up the issue with a new database (8) .... in conjunction with the Trades Union Congress.

1	**A**	habits	**B**	plights	**C**	sites	**D**	conditions
2	**A**	red	**B**	green	**C**	black	**D**	white
3	**A**	few	**B**	least	**C**	most	**D**	furthest
4	**A**	Think	**B**	Remark	**C**	Dwell	**D**	Comment
5	**A**	detection	**B**	expression	**C**	expansion	**D**	exposure
6	**A**	methods	**B**	prosecutions	**C**	regulations	**D**	principles
7	**A**	attendance	**B**	presence	**C**	company	**D**	residence
8	**A**	launched	**B**	embarked	**C**	terminated	**D**	propelled

Part 2

For questions 9-16, read the text below and think of the word which best fits each gap. Use only one word in each gap. There is an example at the beginning (0).
Write your answers in **CAPITAL LETTERS**.

Example:

0	OF

Thousands of nurses out of work

Nearly three-quarters (0) .... newly-qualified nurses cannot find a permanent job in the Health Service, a study has found. Thousands are struggling to get a full-time post as the financial crisis in the NHS has led to job cuts and recruitment freezes. A survey from The Royal College of Nursing questioned (9) .... over 500 newly-qualified nurses and 2,200 students. Of (10) .... who had just graduated, it found that 71 per cent were still searching for a Band Five nursing job - the level at which nurses begin their career. And the majority - 86 per cent - were not confident of finding a permanent position, with more than nine out of ten blaming recruitment freezes and job cuts (11) .... their difficulties.

More than eight out of ten said they would consider retraining or looking for work in another profession if the problem continued. (12) .... it costs more than £50,000 to train each nurse, campaigners have called the situation a 'disgraceful (13) .... of taxpayers' money'. The RCN's secretary, Dr. Beverly Malone, said: "What message are we sending out to the nurses of the future if we spend tens of thousands of pounds training them, only to see them without jobs (14) .... at the beginning of their careers? The period straight after qualification is the single most important time in a nurse's career. (15) .... we welcome them into the profession, we risk losing them forever. Nurses are encouraged to train by this government, (16) .... ministers have let the NHS deteriorate to such a point that they (nurses) are unable to find jobs."

Part 3

For questions 17-24, read the text below. Use the word given in capitals at the end of some of the lines to form a word that fits in the gap **in the same line.** There is an example at the beginning (0).
Write your answers in **CAPITAL LETTERS.**

Example:

0	PREPARATION

JOB HUMOUR: How to get away with doing nothing at work

Avoiding work is fast becoming an art form. Looking busy and achieving nothing takes skill	
and **(0)** .... So if you've ever been caught out by your boss, here's an	**PREPARE**
(17) .... way to make sure it doesn't happen again. The secret	**FAIL**
to spending time doing nothing, is to be able to lie with **(18)**	**CONVINCE**
and the kind of **(19)** .... that suggests that nothing would give you	**ENTHUSE**
more **(20)** .... than to explain what you are doing in the utmost detail.	**PLEASE**
Now, this is the clever bit. Be sure that your explanation is completely	
(21) .... by using as much technical jargon as you can until your questioner	**COMPREHEND**
runs off in either boredom or total **(22)** .... You need to have in your	**CONFUSE**
mind an **(23)** .... list of jobs that just have to be done today, but of course,	**END**
in reality, don't actually exist. Then, if you think that your boss is getting	
(24) ...., change your activity to another equally time-wasting one.	**SUSPECT**

Part 4

For questions 25-30, complete the second sentence so that it has a similar meaning to the first sentence, using the word given. **Do not change the word given**. You must use between **three** and **six** words, including the word given. Here is an example **(0)**.

Example: 0 George should have worked harder if he wanted to pass the exam. **succeeded**
Had George worked harder, ... passing the exam.

Write the missing words **IN CAPITAL LETTERS.**

0	HE WOULD HAVE SUCCEEDED IN

25 I don't intend to stop trying for a career in the police force. **no**
I have .... up on trying for a career in the police force.

26 David praised her exceptionally good choice of venue for the party. **congratulated**
David .... a good venue for the party.

27 It seems that the thieves escaped in a stolen car. **appear**
It .... away in a stolen car.

28 He said that he was sorry that he'd missed the meeting. **apologised**
He .... up at the meeting.

29 She thought she might want to buy some souvenirs so she took some extra money with her. **case**
She took some extra money with her .... some souvenirs.

30 I don't care if she doesn't write to me. **difference**
It makes no .... in touch or not.

Part 5

You are going to read a magazine article about someone who set up their own business. For questions 31-36, choose the answer **(A, B, C or D)** which you think fits best according to the text.

Starting up your own business

My earliest memory is one of incredible trauma. When I was five, my older brother and I crept downstairs on Christmas morning to light candles on the tree, and his pyjamas caught fire. As he ran around the room in flames, I knew I had to fetch a bucket of water, but shock rooted me to the spot and I could do nothing. He's still scarred, and the incident had a lasting impact on me, too. Ever since, I've been driven by a need to help heal other people. When I was 18, I started studying medicine, but I never really got into it. The course wasn't what I'd expected and I took some time out to think about what I really wanted to do. But before I had a chance to start a new course, I'd fallen in love and was married.

I was sad to give up my studies but I put our marriage first. We had three children, but by the time the third was born, our relationship was falling apart. After nearly five years, I realised nothing was going to change unless I made it happen myself, so I persuaded my husband to leave. It was the hardest thing I'd ever done.

So there I was, 29, on my own, with three young children to bring up and very little money. Things were bleak. I knew I had to get on with bringing up the children, but there were times I felt I couldn't cope and then I'd go outside, lie on the grass and cry. My salvation was living in such a lovely place - it was so beautiful that just looking at the landscape was a form of therapy.

But back then, nature also supported us on a practical level. I realised that if I saved a few potatoes and planted them, I could grow my own. I taught myself as I went along, and learned how to use birch leaves and nettles from the garden to make soups. The children and I would go to the woods to pick blackberries and collect mushrooms and firewood. I also kept bees for honey. I'd always loved the outdoors, but for the first time I found myself looking at plants and thinking about what I could use them for. The children still remember those times as idyllic, but I knew I couldn't go on living like that forever. After a few years, as I built up my confidence, I decided I had to start using my brain again. I considered resurrecting my medical ambitions, but in the end I turned down a place to study medicine in Dundee as it would have meant studying 70 hours a week, which was unfair on the children.

Then I heard about a homeopathy course, which was held one weekend a month in Newcastle. It was the mid-Eighties, when homeopathy wasn't so widely accepted, but I had faith in it because my parents had used it. Suddenly I had an energy I hadn't felt for years because I had regained control of my life. Healing people with homeopathy made perfect sense because it is based on the relationship between nature and ourselves, rather than being about automatically prescribing drugs.

For the first few years after I qualified, my surgery was a room in my house. It was exciting - people told their friends about me, so I never had to advertise, but it wasn't easy working from home. The children were very good but I felt guilty telling them they had to be quiet, so I started working from treatment rooms at clinics alongside other complimentary therapists. But before long I found I was working six days a week. It was exhausting travelling between clinics and it dawned on me that with the money I was paying in rent I might as well have my own place.

Eight years ago, I opened my own clinic in the centre of Edinburgh. I was totally out of my depth in the beginning and simply looked around until I found premises and took on the lease. I had no savings; I just planned to pay the rent with the money as it came in. I had no idea how to run a business back then. I was so naive I didn't even know you had to pay rates, until I received a huge bill! But I began to realise that running a business is a creative process, too. I was determined that my lack of business skills wouldn't let me down, so I taught myself the basics, kept things simple and, when things went wrong, I learned from my mistakes.

Running the clinic was my dream. I have three treatment rooms and I treat my patients in one of them, while the other two are rented to other therapists. There's also a shop where I sell natural healthcare products and natural beauty products that I've made. These days I work six days a week - three days spent treating people and the other three in the shop doing the accounts and making products.

I've learned you have to accept the negative things in life and use them to move on. You can't hide from them. It's hard when things go wrong, but it does help to clear out all the things that don't matter and lets you focus on what does. But more than anything, I've realised that it's worth pushing for what you want, because if you are lucky enough to find work you believe in, it can totally transform you.

31. What effect did her brother's accident have on the writer?

A. She blames herself for causing the accident.
B. She felt somehow responsible for the extent of his injuries.
C. She realises now that there was nothing that she could have done to help him.
D. She felt that they were being punished for misbehaving.

32. What initially stopped the writer from following a career in medicine?

A. She decided she would prefer to get married and have a family.
B. She found the course too demanding.
C. She was uninspired by the course.
D. Her husband wanted her to stay home and be a housewife.

33. What happened after the writer split up with her husband?

A. She didn't have enough money to feed her children.
B. She avoided mixing with other people socially.
C. She reverted to a childlike state herself.
D. She became as self-sufficient as she could in order to save money.

34. What was the writer's attitude to studying homeopathy?

A. She was unsure what it involved but believed it might make a good career.
B. She was positive about it because she'd had previous experience of it.
C. She naturally accepted it because her parents had a homeopathy clinic.
D. She was worried that people would be negative about it because it wasn't used much at that time.

35. What does the writer say about her business skills in the beginning?

A. There were more challenges to deal with than she realised at first.
B. She found it fairly simple to deal with the business from day one.
C. She was so well prepared that she managed to deal with problems as they came up.
D. She couldn't afford to pay her first rates bill.

36. How could one describe the writer's approach to life?

A. Sensible and carefully planned.
B. Insecure and negative.
C. Flexible and positive.
D. Unreliable and without commitment.

Part 6

You are going to read four reviews of a film. For questions **37-40**, choose from reviews **A-D**. The reviews may be chosen more than once.

The King's Speech
Four critics comment on the film

A

History and film buffs will delight in Seidler's *The King's Speech*. Its strong historical context might deter those not falling within these two categories, however. The film largely involves the actors Colin Firth, formal and decent, and Geoffrey Rush, large and expansive, in psychological struggle. Helena Bonham Carter, who can be merciless, is here filled with mercy, tact and love for her husband; this is the woman who became the much-loved Queen Mother of our lifetimes, dying in 2002 at 101. As the men have a struggle of wills, she tries to smooth things and raise her girls Elizabeth and Margaret. In the wider sphere, Hitler takes power, war comes closer, and the dreaded day approaches when Bertie (Firth), as George VI, will have to speak to the world and declare war. The director's handling of that fraught scene is masterful. Firth internalises his tension and keeps the required stiff upper lip, but his staff and household are terrified on his behalf as he marches towards a microphone as if it is a guillotine. At the end, what we have here is a superior historical drama and a powerful personal one.

B

Some films turn out to be unexpectedly good. Not that you've written them off, only they ply their craft on the hush-hush. Tom Hooper's *The King's Speech*, looked no more than a well-spoken costume drama, optimistically promoted for Sunday tea-time: decent cast, nice costumes and posh carpets. That was until the film finished a sneak-peak at a festival in deepest America and the standing ovations began. Tweeters, bloggers and Internet spokespeople of various levels of elocution, announced it the Oscar favourite, so it arrives in our cinemas with a fanfare of trumpets. But for all its pageantry, it isn't a film of grandiose pretensions. Much better than that, it is an honest-to-goodness crowd pleaser. *Rocky* with dysfunctional royalty. *Good Will Hunting* set amongst the staid pageantry and fussy social mores of the late 30s. A film that will play and play. A prequel to *The Queen*. Where lies its success? Let's start with the script, by playwright David Seidler, a model for transforming history into an approachable blend of drama and wit. For a film about being horrendously tongue-tied, Seidler's words are exquisitely measured, his insight as deep as it is softly spoken.

C

W. H. Auden wrote his poem "September 1, 1939" while sitting in a New York bar:

> "Uncertain and afraid /
> As the clever hopes expire /
> Of a low dishonest decade."

The King's Speech takes a rather different view of Britain and the 1930s, though it's not entirely inconsistent with Auden's judgment and isn't in any sense what is sneeringly called, 'heritage cinema'. It is the work of a highly talented group of artists who might be regarded as British realists. The film is the private story of a famous public man, King George VI (known in his family circle as Bertie), the woman who loved him and became his queen and the innovative Australian speech therapist Lionel Logue, who helped him control and come to terms with the stammer that had tortured him since childhood. Although the film involves a man overcoming a serious disability, it is neither triumphalist nor sentimental. Its themes, which are of universal appeal, are courage, where it comes from, how it is used, responsibility, and the necessity to place duty above personal pleasure or contentment – the subjects, in fact, of such enduringly popular movies as *Casablanca*.

D

It could have been a bunch of pip-pip, stiff-upper-lip Brit blather about a stuttering king who learns to stop worrying and love the microphone. Instead, *The King's Speech*, a crowning achievement powered by a dream cast, digs vibrant human drama out of the dry dust of human history making it a real crowd-puller. King George VI (Colin Firth), father of the present Queen Elizabeth, found his own *Dr. Strangelove* in Lionel Logue (Geoffrey Rush), a wildly eccentric Australian speech therapist who made it possible for the stammering monarch to go on radio in 1939 and rally his subjects to support the declaration of war on Hitler's Germany. *The King's Speech* plays out on the battlefield of words, not action. Writer David Seidler breathes fresh, urgent life into every frame of this powerhouse. The film's director Tom Hooper, 37, is a prodigious talent. The emotion this film produces is staggering.

Which reviewer

does not make a comparison between *The King's Speech* and another film? **37** [ ]

highlights the work of the film's writer like reviewer D? **38** [ ]

like reviewer D, was forced to re-assess any preconceptions they had had about the film? **39** [ ]

disagrees with the other three reviewers, in saying *The King's Speech* does not have popular appeal? **40** [ ]

Part 7

You are going to read an extract from a newspaper article. Six paragraphs have been removed from the extract. Choose from the paragraphs **A-G** the one which fits each gap (41-46). There is one extra paragraph which you do not need to use.

Up, up and away!

So you think you're inconvenienced by having to put your personal belongings in a clear plastic bag and arrive at the airport three hours before departure? Imagine how recent security changes are affecting aviation personnel. You don't need to be a regular viewer of 'Airport' to know that commercial airport staff are accountable for all sorts of situations both within and outside of their control.

41 ______

Balpa, which has over 9,000 of Britain's airline pilots in membership, wants safety recommendations from pilots to be taken much more seriously. Many pilots feel that the system is making their jobs more difficult rather than improving security. And, of course, with the recent increase in the terrorist threat, a career in aviation might not be the first thing on the mind of the nation's graduates.

42 ______

North, from Cambridge, is a first officer with KLM. Her job involves flying from Amsterdam to various European destinations, checking flight planning and fuel measures. She has wanted to be a pilot since she was very young. "I went on holiday with my family and was allowed a flight deck visit," she says. "When I saw all the screens and dials I thought, Wow, I want to do that!"

43 ______

She says one of the best things about being a pilot is "the feeling you get when it's pouring with rain and freezing cold on the ground, then when you go flying and pop up through the clouds and it's warm and sunny." She continues: "Sometimes, you have to get up at 2.30 a.m. to get to work and if you are really unlucky you'll get that scheduled six days in a row. There are rules about how long you can work, but after 14 hours on day six ... it's exhausting."

44 ______

However, despite the cost of training, competition for training positions at flight schools is normally fierce. The RAF offers university and sixth form sponsorship for certain RAF careers, and you can receive up to £4,000 a year as an undergraduate.

45 ______

Thirty-two-year-old Zoe Goldspink is a senior flight attendant for Virgin Airways. She trained for 6 weeks at the Horley Flight Centre near Gatwick Airport, learning safety, security, customer service and medical training. It's a comprehensive training programme and entry requirements vary from airline to airline. None require a degree but some prefer a European language, most have minimum GCSE requirements and some like experience in a customer service role.

46 ______

She believes that since 9/11 there are more security measures in place and she doesn't feel personally threatened. "There's passenger profiling, baggage screening at the airports, and preventative measures onboard like cockpit CCTV and strengthened cockpit doors. The safety and security of the crew and passengers is the number one priority of all airlines today.

A Training as a pilot can be a pretty pricey exercise. Costs vary but potential flyers need to have around £60,000 in sponsorship or private wealth. Some airlines offer sponsorship, and some offer methods for borrowing and repaying this money that may be linked to a starting salary.

B One of the most annoying things is delays at check-in. In high season these can be unacceptably long and many people get irate at having to hang around. Terrorist threats have added to this problem of course and I appreciate that, but I still don't see why it takes quite so long. It drives me mad and so I never fly anywhere unless I really have to. I'm also slightly nervous of flying, so for me it's just a necessary evil.

C Brunel University is offering a BA and MA in aviation engineering and pilot studies. There are also several aviation schools, such as Oxford Aviation Training, which offer full flight training as well as post-qualification selection preparation. All of these courses offer qualifications which are recognised worldwide.

D North won a flying scholarship with the Air Training Corps (Air Cadets) when she was seventeen and used it to get her private pilot's licence. She left the RAF when she won a sponsorship with civilian commercial flying school, Cabair, before joining KLM as a first officer on the Fokker 50.

E Goldspink says the benefits are obvious. "One minute you can be in New York and then the following week in Hong Kong or on a beach in Barbados. It does disrupt your social life and sometimes it can be a bit tiring, but there are far more pluses to the job. I love being cabin crew. It's the endless variety that appeals so much to me."

F But it's not all terrifying, says Kate North. "Exciting, perhaps. Thankfully, confidence in the industry remains strong and it seems more people are flying than ever before. Obviously, there is increased security at UK airports but that is necessary for the safety and wellbeing of all passengers. I think most passengers appreciate that."

G Other than doctors and nurses, there are few people whose hands we put our lives in so readily. We are not in control of our fate when we are passengers on a plane. Travelling 30,000 feet in the air with nothing for company except an in-flight magazine, tensions can run high.

Part 8

You are going to read some extracts of people talking about their jobs. For questions 47-56, choose from the extracts (**A-F**). The extracts may be chosen more than once.

In which extract is the following mentioned?

A situation that makes you realise you are ageing.	47	
Initial hostile behaviour that can be changed.	48	
Treating people as you wish to be treated yourself.	49	
People anxious for news.	50	
A family member taking credit for someone's success.	51	
Longing for a more conventional life.	52	
The risk of being physically attacked.	53	
Needing a certain amount of courage.	54	
Not intending to follow the career they have ended up doing.	55	
Putting other people at risk.	56	

JOBS

A The writer

I'm often accused of living in a parallel universe. The nature of my job demands a natural inclination to all things weird and wonderful. After all, I'm creating an unreal world based on what I see, feel and experience. I don't remember a time when I didn't write but I never had aspirations to earn a living from it until a cousin of mine entered a short story I'd written into a national competition and I won! It was a bolt out of the blue seeing as I knew nothing about the competition. The cash prize was substantial so I shared it with my enterprising cousin. Now she tries to claim commission on the royalties of every book I have published, not that she has any luck!

B The postal worker

I love the freedom of my job. You are out on the streets delivering and there is no one to bother you. Well, with the exception of the local wildlife of course. I've had a few close encounters with a canine jaw or two but no actual bites. I'm a fast runner when need be. I'm not so sure that some of the letters I deliver survive some of the cuddly dogs that rip them out of my hand as they go through the letter box. In some houses I can hear great snarling and ripping noises as I walk away from the door. Still, once they are through that box, they're no longer my responsibility. Seriously though, it can give you a warm feeling inside sometimes when someone is waiting for something special and they look so happy when you deliver it. Exam results time, now that's an emotional one. Poor kids, you see them looking out of a window or even hanging around outside their house, just waiting for me to come along with that dreaded envelope that will affect their whole future.

C The teacher

It's not a job for the fainthearted that's for sure. But on the other hand, I think people make it out to be worse than it is. The majority of the time, things run very smoothly, well as smoothly as they can with a building containing over a thousand kids. It's a fascinating job when you think about it, all those little personalities developing in front of your eyes. The wonderful thing is when they stay in touch and come back on regular visits to keep you up to date on how their life is panning out. And then you feel really old as their children come along and you end up teaching the next generation.

D The actor

My brothers always say that I've never had a proper job in my life. That's just because they are jealous since they are stuck in nine-to-five jobs. We were always competitive with each other as kids and I guess we still are in some ways. They crave my freedom but I admire their skills as fathers. I love acting but I sometimes wonder if I've missed out on the traditional way of life. Maybe the stability of a 'proper' job would be more rewarding in the long run. It must be great to have workmates that you've known for years and joked with day in, day out. And office Christmas parties, now they sound like fun.

E The au pair

My job is quite strange if you think about it. I move into the home of complete strangers and overnight I become an integral part of the family. It can often be hard for the children to adjust to a new au pair. Sometimes they are a bit resentful because they want more of their parents' attention and the au pair is considered, at best, a poor substitute and at worst, an invader in the family home. We are trained to deal with such issues though and have techniques to help us win the trust of the children and to make them see that having an au pair is a positive thing in their life. Usually things turn out well in the end and it can be a real wrench when you leave a family. I've stayed in touch with all the families that I've worked for.

F The bus driver

I wouldn't say my job is particularly stressful. Some of the other drivers grumble about traffic and rude passengers but I think that you get what you give and if I give people a cheery good morning they are going to respond in a positive way towards me. That's not to say there aren't a fair few idiots on the road. Some drivers think they have a divine right to go wherever they want without paying any attention to fellow road users and others have a thing about buses and feel obliged to overtake them at all costs and in any situation, whether it is safe or not. There's a real sense of camaraderie among the drivers and we have a good laugh together in the depot canteen. With this job you've got to keep a smile on your face.

WRITING - Part 1

You **must** answer this question. Write your answer in **220-260** words in an appropriate style.

1. You have watched a TV debate about which charity organisations should receive funding from the government. You have made the notes below:

Which charities should receive funding from the government?
- Sports & Recreation Charities
- Health Charities
- Human Rights Charities

Some opinions expressed in the discussion:
"We should not spend money on sport but on health."
"Cancer charities have helped lots of people and need our support."
"Human rights issues should be addressed."

Write an essay discussing **two** of the charities in your notes. You should explain **which charity is more important** for the government to give money to, **giving reasons** in support of your answer.

You may, if you wish, make use of the opinions expressed in the discussion, but you should use your own words as far as possible.

WRITING - Part 2

Write an answer to **one** of the questions **2-4** in this part. Write your answer in **220-260** words in an appropriate style.

2. You are interested in becoming a food critic and have been given an assignment by your school newspaper to review a newly-opened Chinese restaurant. The editor of the publication instructs you to consider the following when developing your review:
   - What did you eat and how was the quality of the food?
   - What was the decor like and did it enhance or lessen the overall dining experience?
   - How attentive and helpful were the staff in serving you?
   - Would you recommend this place to people you know? Why or why not?

   Write your **review**.

3. You have decided to go backpacking around Europe. One of your best friends did exactly that last year. Write to your friend asking for advice. Look at the notes you have made below of all the things that you need to ask your friend.

   Notes
   - plan route or just go for it?
   - accommodation?
   - places not to miss?
   - best way to travel?
   - insurance?
   - possible problems?

   Write your **letter**. You do not need to include postal addresses.

4. The city council that you work for has received funding to start a new careers service for young people. Read the notes below and write a proposal giving your suggestions as to what the service could offer and how it could be run.

   Notes
   - opening hours: 11.30am to 8.00pm or even later when students can visit the office
   - provide information on higher education and part-time / temporary work opportunities
   - maintain a job notice board that companies can advertise on

   Write your **proposal**. You should use your own words as far as possible.

LISTENING - Part 1

You will hear three different extracts. For questions 1-6, choose the answer (**A**, **B** or **C**) which fits best according to what you hear. There are two questions for each extract.

Extract One

You will hear two people talking about a problem at work.

1 What is the man's problem?

A Nobody will listen to his complaints at work.
B There is friction between him and a colleague.
C He's fallen out with his boss.

1	

2 What does the woman think?

A He needs to approach the problem in a different way.
B He has to accept that there will be problems in any office.
C He is the main cause of all the office problems.

2	

Extract Two

You will hear two people talking about how the woman got her job.

3 What were Janet's expectations of the recruitment fair?

A She was hoping to get some ideas for a career.
B She was sure that someone would offer her a job in Public Relations.
C She had incorrect preconceptions as to what she would gain from it.

3	

4 How did Paul gain from the recruitment fair?

A He passed an interview there and got a job.
B He impressed someone who then recommended him for a job.
C He applied for several jobs there and was successful.

4	

Extract Three

You will hear two people talking about the man's job as a prison officer.

5 What does the man say about his job?

A You need to have a degree to get a promotion.
B If you want a promotion you will have to go into management.
C It's a career that offers incentives for industrious people.

5	

6 What is the woman's opinion of the man?

A He is both courageous and mad.
B He must have a cruel side to him.
C His desire to get a promotion is more important than anything else.

6	

LISTENING - Part 2

You will hear a woman talking about her job as a probation worker.
For questions 7-14, complete the sentences.

The Probation worker

Georgia grew up on a **7** ______ .

Georgia didn't think she had enough **8** ______ for a career in probation work.

While studying for her degree, Georgia worked as a **9** ______ in three different places.

Being able to work out which **10** ______ is the most urgent is an important skill.

While working face to face with an offender, you both have **11** ______ to deal with.

Georgia works in the prison, **12** ______ and her office.

The worst part of Georgia's job is dealing with **13** ______ .

Georgia has to work with the courts to decide on a fair **14** ______ for each offender.

LISTENING - Part 3

You will hear part of a radio interview with an economist. For questions 15-20, choose the answer (A, B, C or D), which fits best according to what you hear.

15 According to the Fawcett Society,

A women would need to work into their eighties to earn as much money as men.
B good qualifications aren't necessarily rewarded with high wages.
C women will never earn as much as men.
D more women have degrees than men.

16 What is said about careers advice in schools?

A It has been improved but it is still inadequate.
B It is now quite good for girls but boys are being neglected.
C There is no advice for girls that are ambitious.
D Girls are always encouraged not to be ambitious.

17 According to Jim,

A women are to blame for not insisting on higher wages.
B new government policies have solved most of the problems.
C there is nothing more the government can do.
D women shouldn't necessarily be encouraged to change their choice of career.

18 A London School of Economics report showed that

A women who worked part-time found it difficult to get a full-time job later on.
B after having children, women find it harder to earn as much money as men.
C women find it hard to find a job after having children.
D most women want a full-time job after having a child.

19 What does the 'stuffed shirt' policy mean?

A Women are being forced to choose between family commitments and work.
B Only men can have part-time senior positions.
C Women don't get the opportunity to train for high-powered jobs.
D No woman can have a senior position.

20 Jim seems to believe that

A women should stay at home and look after their children.
B women now earn as much money as men in the workplace.
C women have been disadvantaged by outdated work ethics.
D having children will soon be an advantage for working women.

LISTENING - Part 4

You will hear five short extracts in which people are talking about work.
While you listen you must complete both tasks.

TASK ONE

For questions 21-25, choose from the list A-H the person who is speaking.

A	a receptionist		
B	an apprentice	Speaker 1	21
C	a temporary worker	Speaker 2	22
D	a manager	Speaker 3	23
E	a caretaker	Speaker 4	24
F	a secretary	Speaker 5	25
G	a courier		
H	a pensioner		

TASK TWO

For questions 26-30, choose from the list **A-H** what each speaker is expressing / talking about.

A	a suspicion that people like to find excuses not to do work		
B	the view that you should never ask for a pay rise	Speaker 1	26
C	the feeling that helping an understudy may go unappreciated	Speaker 2	27
D	an intimate knowledge of other people's affairs that could be profitable	Speaker 3	28
E	the view that you should never take work home with you	Speaker 4	29
F	a distrust of colleagues who are nice to you	Speaker 5	30
G	a feeling of having been taken advantage of on account of inexperience		
H	the wisdom of prioritising tasks		

Test 3

Part 1

For questions 1-8, read the text below and decide which answer (**A**,**B**,**C** or **D**) best fits each gap. There is an example at the beginning (0).

Example:

0 **A** otherwise **B** instead **C** despite **D** although

0	A	B	C	D
	▭	▭	▬	▭

Drunk-driving soars in the pre-Christmas period

Four million motorists will drink and drive over the festive period **(0)**............ high-profile campaigns **(1)**............ them against it, new research suggests. The research, by a national car insurance company, also **(2)**............ alarming ignorance of the effects of alcohol. Three million believe leaving the windows open while they drive will help them sober up and at least 600,000 think that chewing gum will foil a breath test. One million car drivers actually admitted they would climb behind the wheel this Christmas even if they were over the limit, with many thinking this is okay if they can walk straight. More than thirteen million people have been in a car with a driver they **(3)**............ of having drunk too much, but just two million have taken the keys and driven themselves.

Of the four million who will drink and drive over the festive period, almost half of these admit it's because they don't want to pay for taxis or can't be **(4)**............ to wait in the cold for public transport. A spokeswoman for the insurance company said: "Drivers should seriously **(5)**............ the need to take the car before heading out for a Christmas drink. If they do end up drinking alcohol and have the car with them, they must find an alternative mode of transport to get home."

The research showed 500,000 drivers will hit the road **(6)**............ of how much alcohol they have **(7)**............ . A further 100,000 drivers will **(8)**......... off home after downing between four and five pints of beer, despite the fact that they have experienced some kind of accident while driving under the influence of alcohol.

1	**A**	tempting	**B**	inspiring	**C**	resisting	**D**	urging
2	**A**	invents	**B**	obscures	**C**	reveals	**D**	conceals
3	**A**	convinced	**B**	suspected	**C**	distrusted	**D**	considered
4	**A**	hindered	**B**	bothered	**C**	disturbed	**D**	cared
5	**A**	consult	**B**	confer	**C**	aspire	**D**	consider
6	**A**	nonetheless	**B**	moreover	**C**	however	**D**	regardless
7	**A**	purchased	**B**	consumed	**C**	employed	**D**	squandered
8	**A**	make	**B**	set	**C**	leave	**D**	put

Part 2

For questions 9-16, read the text below and think of the word which best fits each gap. Use only one word in each gap. There is an example at the beginning (0).
Write your answers in **CAPITAL LETTERS**.

Example:

0	IN

The delights of Italy's Abruzzo

When Edward Lear visited Abruzzo **(0)** .... the 1840s, it was a little-known region of Italy, shunned by most tourists, who were more taken **(9)** .... the delights of Tuscany and cities **(10)** .... as Venice, Rome and Milan. But the poet and artist was drawn by its sense of isolation and old-fashioned ways. In his 1846 travel book, Lear captured sights that many in Britain had never seen before, describing the sleepy feel of the region and complaining about the local wine.

Yet Abruzzo, all these years on, still lags way **(11)** .... Tuscany in the tourism and second home popularity stakes. **(12)** .... there has been more interest - the number of tourists to the area has risen by a third in five years, **(13)** .... to new low-cost flights - property opportunities have been thin on the ground.

According to Lucio Forgione, who works for Overseas Homesearch and who is a big fan of Abruzzo, its time, he believes, has come. The area has several selling points. The **(14)** .... is its isolation and peacefulness. It is truly tucked away. There is virtually no traffic and the main sound is that of birdsong. The village of San Donato is a good place for outdoor types and it is **(15)** .... an hour's drive to beaches on the Adriatic. The food at local restaurants is first rate and the wine's not bad either. For a back to nature holiday, Abruzzo is second to none and it is astonishing that so **(16)** .... holiday companies have developed an interest in the region.

Part 3

For questions 17-24, read the text below. Use the word given in capitals at the end of some of the lines to form a word that fits in the gap **in the same line.** There is an example at the beginning (0).
Write your answers in **CAPITAL LETTERS.**

Example:

0	FOOTSTEPS

The Silk Route

Follow in the **(0)** .... of the pioneering traders to experience one of the world's	**FEET**
most **(17)** .... overland journeys. This route goes through harsh deserts and up	**SPECTACLE**
into mountainous lands. A greater variety of landscapes would be difficult to find.	
Although the silk route is strictly a land-based route, it is worth making an **(18)**	**EXCEPT**
in Cappadocia as this area is firmly established as one of the prime hot-air balloon destinations	
in the world because of its **(19)** .... wind conditions and agreeable geography.	**FAVOUR**
The bird's eye views of the valleys are **(20)** .... and the skill of the balloonists	**FORGET**
is breathtaking. In theory you can now travel the entire silk route by train but in **(21)**	**REAL**
few foreign visitors use trains outside of China because they are slow and **(22)**	**RELY**
Some intrepid travellers take the brave decision to do the route by cycling.	
One advantage of this is that you can stop whenever you like and enjoy your surroundings.	
There are however, drawbacks to cycling, not least the fact that it can be very	
(23) .... on some of the rough tracks and bumpy roads!	**COMFORT**
Bizarre as it may seem, it is actually **(24)** .... to have more than one person	**LEGAL**
on a bike in China, so think twice before deciding to ride a tandem with a friend!	

Part 4

For questions 25-30, complete the second sentence so that it has a similar meaning to the first sentence, using the word given. **Do not change the word given**. You must use between **three** and **six** words, including the word given. Here is an example **(0)**.

Example: 0 George should have worked harder if he wanted to pass the exam. **succeeded**
Had George worked harder, ... passing the exam.

Write the missing words **IN CAPITAL LETTERS**.

0	HE WOULD HAVE SUCCEEDED IN

25 They say this company is one of the most reliable in the country. **reputed**
This company .... of the most reliable in the country.

26 We were all surprised when she announced that she was engaged to be married. **announcement**
The .... all by surprise.

27 Finding the survivors is our number one priority. **utmost**
It is of the .... the survivors.

28 Whatever happens, I will never trust him again. **ever**
Under .... trust him again.

29 George had to try for months before he finally got a job. **did**
Only after .... George finally get a job.

30 Tom didn't feel like dancing that night. **mood**
Tom .... dancing that night.

Part 5

You are going to read a magazine article about two women who walked up mount Kilimanjaro. For questions **31-36**, choose the answer **(A, B, C or D)** which you think fits best according to the text.

We climbed a mountain

When I set off to climb Kilimanjaro, I was 45, overweight, stressed out and trapped in an unhappy marriage. My best friend, Siobhan, had heard about a fundraising trip, organised by the charity Whiz Kidz, on the radio. As we were pounding the treadmill in the gym, she said, "Hey Tracey, let's climb a mountain." I said, "You must be mad," but the idea was firmly planted in our minds from that moment. Like so many women in my situation, I felt I had no time for me, and no time to make choices. I worked full time for an advertising agency; a stimulating but stressful job that left me mentally exhausted. My husband David was, and is, a fantastic father but, like many men, he has no idea about tidying up and day-to-day chores like washing and cleaning. So I ran our home almost single-handedly. When I wasn't at work I was rushing about trying to get everything sorted out, and weekends were spent ferrying my two daughters to all their activities - trying to make up for not being there during the week.

Siobhan set the ball rolling on the trip, and our first hurdle was raising £3000 each. We had a fantastic time doing it, because it was so different from the rest of our lives - organising a ball for 150 people, going carol singing and running a school disco. When we started training for the trip I was about three stone overweight, so we hired a personal trainer, went to the gym and took long walks in the hills.

There were 35 of us on the trip, and Siobhan and I were the only middle-aged women. There were young guys who'd run marathons and girls in their 20s, but the age gap didn't matter. In fact, we were the practical ones, the leaders. The climb took four days going up, two days coming down. After just two days we were filthy. Sometimes the young girls would be in tears because they couldn't get anything clean and Siobhan became like a mother hen.

It was hot during the day and freezing at night, and we slept six to a hut. My lips blistered so badly I could hardly speak, and my feet were in agony. I kept up with the others until the very last climb, which you had to do at night because otherwise the sun was too strong. We pitched camp at about 18,000ft - just a thousand feet from the summit. But the going was very tough, over loose scree, and you literally had to scramble hand over hand. We set off in the dark wearing head torches, in a long straggling line.

A full moon lit our path, but as we climbed I felt worse and worse. It was so cold, I couldn't feel my fingers, and I felt so dizzy I was staggering about like a drunk. After six hours I passed out. I had altitude sickness really badly and a porter had to lead me back down gently. They wanted to put me in a decompression chamber, but I refused - I didn't think I was that ill. It was only later I realised I could have died from a cerebral oedema, where excess fluid collects on the brain, making it swell up. The walk back to the hut should have taken two hours but it took four - possibly the hardest four hours of my life. When I got back I collapsed on my sleeping bag and slept. Siobhan, meanwhile was making her way up to the top. When I woke I was crying because I hadn't made it and she was up there. I was determined to be on my feet to welcome her back. Against the guide's wishes, I managed to climb back up the trail for an hour and stand on the side of the trail, crying and emotional as she came back. Even though I hadn't made it to the top, I didn't feel like I'd failed. I realised that I had achieved something just for me.

We ended up raising £9,000 for Whiz Kidz which was fantastic and the personal achievement put everything else into perspective. It made me realise you don't have to put up with situations - you do have a choice. There are infinite opportunities out there, and women are brilliant at seizing them. You don't have to have a man by your side to feel complete. I now feel that I'm really living, and getting what I want out of life. And next year Siobhan and I are planning to walk the Inca Trail together.

31. Tracey and Siobhan's decision to climb Kilimanjaro can be described as

A. practical.
B. desperate.
C. unrealistic.
D. impulsive.

32. In order to prepare for the trip Tracey and Siobhan

A. had to be a specific weight.
B. had to tackle new challenges.
C. did a lot of socialising with the people they were about to travel with.
D. joined a choir.

33. How did Tracey and Siobhan fit into the group dynamics?

A. They were outsiders because they were so much older than the others.
B. They were envious of the younger girls.
C. Their maternal instincts led them to support the younger members.
D. They had to make a big effort to be accepted into the group.

34. What happened to Tracey towards the end of the trip?

A. She refused to give up even though she was very ill.
B. She was forced to admit defeat due to ill health.
C. She was too emotional to carry on to the top.
D. The others refused to help her to the summit.

35. When Tracey didn't reach the summit she

A. accepted that the experience had been of value.
B. was envious of Siobhan.
C. could not get over her sense of failure.
D. felt relieved that the experience was at last over.

36. The writer seems to intend this piece to be

A. cautionary.
B. pretentious.
C. inspirational.
D. cultural.

Part 6

You are going to read four reviews of a novel. For questions 37-40, choose from reviews A-D. The reviews may be chosen more than once.

Atonement
Four critics comment on the novel

A

Atonement does not feel, at first, like a book by McEwan. The opening is almost perversely ungripping. Instead of the expected sharpness of focus, the first 70 or so pages are a lengthy summary of shifting impressions. One longs for a cinematic clarity and concentration of dialogue and action, but such interludes dissolve before our - and the participants' - eyes. Unlike Martin Amis, say, or Salman Rushdie, McEwan is an invisible rather than a flamboyant stylist. Even so, the pallid qualifiers and disposable adverbs (a 'gently rocking sheet of water, the 'coyly drooping' head of a nettle) come as a surprise. The language used to distil the scene - a gathering of the Tallis family at their country house on a sweltering day in 1935 - serves also as a wash that partially obscures it.

B

Ian McEwan's remarkable novel *Atonement* is a love story, a war story and a story about the destructive powers of the imagination. It is also a novel that takes all of the author's perennial themes - dealing with the hazards of innocence, the hold of time past over time present and the intrusion of evil into ordinary lives - and orchestrates them into a symphonic work that is every bit as affecting as it is gripping. It is, in short, a tour de force. The story that *Atonement* recounts, concerns a monstrous lie told by a 13-year-old girl, a lie that will send her older sister's lover away to jail and that will shatter the family's staid, upper-middle-class existence.
As in so many earlier McEwan's novels, this shocking event will expose psychological fault lines running through his characters' lives and force them to confront a series of moral choices. It will also underscore the class tensions that existed in England of the 1930s and the social changes wrought by World War II.

C

If you knew for a fact that you'd ruined someone's life - two lives, really - how would you make amends? That's the question the stark title of Ian McEwan's beautiful but wrenching, well-paced new novel refers to. *Atonement* is about a crime and its consequences over the course of six decades: In the mid-thirties, a precocious young girl with an overactive imagination helps to wrongly accuse an innocent man, and it is not until 1999 that she finds a kind of absolution. But this book, McEwan's grandest and most ambitious yet, is much more than the story of a single act of atonement. In his compact and clockwork-precise earlier fictions, McEwan, whose previous novel Amsterdam won the Booker in 1998, liked to show how relationships and people can disintegrate in ways that manage to seem both shocking and inevitable.

D

Minor resemblances between this novel by Ian McEwan and Henry James's *What Maisie Knew* have already been noticed and are of some interest. McEwan's new novel, which strikes me as easily his finest, has a frame that is properly hinged and jointed and apt for the conduct of the 'march of action', which James described as 'the only thing that really, for me, at least, will produce *L'Oeuvre*.' Not quite how McEwan would put it, perhaps, but still the substance of his method, especially if one adds a keen technical interest in another Jamesian obsession, the point of view. His central character is a 13-year-old girl called Briony, already a maker of stories and plays and so already a writer of fictions that have only their own kind of truth and are dependent on fantasies which readers are invited to share, with whatever measure of scepticism or credulity they can muster.

Which reviewer

like reviewer A, makes comparisons between McEwan and other writers?	37
disagrees with the other three reviewers, by finding the novel's structure unsatisfactory?	38
believes this to be the author's best work to date?	39
examines the question of morality in the piece like reviewer C?	40

Part 7

You are going to read an extract from a newspaper article. Six paragraphs have been removed from the extract. Choose from the paragraphs **A-G** the one which fits each gap (41-46). There is one extra paragraph which you do not need to use.

Alexandria

Smoke and the fragrance of roasting quail float up from long charcoal grills lining the perimeter of Suq el-Attarine, the Market of Scents, in Alexandria, Egypt. It is October, the season when quail fly south from Europe, tire over the Mediterranean Sea, land on beaches, and are easily trapped. Along pavements men sit on benches and puff apple-cured tobacco through water pipes. Some play dominoes. Above us hang the purple flowers of jacaranda trees.

41 ______

Nearly half the world's population lives in cities. The number of megacities - those with populations of more than ten million - will exceed two dozen by 2015, up from fourteen in 1995. But what is it that draws people to cities like bees to pollen?

42 ______

I decided to commence my investigations here because this was one of the few international cities in the world. It was part of Africa, close to Arabia, and home to Europeans from Greece and Rome. Alexandria was a crossroads for trade that ranged from China to Britain. Strabo, a geographer in the first century A.D. called Alexandria "the greatest emporium in the inhabited world." After Alexandria, I will visit Cordoba, Spain, western Europe's largest city in A.D. 1000, now a modest town supported mainly by agriculture. In its prime Cordoba was, in the words of one observer, "the mother of towns, the abode of the good and godly, the homeland of wisdom." My travels will end in New York City, a modern epicentre of finance and culture. New York, writes Joan Didion, is "an infinitely romantic notion, the mysterious nexus of all love and money and power."

43 ______

Alexander's engineers realised that Mediterranean currents running west to east would keep the port navigable and free of Nile River silt. They also knew that the Island of Pharos, if joined to the mainland by the construction of a pier, would offer an effective wave breaker.

44 ______

In the 14th century it collapsed during an earthquake, and the Egyptians built a fortress here using, some accounts say, stones from the lighthouse. From my waterside cafe table I can see the fortress where team members from the Alexandria-based Centre d'Etudes Alexandrines are easing into wet suits. They will dive down 20 feet where they are cataloguing statues, columns, and other architectural elements near the lighthouse site.

45 ______

The idea of a place of records was not new. A building was constructed in 3200 B.C. to house a collection of Egyptian papyrus scrolls, and Athens had a similar building in the fourth century B.C. But Alexandria's library was on a scale new to the Mediterranean world, and the city was notorious for its aggressive pursuit of texts. Mohen Zahran the project manager talks about reviving "the lighthouse of knowledge". The new library, he says, "will encourage the peace and exchange of ideas throughout the region and provide a place for scholars of diverse backgrounds to meet."

46 ______

Scholarly pursuits had immediate commercial applications. Translations helped Alexandrians to better understand their trading partners, and new maps enabled traders to calculate distances more accurately. It was this wealth of knowledge that helped Alexandria to establish itself as one of the richest cities of its day.

A The city grew steadily as a centre for trade. About four decades after Alexander's death in 323 B.C. Ptolemy II built a lighthouse, known as one of the seven wonders of the world. It rivalled the Pyramids in height at about 400 feet and had as many as 300 rooms. Fires, reflected in mirrors on top of the lighthouse, could be seen for some 35 miles, alerting ships to Egypt's reefs and shifting coastline.

B Little is known about how the ancient Mouseion operated because so few written records have been found. But we do know that it was a place for scholars to meet. From throughout their known world Alexandria's rulers invited nearly a hundred learned men to the Mouseion where they lived in a communal residence and ate together in a dining hall. From these scholars came Euclidean geometry, the first scientific dissections of human bodies, a translation of the Hebrew Bible into Greek and a compilation of Homer's epic poems.

C The tranquil scene recalls earlier times in the city that Alexander the Great founded more than 2,300 years ago. But as I stroll from the marketplace toward the harbour, I am clearly in a modern city. Apartment buildings, home to nearly three and a half million people, surround me. Traffic jams the streets. Supermarkets, cell phones, motorcycles, and teenagers in baseball caps are everywhere.

D But, back to Egypt and the hustle and bustle of Alexandria. Dodging cars speeding along El-Horreyah Avenue, Alexandria's busiest street, I arrive at the waterfront. I see small fishing boats at anchor, young boys jumping off rocks into the water, and, beyond, the natural harbour that Alexander the Great saw in 331 B.C..

E The past - and the answers it might hold - feels impossibly distant as I wander up the coast near where Cleopatra's palace once stood. Somewhere in this area, perhaps beneath my feet, lies the sarcophagus holding Alexander the Great. It disappeared from recorded history in the third century A.D. Also buried here in a site yet to be located is the famous Alexandria library, founded early in the third century B.C. as part of the Mouseion, the great research centre of its day.

F All cities share certain characteristics. They are places to buy and sell, to worship, to share companionship. They are where new ideas trigger changes in sciences and art, where cultures meet and evolve. But why and where do cities, these centres of trade and knowledge, grow? What causes some to flourish and others to fade? I am in Alexandria at the beginning of my journey to three great cities to seek the answers.

G The United Nations and other international agencies are co-operating with the Egyptian government to finance a new 200-million dollar Alexandria library near a possible site of the old one. Cranes swing steel beams overhead, and workers scamper up the scaffolding surrounding the building's circular framework.

Part 8

You are going to read some extracts from a travel magazine about places to visit. For questions 47-56, choose from the extracts (**A-F**). The extracts may be chosen more than once.

In which extract is the following mentioned?

People of different social classes are working together to improve the community.	47	
There are no buildings to spoil this area.	48	
There are specific things that you must take with you on this trip.	49	
There is a slight risk of serious injury or even death on this trip.	50	
Different eras can be compared in this place.	51	
A political change had an unexpectedly good outcome.	52	
A place used by several monarchs.	53	
A remarkable form of transport.	54	
The near total destruction of a population in one area.	55	
A trip for artistic people.	56	

Places to visit around the world

A Preah Vihear, Cambodia

This enigmatic temple/fortress near the Thai/Cambodian border welcomed tourists until, in 1993, the Khmer Rouge settled here. Though they soon left, it was ten years before Preah Vihear was completely reopened - Cambodia finally finished the access road in 2003. The original temple was started in the 9th century, although it was subsequently maintained and enlarged by many different kings. For the makers, the cracking views were incidental: building the temple on a mountain was designed to encourage religious meditation.

The best way to reach Preah Vihear is to hire a driver or join a coach party from Siem Reap. If you go under your own steam you might want to stay overnight in the basic accommodation at the foot of the mountain or the even more primitive accommodation atop the 550m peak. The area has been largely cleared of land mines but it's probably best to stick to the main paths.

B Gorgongosa National Park

Ten years ago, this magnificent wildlife park in central Mozambique was an environmental disaster area. In 1971, 12,000 visitors came here, attracted by the greatest lion population in Africa. From 1983 to 1992, the park was the stage for many battles in Mozambique's civil war. By 1992, when peace arrived, the park's stock of large mammals had fallen by 95%.

The park, a day's drive from the capital Maputo, was partially reopened in 1998. Gorgongosa's recovery has gathered momentum this year. Buffalo have been reintroduced and the park has received donations from internet mogul Greg Carr and rock star Ronnie Wood. It may be a while before the cheetah and rhino return but 1,862m-high Mount Gorgongosa is still an unforgettable hike.

C Johannesburg

Johannesburg is a bustling modern city set against the grandeur of African horizons. It was here Nelson Mandela began the revolution that destroyed apartheid, and today the same spirit lives on in the diverse population - they are now living the new South African dream.

After the end of Apartheid in 1994, many felt the change to democratic government would spell decline. That simply hasn't happened - instead, the negative image of the city has taken a turn for the better. Johannesburg has an edge, no-one can deny that, but recently it has shaken off its reputation for grime and crime. The centre of town is beginning a hesitant renaissance - restaurants are multiplying, the theatre is booming - while its outer suburbs are flourishing. This is a city where, against all odds, people from all walks of life are coming together and forging something new.

D Northern India

Palanquin Traveller has a new programme of cultural studies on location, designed to satisfy the seriously inquisitive traveller. *Origins of the Buddha* is a journey across northern India travelling in the Buddha's footsteps. Visiting important sites in Buddha's life is not just for pilgrims - this expedition stays in rural villages and homes to get a better understanding of how modern and traditional India strive to co-exist. The tour is led by scholar Shantum Seth, who is not only a charismatic companion and fascinating guide, but also an adviser to the UN and Unesco.

This thirteen-day trip involves some challenging trekking and basic mountain climbing so appropriate clothing and footwear is essential. Accommodation and all food included in holiday price.

E Estonia

Would you like to spend your next holiday in an Eastern European bog? This may seem like a daft idea, until you realise 50% of Estonia is made up of virgin forest, including some of the most glorious and pristine bogs in Europe. The landscape is unmarred by human construction, save the boardwalks that penetrate this soggy countryside as shown on 'Light and Land's' new photography trip to Estonia. Mineral islands amongst the murky pools provide a haven for wildlife - bears, lynx, flying squirrels and elk - and denning sites for Estonia's thriving wolf population.

Point your lens upwards to the peaks of the ancient pines and you'll find an array of birdlife from golden eagles to white-backed woodpeckers. On the ground, there's a host of curious flora and wild flowers including orchids, bittercress and lady's slipper. Led by wildlife enthusiast and photographer Niall Benvie, this is an unusual and rewarding trip to a wilderness in Europe.

F Sail the Galapagos

This really is the trip of a lifetime. This seven-day expedition is in association with the Galapagos Conservation Trust. Sailing on the *Sagitta* is an experience in itself - three masts tower above this handsome tall ship and sails ripple into action as she sets off around the archipelago to mingle with the world's friendliest wildlife. This trip is led by Galapagos naturalist, author and photographer David Horwell. Pick his brains on the local fauna and flora over the scrumptious Ecuadorian food on board.

Help collect data for the Trust and be part of a team of select scientists for a fortnight. Contribute to the effort to conserve this magical part of the world. This truly is a 'green holiday' where tourist becomes conservationist rather than destroyer of the planet.

WRITING - Part 1

You **must** answer this question. Write your answer in **220-260** words in an appropriate style.

1. You have listened to a radio programme about which courses should be included in secondary schools' curricula. You have made the notes below:

Which courses should be included in secondary schools' curricula?
- Ancient Greek and Latin
- computer course
- plumbing course

Some opinions expressed in the discussion:
"Computer Science is more important than ancient languages."
"All students need to know about Latin and Ancient Greek authors."
"We should include courses that teach something useful and practical to students!"

Write an essay discussing **two** of the courses in your notes. You should **explain which course should be included** in secondary schools' curricula, **giving reasons** in support of your answer.

You may, if you wish, make use of the opinions expressed in the discussion, but you should use your own words as far as possible.

WRITING - Part 2

Write an answer to **one** of the questions **2-4** in this part. Write your answer in **220-260** words in an appropriate style.

2. You work as an environmentalist for the local council. A large shopping centre has recently been built in your area. You have been asked to visit the shopping centre and to write a report saying what effect the shopping centre might have on the local environment and the community.

   Your report should state both the positive and the negative aspects of the shopping centre. Finally, you should make some suggestions as to how the more negative aspects could be improved.

   Write your **report**.

3. You recently had an unpleasant experience when you were shopping in a department store. One of the assistants wrongly accused you of shoplifting. Although you were able to prove that you had paid for the item in question, you received no apology.

   Write a letter to the manager of the shop, saying why you are angry and disappointed and asking for some kind of compensation for the way you were treated. Say that you will take further action if you do not receive an official apology.

   Write your **letter**. You do not need to include postal addresses.

4. Your boss at work has asked you for ways to improve the overall wellness of your colleagues. He has asked you to come up with a proposal with recommendations for what and how to encourage people to improve their health. Other companies have encouraged employees to eat right, sleep well, exercise regularly, socialise with friends and family and to take holidays.

   You may use these suggestions in your proposal, but feel free to incorporate others. Be sure to provide reasons to support your recommendations.

   Write your **proposal**.

LISTENING - Part 1

You will hear three different extracts. For questions 1-6, choose the answer (**A**, **B** or **C**) which fits best according to what you hear. There are two questions for each extract.

Extract One

You will hear part of a radio interview.

1 What does Bob Aldridge do currently?

A He's an executive.
B He's a politician.
C He's probably retired.

1	

2 What does Bob think about air travel?

A It can be justified but travellers should pay more tax.
B Airports are big enough to cope with the number of air travellers.
C Rail travel could eventually replace air travel.

2	

Extract Two

You will hear two friends talking about a trip one of them went on.

3 What does the woman feel about travelling alone?

A She gets a thrill out of taking big risks abroad.
B She believes that positive common sense keeps most people out of trouble.
C She believes that being abroad is bound to be more dangerous than being at home.

3	

4 When the woman was in Thailand, she

A thought her life was in danger.
B was too interested in the coup to be frightened.
C realised immediately that there was nothing to be afraid of.

4	

Extract Three

You will hear two people talking about digital cameras.

5 What does the woman want a new camera for?

A To take holiday snaps to show her friends and family when she returns.
B To take photographs to sell as cards in an art gallery.
C To try to create an original impression of the countries she visits.

5	

6 What does the man say about digital cameras?

A Compact cameras are convenient for the casual photographer.
B More creative photography demands a film camera.
C The bigger the camera, the better the quality of picture.

6	

LISTENING - Part 2

You will hear a radio report about British people buying holiday homes abroad.
For questions 7-14, complete the sentences.

Brits head for foreign lands

There has been a **7** ______ increase in the number of Brits with homes abroad.

8 ______ are inspiring people to buy homes abroad.

The main reason people are buying foreign homes is to live in a **9** ______ .

People can borrow easily now due to the **10** ______ .

Only a **11** ______ of people buy a property in eastern Europe.

Bulgaria has some of the **12** ______ property opportunities in Europe.

Buying a property abroad isn't necessarily a good **13** ______ .

You may not be able to pass on your property to your children due to foreign **14** ______ laws.

LISTENING - Part 3

You will hear an interview with a man who enjoys ice-skating in the Netherlands. For questions 15-20, choose the answer (**A, B, C** or **D**), which fits best according to what you hear.

15 What does Conrad mean when he says that he 'studied' skating?

- **A** He'd had some lessons when he lived in Delft.
- **B** He'd looked at images of skaters and the poses they adopted.
- **C** Some skaters had helped him out when he first tried to skate.
- **D** He'd read up on skating techniques before he went on to the ice.

16 How does Conrad describe his own style?

- **A** rough, even after a lot of practice
- **B** a bit like a duck on ice
- **C** just as good as the skaters in the paintings he'd looked at
- **D** clumsy but acceptable

17 What happens when there's ice in the Netherlands?

- **A** Most businesses are forced to close down because staff can't get to work.
- **B** Most of the population goes on the '11 Cities Course'.
- **C** Parents reluctantly take their children out of school so that they can skate.
- **D** Skating mania takes over the country.

18 How does Conrad view the traditional Netherlands when it's icy?

- **A** as a rather sober and depressing place
- **B** as a hazardous landscape to be avoided
- **C** in a poetic and romantic way
- **D** in a critical and negative way

19 Which of the following does Conrad not mention?

- **A** having a map
- **B** skating with a companion
- **C** precautionary action against the cold
- **D** thin ice

20 What is Conrad's general attitude to skating?

- **A** excited but apprehensive
- **B** cautionary and slightly negative
- **C** enthusiastic and knowledgeable
- **D** reckless and excitable

LISTENING - Part 4

You will hear five short extracts in which people are talking about holidays and travel.
While you listen you must complete both tasks.

TASK ONE

For questions 21-25, choose from the list **A-H** the person who is speaking.

A	a travel writer		
B	a hotel owner	Speaker 1	21
C	a chef	Speaker 2	22
D	an inadvertent adventure tourist	Speaker 3	23
E	a farmer	Speaker 4	24
F	a tour guide	Speaker 5	25
G	a politician		
H	a pilot		

TASK TWO

For questions 26-30, choose from the list **A-H** what each speaker is expressing / talking about.

A	a lack of certainty over whether or not a goal would be achieved		
B	a hesitancy when it comes to trying new and different foods	Speaker 1	26
C	doubt about whether or not to journey somewhere new	Speaker 2	27
D	the requirement to have a good head for heights on a visit somewhere	Speaker 3	28
E	discomfort with a mode of travel	Speaker 4	29
F	failure to be persuaded not to do something by family members	Speaker 5	30
G	a requirement to trust one's life to others		
H	the need to convince others something was safe		

Test 4

Part 1

For questions 1-8, read the text below and decide which answer (**A**,**B**,**C** or **D**) best fits each gap. There is an example at the beginning (0).

Example:

0 **A** primitive **B** limited **C** rare **D** basic

0	A	B	C	D
	▭	▭	▭	▬

Home sweet home

Having a roof over your head is a (0) .... necessity that we in the western world have (1) .... into an art form - a stylish place to dwell is now intrinsic to our happiness. But the way we live also has to keep pace with rapidly changing lifestyles and as our (2) .... towards the environment change, we're becoming more aware that our homes need to tread more lightly on the earth.

Architects are (3) .... to this creative challenge, designing inspiring buildings that respond both to our modern lives, and to our growing sense of environmental responsibility. These new buildings boast contemporary aesthetics while encouraging us to live more responsibly by using (4) .... resources. From innovative designs of tiny capsule dwellings to elegant family homes with robust green features, sustainable ideas are permeating modern design. And it seems we're on the verge of a seismic shift.

One idea doing the rounds is that because our aspirations have changed, we can now be content with far fewer possessions. This concept (5) .... Horden Cherry Lee to design the micro-compact home, a sleek pad only two cubic metres in size, (6) .... spacious enough for two people to live in for short periods. Professor Horden justifies these compact proportions in (7) .... of our modern habits: status is (8) .... gained by having a high degree of mobility rather than merely owning things.

	A	B	C	D
1	**A** produced	**B** assembled	**C** turned	**D** caused
2	**A** attitudes	**B** concepts	**C** ideas	**D** schemes
3	**A** climbing	**B** rising	**C** soaring	**D** swelling
4	**A** shorter	**B** greater	**C** grander	**D** fewer
5	**A** assured	**B** inspired	**C** imposed	**D** created
6	**A** despite	**B** how	**C** whatever	**D** yet
7	**A** means	**B** reasons	**C** terms	**D** plans
8	**A** accurately	**B** increasingly	**C** highly	**D** extremely

Part 2

For questions 9-16, read the text below and think of the word which best fits each gap. Use only one word in each gap. There is an example at the beginning (0).
Write your answers in **CAPITAL LETTERS**.

Example:

0	WITH

Embarrassing moments

'As soon as I'd said it, I realised my mistake,' says Bella, 36. 'I was having a drink (0) .... a friend and we were gossiping about this woman we know. I made a joke about her haircut (9) .... her look like an escaped convict. As we were laughing, I looked around and realised she was in the bar. I (10) .... have died. I still have no idea if she heard me but I can't think about it now (11) .... cringing.'

It's easy to sympathise with Bella's situation. (12) .... hasn't had a moment of awkwardness that has somehow grown out of (13) .... proportion, so much so that even the memory of it makes us feel sick? Our shame when we make a faux pas is so strong it makes us irrational. We know that, if it happened to anyone else, we'd advise laughing it off, but when it's our own mistake we torture (14) .... by replaying the moment over and over again. Why is it that little incidents can cause us (15) .... agony?

Studies show that we consistently overestimate our real worth and abilities. When we make a mistake we're shocked by the reality of our faults. It's as (16) .... we suddenly catch a glimpse of how we actually are, rather than how we like to think we are, and this sits uncomfortably with our perception of ourselves.

Part 3

For questions **17-24**, read the text below. Use the word given in capitals at the end of some of the lines to form a word that fits in the gap **in the same line.** There is an example at the beginning **(0)**.
Write your answers **IN CAPITAL LETTERS**.

Example:	0	INVITATIONS

Modern manners

Dress down Fridays, emailed **(0)**.................................. and texting your boss - British society is	**INVITE**
(17) .... loosening up and the famous British etiquette is fast eroding.	**APPEAR**
Jeans are **(18)** .... in many smart restaurants and casual buffets have started	**ACCEPT**
to replace three-course dinner parties. Increased **(19)** .... might, for some,	**FORMAL**
be a sign of national liberation, but for others, it could be a cause of anxiety.	
It might be that it is an **(20)** .... that the stiff-upper-lip Brits are finally	**INDICATE**
responding to fast-forward, modern, multi-cultural life by becoming less inhibited.	
However, while we are social creatures, we are also **(21)** .... Over the years	**RITUAL**
we have evolved certain social codes for our **(22)** .... with others.	**INTERACT**
We create little boxes around ourselves to make us feel secure. But for some, this new era	
is one of despair where standards of presentation have slipped and common	
(23) .... is fast disappearing. People who hold this belief try to rationalise	**COURTEOUS**
their resistance by saying it amounts to **(24)** .... , ignorance or loss of respect.	**LAZY**

Part 4

For questions **25-30**, complete the second sentence so that it has a similar meaning to the first sentence, using the word given. **Do not change the word given**. You must use between **three** and **six** words, including the word given. Here is an example **(0)**.

Example: 0 George should have worked harder if he wanted to pass the exam. **succeeded**
Had George worked harder, ... passing the exam.

Write the missing words **IN CAPITAL LETTERS**.

0	HE WOULD HAVE SUCCEEDED IN

25 Her boyfriend impressed her parents on their first meeting. **made**
Her boyfriend .... her parents when they first met.

26 Thomas didn't feel like going to the party. **mood**
Thomas was .... to the party.

27 They didn't trust each other at all. **complete**
There .... between them.

28 The ferry timetable can alter depending on the weather. **subject**
The ferry timetable .... depending on the weather.

29 I hope his story will help us to understand what happened. **shed**
Hopefully when he tells us his story it will .... what happened.

30 They concluded that there was nothing more they could do to save the business. **came**
They .... the business was beyond help.

Part 5

You are going to read a newspaper column written by an artist. For questions **31-36**, choose the answer **(A, B, C or D)** which you think fits best according to the text.

A week of letters

This week I've been showered with accolades. It's been a week of extremely strange, wonderful letters. One letter I received was from the University of Kent, inviting me to accept an honorary PhD, to be made a Doctor of Letters this summer. I was really chuffed and quite taken aback. I kept having to explain to people: "But you're not a real doctor. People don't actually call you a doctor." The other week I was on a plane where they actually asked: "Is there a doctor on board?" And then quickly followed with the words: "Medical doctor". I said to my friend: "Lucky they got that in quick or half the plane would be on their feet."

A few years ago, I was made an Honorary Fellow by Kent Institute of Art and Design. My gown and puffy hat really suited me and I was quite proud of them. Once when I was a guest speaker at the Oxford Union, I said to the union President, about half-an-hour before the talk: "Is there somewhere where I can change into my gown?" At which he just presumed I meant a dress by some top fashion designer. When I appeared in my university gown and hat he said: "Where did you get that from?" I replied: "What? Do you think I stole it?" and I remember, when I walked into the grand hall, I'd never heard so many wolf whistles. But it is odd that if you are a little bit rough around the edges, and you have a good education, let's say you went to a good university, people somehow think that your dad must have pulled a few strings to get you there. I must admit it really winds me up the way that people make assumptions about you just from the way that you speak. It's not so much about a regional accent, it's more a class thing. I try to take people as I find them. You never know what you might miss out on if you dismiss somebody from the first moment you meet them.

I like being a doctor of letters. I think it suits me. And people who know me really well know that I like sending all manner of missives and notes through the post. I like it in an old-fashioned kind of way. It's how I imagine myself being when I am old and happy, sitting cosy by the fire with a cat who has broken the *Guinness Book of Records* for being the oldest cat on the planet. Happily sitting there, writing letters and sending them out into the ether. I love that familiar plop as a letter or package lands on the floor by my front door. There's always the excitement of the unknown as you go to open it. I guess I'm just like a kid at Christmas wondering what's inside the sparkling parcel.

I have received some cracking letters this week. One from Africa - an ex-mercenary putting me straight. It's a fascinating letter that describes the whole history of the mercenaries. It was a very thoughtful, sophisticated letter - something which would be quite hard to achieve in conversation. That's what is so amazing about letters, there's a timelessness about them, where the thoughts hang in space and then you have time to deal with these thoughts. Especially in terms of an argument which, for the record, I am absolutely useless at. I have no chance of ever winning an argument. I am too emotional and react very immaturely to certain situations.

Back to the letters. I had a lovely one from the NSPCC who want to induct me into the third NSPCC Hall of Fame for the support I have given them over the last few years. I became all teary when I read the letter. When you speak on behalf of people or children who don't have a voice, that's the reward in doing it, hoping that you are making a difference somewhere. But to be honoured for doing it is really lovely.

Even my cat received a letter today with a big pack of cat food. The letter was really cute and put a smile on my face. But not as half as big a smile as the letter I received last Friday. "May I offer my sincere apologies that you did not receive the letter of 28th November. I have the greatest pleasure in inviting you, on behalf of the Council and Senate of the College, to accept an Honorary Doctorate of the Royal College of Art" - a double doctorate! Now who shall I write to tell them my news?

31. How did the writer feel about receiving the letter from the University of Kent?

A. She had been expecting to receive something like that.
B. She was quite arrogant about it.
C. She wasn't quite sure what it entailed.
D. It came out of the blue.

32. The President of the Oxford Union

A. assumed that she only wore fashionable clothes.
B. deliberately offended her.
C. thought she looked ridiculous in her gown.
D. had preconceptions about her.

33. The writer believes that

A. too many people rely on their parents to help them out in life.
B. she lives in a generally classist society.
C. her father could have done more to help her.
D. she has missed out on a lot of opportunities in the past.

34. Why did the ex-mercenary write to her?

A. To introduce her to his particular field of interest.
B. To inform her on a subject that she had misunderstood.
C. To try to persuade her to support a particular cause.
D. To help her with an educational study.

35. The writer believes that letters

A. are the most sophisticated form of modern communication.
B. will remain when all other forms of communication no longer exist.
C. let the reader absorb information and formulate a response.
D. incite argument more than speech does.

36. Why is the writer so pleased in the final paragraph?

A. Because she has gained more public recognition.
B. Because she has finally received an apology from The Royal College of Art.
C. Because she finds the idea of her cat getting a letter very amusing.
D. Because she doesn't know if she should write lots of letters.

Part 6

You are going to read four reviews of visiting Venice during Christmas time. For questions 37-40, choose from reviews A-D. The reviews may be chosen more than once.

Venice for Christmas

Four critics comment on the experience

A

I first saw Venice in June 1984. It was a sewer. I had arrived in Rome with an insane man (a misanthropic friend with all the composure of a bag of cats), his new wife, and an image of myself sitting in a white suit in the Piazza San Marco listening to violins while pigeons flew. Lord knows where this image came from. I had never read Thomas Mann's *Death in Venice* nor seen Katharine Hepburn in *Summertime*. I picked up the suit in Rome, ditched my friends and drove to Florence and on to Venice. At a mediocre trattoria on my first evening, I met a photographer, a young woman from Mexico travelling through Italy. After snapping a picture of me in the suit, standing among the pigeons in the Piazza San Marco while violins whined the Beatles, she skipped town. Following a quick tour of the Doge's Palace, I also fled the hordes for an Orient-Express train through the quiet Tyrol.

B

My dream has always been to spend Christmas in Venice, during the off-peak season. This was brought on by reading a travel article about a writer who did just that years ago - it sounded just magical. This year my dream came true. I have always had a real passion for Venice and with my love of photography, it's a totally unique destination. My husband Brian and I spent 12 days in Venice for Christmas and New Year and we revelled in the absence of ostentatious decorations that are unfortunately, so common, back home. We left home on the 21st of December arriving in glorious sunshine that lasted for the whole holiday. There is nothing more pleasurable than arriving by water taxi, especially with the light streaming onto the palazzi of the Grand Canal, turning them to burnished gold with the light once again reflected back into the canal streaked gold and blue; just divine, and the thing of Venice legends. Speeding along towards the Grand Canal it's the light that seduces you every time and makes you feel so very alive.

C

Venice at Christmas time is truly magical. The misty grey weather makes Venice hauntingly beautiful and absolutely enchanting. Canals seem to belong, once again, to those long lost centuries; past and ancient palaces seem to float upon white clouds. Ancient history and magical kingdoms meet in a delightful experience you'll never forget. Venice at Christmas is surprisingly lacking the tourist crowds. Instead you'll find it full of locals and Christmas markets. Most of the main squares or campos have a market. Plenty of delightful Christmas concerts are held throughout Venice. They are easily discovered by reading the posters around the city or asking your hotel for advice. La Pieta church on the Riva degli Schiavoni, where Vivaldi was once choir master, hosts some of the best. If you would like to experience Venice in all its magnificence and you have a big budget for sumptuous luxury, then the following hotels are the ones I can recommend.

D

True to its authentic nature, Christmas is not a big commercial event in Venice. Typical Christmas decorations such as lights, garlands and trees are confined to the busiest parts of the city: the Merceria, the Rialto and San Marco - mercifully not thronged with masses of tourists at this time of year. Occasionally, one can see a window or a balcony timidly decorated. Nativity scenes, or presepi, on the other hand, are much dearer to the Italians. After all, the first Nativity scene is said to have been the creation of Saint Francis. It was a living one and took place in Greccio, a small town south of Assisi, in 1223. Christmas trees, Germanic in origin, came to Italy, and the rest of the world, via England and the United States and much later than the presepi. You can find Christmas trees in Venice, even natural ones, but only rarely in public areas.

Which reviewer

disagrees with the other three reviewers, finding Venice over-crowded and unpleasant?	37
like D, refers to the understated way that Venetians celebrate Christmas?	38
like C, refers to the captivating nature of Venice?	39
comments on the lack of tourists at Christmas time in the city?	40

Part 7

You are going to read an extract from a newspaper article. Six paragraphs have been removed from the extract. Choose from the paragraphs **A-G** the one which fits each gap (41-46). There is one extra paragraph which you do not need to use.

Bad moods aren't necessarily bad for you

A two-minute film of penguins is a sure-fire way to improve a person's mood. There's something about penguins slip-sliding on the ice that seems to make everyone smile, a fact that psychologists have put to good use in their laboratory investigations of mood.

41 ______

Moods, and bad moods in particular, often appear to come from nowhere. We all have a tendency to notice the negative feelings rather than the positive feelings, but the good news is that we are happier than we tend to think. When a leading Canadian psychologist asked people to keep a diary of every mood they experienced throughout the day, it was the negative moods that predominated. But when he paged the people at random intervals and asked them how they were feeling at that exact moment, it was clear that they felt good most of the time.

42 ______

Moods are not just feelings we experience; they affect the way our minds work. When we are feeling happy we notice a lot of what's going on around us, but the moment anxiety strikes our attention narrows. If you're phobic about spiders, once you realise you're in a room with a spider, you focus on that and disregard almost everything else.

43 ______

Moods even influence the way we retrieve memories. A person feeling sad finds it easier to remember other sad occasions, while a happy person remembers other happy times. This can make it hard to shake off a bad mood. While you sit fuming with anger that a friend of yours has upset you, happy events do not tend to pop into your head. Instead you are more likely to think of other times when friends have let you down.

44 ______

Hope - the feeling that good things might happen in the future - is so powerful that it can even affect our health. Hope gives us energy, and research has shown that hopeful people are more likely to succeed in work, in sport, in academia and in politics. They are also happier and better at both persevering with a task and solving problems.

45 ______

Positive emotions have clear and tangible benefits - hope can even make you live longer. But however destructive they seem, even temper tantrums and sulks have their uses. Emotions are all about communication. They give us information about the way other people feel. If no one ever got angry with you or stopped talking to you, you might never know you had upset them.

46 ______

Looking at the research on moods, it is clear that we don't need to be afraid of our negative emotions. We imagine that it's essential to get control of our bad moods, and it's true that emotional management is a crucial part of our personal development and relationships. But there is another aspect to our emotional ups and downs: our feelings have important things to tell us, and we do well to listen to them.

A In one study, which shows just what sort of ramifications this could have, job interviewers who were feeling happy (because they'd just been told they had done well on a test) rated applicants more positively and were more likely to say they would hire them. Meanwhile, the interviewers who were told they had done badly on the test viewed applicants less favourably.

B Now, it could be argued that this is all a media stunt. Following a thoroughly frustrating half hour listening to unbearable music while you wait to get through to a call centre, only to find that they cannot solve your problem, you might well feel pretty angry. But eventually, and probably without consciously thinking about it, you will distract. You are employing coping strategies to help to change your mood.

C If words are flashed up on a computer screen it takes us longer to read a word associated with our anxieties than other words. So people with eating disorders take a fraction of a second longer to read words such as 'food' and 'meal' than everyone else. Because these words make a person anxious, they actually slow down their thinking.

D Also, anger readies our bodies for attack, giving us extra vigour that might prove essential in a fight. No other emotion is able to keep the body at a high pitch for such long periods. Energy is diverted towards the muscles, a feature that many sports people use to their advantage, deliberately stoking up their anger towards their opponent.

E One reason why hopeful people succeed is that they set themselves higher goals and more goals at a time, which buffers them against disappointment if one plan does not work out. In one extraordinary study, students' feelings of hope when they started college were a better predictor of their final results six years later than their entrance exam marks. Levels of hope even foretold the students who were later to drop out.

F Indeed we are far more likely to notice and remember negative moods. Whether it's anger, fear or pure joy, moods can feel overwhelming and beyond our control. Just one careless comment or email can trigger a new mood. They change very fast.

G Take part in an experiment on mood and the chances are that you will be shown a video of penguins. Over the past decades, in particular, psychologists have been using such laboratory experiments to investigate what moods are and why it is that they can fire us up one moment and drain us of energy the next.

Part 8

You are going to read some horoscopes. For questions 47-56, choose from the horoscopes (**A-F**). The horoscopes may be chosen more than once.

In which horoscope is the following mentioned?

There's a hidden side to something someone says.	**47**	
Boring people seem to have featured in your life lately.	**48**	
More is less in some situations.	**49**	
Don't let someone force you to make a hasty decision.	**50**	
Your finances are your own business.	**51**	
Someone special needs your undivided attention.	**52**	
To take advantage of a situation you need to be adaptable.	**53**	
Don't get carried away by your positive feelings.	**54**	
People tend to be cautious of positive things.	**55**	
It's time to recharge your batteries.	**56**	

Horoscopes

A

At times you'll wonder how many major roles you're meant to play in the lives of others. Instead of trying to keep everybody happy, focus on a one-to-one relationship that's suffering from neglect. Do whatever it takes to rejuvenate it. A close relationship is about to go through a magical phase, and although you should relax and enjoy it, there will still be tricky topics to tackle. Remember: too many words can weaken even the strongest argument. As a certain situation becomes untenable, it's not your job to make everything perfect for everybody. You could try detaching yourself, as long as those concerned don't start wondering why they're being given the cold shoulder. Be tactful.

B

It may not be until you look back on this week that you realise it was a watershed. That's mostly because you'll be so absorbed by sudden offers and the dilemmas left over from recent events. With things moving so swiftly, you'll have to leave details for later. But you'll soon realise that developments are only the first stage in a series of brilliant ideas and changing situations that lasts until the end of the month. Knowing that, you can afford to aim higher than you would otherwise. Be sure to get to grips with minor problems now - you're in line for one or two wonderful experiences and mustn't be preoccupied with mundane concerns. And certainly don't allow anyone to question how much you're spending on yourself.

C

Most people are wary of offers that seem too good to be true. However, by now you've probably realised that what came your way last week could change your life. This fantastic trend continues this week, the only problem being that you must respond swiftly, probably before midweek. From that point onwards the mood changes. This might not be much fun but it gives you a chance to investigate what you've got yourself involved in and undertake the first of many sessions of fine-tuning future arrangements. Don't be unnerved by unexpected developments - you'll find strengths you never knew you had. You'll develop an air of optimism. Just remember to take a reality check once in a while.

D

You don't regard yourself as a control freak, or you didn't, until recently, when numerous decisions were taken out of your hands. Things haven't been that bad. You've just been cornered into dealing with tedious people, being dutiful and doing what you dislike. However, as you're now discovering, each cleared up a potential obstacle. By the end of the month, not only will the tide turn your way, some of what you have learnt dealing with those loathsome tasks will prove to be unexpectedly handy. If others tell you something serious, don't freak out, and certainly don't feel you have to provide instant solutions if you're suddenly offered an ultimatum. You're sometimes seen as a bit of a pushover - prove that you're anything but.

E

Exciting developments earlier this month made you realise that to make the most of what's coming your way, you'll have to be flexible about existing arrangements and future plans. Exhausting as the resulting juggling of plans is, you can't help but be intrigued by what - and who - has come your way. Taking advantage of this requires a serious rethink of elements of your life you'd regarded as set in stone. This takes you in new directions that shake things up. If this seems too much trouble, think of times in the past when you gave similar things a go and, ultimately, were relieved you did. Try to build into your routine regular intervals during which you can be as light-hearted as you want. You may feel that others are trying to make you work non-stop. They're not.

F

You'll feel on top of the world at times, but if certain colleagues or associates swear they're on your side, watch out. Some people will try to use words that disguise their true motives, rather than reveal them, don't fall for it. This might be a good time to take a well-earned break and I don't just mean a day or two off work to catch up with the housework. Why not book yourself a last-minute cheap flight to somewhere that you've never been to before. Experience something new and put something back into your creative system instead of giving out all the time. We all need inspiration every now and again and you are well overdue a refuelling session. You'll bounce back with a strength that you haven't felt for years.

WRITING - Part 1

You **must** answer this question. Write your answer in **220-260** words in an appropriate style.

1. You have watched and listened to a video on Youtube about which form of renewable energy would be best for a tourist island. You have made the notes below:

Which form of renewable energy would be best for a tourist island?
- wind turbines
- solar panels
- nuclear power

Some opinions expressed in the discussion:
"Nuclear power is a sustainable energy source that reduces carbon emissions."
"Wind turbines would destroy the landscape of the island."
"We couldn't be 100% powered by solar panels."

Write an essay discussing **two** of the renewable energy forms in your notes. You should explain **which form of renewable energy would be best** for a tourist island, **giving reasons** in support of your answer.

You may, if you wish, make use of the opinions expressed in the discussion, but you should use your own words as far as possible.

WRITING - Part 2

Write an answer to **one** of the questions **2-4** in this part. Write your answer in **220-260** words in an appropriate style.

2. You have recently visited a museum or gallery, either in your country or abroad. Write a review for a tourist information magazine describing the building, where it is located and if it has any facilities such as a shop or cafe.

   Describe the contents of the museum or gallery and mention any exhibits that you were particularly impressed by. Say whether it is worth visiting and mention who might be interested in it and why.

   Write your **review**.

3. You have read an opinion on a blog about a new mobile application for finding nightspots in a given postal code. The author of the piece presents a negative picture of the application criticising its speed, accuracy, and usability. You, however, have used the application regularly and believe it to be excellent.

   Write a response to the blogger expressing how the application has served you well, highlighting its user-friendliness, design, accuracy and speed. Feel free to address other points in your letter to be sent by e-mail.

   Write your **letter** in reply. You do not need to include postal addresses.

4. The University is building a new recreation centre for students and is looking for input as to what the facility should include. The institution has asked students to write a proposal of what they would like to see in the centre. Past facilities there and at other universities have included restaurants, computer facilities, games and cinemas, among other services and attractions.

   Discuss what you think should be included and why, in order to improve the overall experience of the student population.

   Write your **proposal**.

LISTENING - Part 1

You will hear three different extracts. For questions 1-6, choose the answer (**A**, **B** or **C**) which fits best according to what you hear. There are two questions for each extract.

Extract One

You will hear two people talking about their grandparents.

1 What kind of character is the man's grandfather?

A unsociable
B quiet but friendly
C moody but lively

1	

2 What did the woman's grandparents use to do?

A try to upset the children by exhausting them
B get very tired when the children stayed with them
C laugh because the children weren't as fit as they were

2	

Extract Two

You will hear two people talking about their childhood.

3 What is the relationship between the speakers?

A school friends
B mother and son
C siblings

3	

4 We learn that

A the man is more highly qualified than the woman.
B the woman failed her degree.
C the man failed all his school exams.

4	

Extract Three

You will hear two people talking about their partners.

5 Jenny

A is engaged.
B is married.
C will probably get a divorce.

5	

6 Paul thinks

A Brian needs to make a decision soon.
B Jenny needs to be more positive.
C they should change their careers to make time for each other.

6	

LISTENING - Part 2

You will hear a report about the 11-plus exam in Britain. For questions 7-14, complete the sentences.

Studying for the 11-plus exam

According to experts, the **7** ______ of children does not significantly help them to pass exams.

English grammar schools receive **8** ______ on average for every place they have.

Mike Walker says that the 11-plus questions are **9** ______ .

Every year approximately **10** ______ children take the 11-plus exam.

According to a recent study, grammar schools tend to have more children from fairly wealthy families than children from **11** ______ backgrounds.

In schools that aren't grammar schools, 12 per cent of children receive **12** ______ .

You have to pay nearly £300 in extra costs for **13** ______ for the internet tutoring course.

Opinions on the effectiveness of courses as preparation for the 11-plus exam are **14** ______ .

LISTENING - Part 3

You will hear two psychologists talking about modern childhood. For questions 15-20, choose the answer (**A**, **B**, **C** or **D**), which fits best according to what you hear.

15 What does Daniel imply about past images of childhood?

A They are entirely fictional.
B They all show the misfortunes of childhood.
C They are diverse.
D They represent the innocence of childhood.

16 When mentioning the children throwing bags on the bus-stop, Louise is

A critical.
B amused.
C angry.
D sarcastic.

17 According to Daniel,

A children are failing to learn adequate social skills.
B children do not eat a balanced diet.
C children are becoming involved in political scandals.
D children are far more sociable than they used to be.

18 Louise believes that

A parents are no longer interested in their children.
B children should study harder to pass school exams.
C modern life has a negative effect on children.
D most parents are emotionally unstable.

19 What does Louise say about the media?

A Manipulative actors have a negative effect on children.
B It encourages celebrities to inspire young children.
C Adverts are aimed more at young people than adults.
D It glorifies unrealistic ideals.

20 Daniel implies that

A children would be happier if their parents taught them at home.
B machines are more of a menace to children than people are.
C teachers aren't helping children to be competitive enough.
D most teenage problems stem from an unbalanced diet.

LISTENING - Part 4

You will hear five short extracts in which people are talking about workaholism.
While you listen you must complete both tasks.

TASK ONE

For questions 21-25, choose from the list A-H the person who is speaking.

A	a police officer		
B	a teacher	Speaker 1	21
C	an advertising agent	Speaker 2	22
D	a translator	Speaker 3	23
E	a journalist	Speaker 4	24
F	a banker	Speaker 5	25
G	a tax inspector		
H	a cleaner		

TASK TWO

For questions 26-30, choose from the list **A-H** what each speaker is expressing.

A	a desire to change their lifestyle but realising this isn't possible		
B	the view that a sense of duty to society should not be taken to extremes	Speaker 1	26
C	regret at having spent too much time playing golf with a superior	Speaker 2	27
D	the view that workaholism is a class issue	Speaker 3	28
E	the belief that work ethic is linked to and varies by culture	Speaker 4	29
F	the view that the main cause of marital breakdown is workaholism	Speaker 5	30
G	how, for them, the lure of financial reward led to workaholism		
H	the view that the government should intervene to grant more holidays		

Test 5

Practice Test 5

Part 1

For questions 1-8, read the text below and decide which answer (**A,B,C** or **D**) best fits each gap. There is an example at the beginning (0).

Example:

0 **A** methods **B** theories **C** causes **D** consequences

0	A	B	C	D
			▬	

The Return of El Nino

Aside from the seasons, El Nino and its twin, La Nina, are the two largest single (0) .... of variability in the world's climate from year to year. Both are dictated by shifts in water temperature in the tropical Pacific basin between Australia and South America. (1) .... after the Spanish words for "Christ child" and "the girl" because of their (2) .... to Christmas, they lead to dramatic shifts in the entire system of oceanic and atmospheric factors from air pressure to currents.

A significant rise in sea temperature leads to an El Nino event whereas a fall in temperature leads to La Nina. The cause of the phenomenon is not fully understood but in an El Nino "event" the pool of warm surface water is forced eastwards by the loss of the westerly trade winds. The sea water evaporates, (3) .... in drenching rains over South America, as well as western parts of the United States, such as California. The effects can (4) .... for anything from a few weeks to 18 months, causing extreme weather as far afield as India and East Africa. The correlation with global warming is as (5) .... unclear. Archaeological evidence shows El Ninos and La Ninas have been (6) .... for 15,000 years. But scientists are investigating whether climate change is leading to an increase in their intensity or duration.

The weather pattern is already having early and intense effects and El Nino could bring extreme rainfall to parts of east Africa which were last year (7) .... by a cycle of drought and floods. It's difficult to (8) .... what will happen to the weather in the British Isles, but it will probably add to the likelihood of record-breaking temperatures in the UK.

1	**A** Elected	**B** Called	**C** Nominated	**D** Named
2	**A** proximity	**B** neighbourhood	**C** attachment	**D** bond
3	**A** producing	**B** resulting	**C** stemming	**D** refreshing
4	**A** persist	**B** keep	**C** conserve	**D** assert
5	**A** still	**B** yet	**C** present	**D** now
6	**A** dawning	**B** obtaining	**C** occurring	**D** securing
7	**A** hit	**B** shoved	**C** punctured	**D** punched
8	**A** predict	**B** imply	**C** entail	**D** point

Part 2

For questions 9-16, read the text below and think of the word which best fits each gap. Use only one word in each gap. There is an example at the beginning (0).
Write your answers in **CAPITAL LETTERS**.

Example: | 0 | JUST |

A sting in the tale

A scorpion stung Peter Marks on the back of his right leg, (0) .... below the knee, then continued up that leg and down the (9) ...., he believes, before getting him again in the shin. It wasn't (10) .... he was expecting on a flight from Chicago to Vermont. Marks, a 46-year-old builder, was aboard the United Airlines flight on the second leg of his trip home from San Francisco where he and his wife Helena had been visiting their sons. He awoke (11) .... a nap shortly before landing and noticed something strange.

"My leg felt like it was asleep, but that was isolated to one spot, and it felt as (12) .... it was being jabbed with a sharp piece of plastic (13) .... something. The second sting came after the plane had landed and the Marks were waiting for their bags at the luggage carousel. Peter rolled up his cuff to investigate, and the scorpion fell out.

"It felt like a shock, a tingly thing. Someone screamed, "It's a scorpion," Peter recalled. Another passenger stepped on the 5-centimetre arachnid, and (14) .... else suggested Marks seek medical help. "The airlines tell you that you can't bring water on a plane", Helena Marks said, "but the scorpion did make it aboard". A United spokesperson said the incident "is something that we will look (15) .... We're very sorry for what happened. Our customers' safety and security is our number one priority." Such incidents are not unheard of. An American Airlines flight was delayed for an hour in Toronto on Sunday after a passenger was stung by a scorpion that had (16) .... its way on board. Paramedics treated the man when the flight landed.

Part 3

For questions 17-24, read the text below. Use the word given in capitals at the end of some of the lines to form a word that fits in the gap **in the same line.** There is an example at the beginning **(0)**.
Write your answers **IN CAPITAL LETTERS**.

Example:

0	GEOGRAPHICAL

Ode to the ocean

Of all our planet's **(0)** .... features, the ocean is probably the most schizophrenic.	**GEOGRAPHY**
In one moment it can be a source of **(17)** .... and comfort, in the next a capricious	**SERENE**
and threatening force that unleashes a barrage of unimaginable power onto coastlines.	
It is this **(18)** .... that attracts photographer Philip Plisson to the world's waters,	**PREDICT**
prompting him to live his life travelling the seas. He has produced a book, *The Sea,* and has now	
(19) .... his lens to provide more global focus in *The Ocean.* In nearly 200 images	**WIDE**
taken in more than 50 countries, the book celebrates Plisson's **(20)** .... for the variety	**FASCINATE**
and beauty of the sea. He honours the sea through his lens and tries to raise **(21)**	**AWARE**
of its importance to the survival of the planet. 60% of the world's population lives on a	
(22) .... strip that is 60km wide. By 2025, 75% will be living on the same strip,	**COAST**
but it will be 75% of 8 billion instead of the present 6 billion. Images of extravagant	
reclamation projects like 'The Palm' and 'The World' in Dubai point towards man's	
attempts to defy nature and expand the coastline for further **(23)**	**URBAN**
Through Plisson's extraordinary photographs, it is the portrayal of the ocean's simultaneous	
power and **(24)** .... that makes this book so enthralling.	**FRAGILE**

Part 4

For questions 25-30, complete the second sentence so that it has a similar meaning to the first sentence, using the word given. **Do not change the word given**. You must use between **three** and **six** words, including the word given. Here is an example **(0)**.

Example: 0 George should have worked harder if he wanted to pass the exam. **succeeded**
Had George worked harder, ... passing the exam.

Write the missing words **IN CAPITAL LETTERS.**

0	HE WOULD HAVE SUCCEEDED IN

25 It is unlikely that Jim will get the promotion. **chance**
There is .... promoted.

26 Graham phoned his wife as soon as he arrived in Brazil. **lost**
Graham .... wife on his arrival in Brazil.

27 The government is so powerful that it can control people's lives. **power**
Such is .... that it can control people's lives.

28 You should never leave the baby alone under any circumstances. **is**
Under .... be left alone.

29 In the end we did all the housework on Sunday. **up**
We .... all the housework on Sunday.

30 Bob often mistrusts people when he first meets them. **tendency**
Bob .... people when he first meets them.

Practice Test 5

Part 5

You are going to read a magazine article about a woman who looks after orphaned gorillas and monkeys. For questions 31-36, choose the answer **(A, B, C or D)** which you think fits best according to the text.

A day in the life of a wildlife conservationist

At half five, bang! I'm awake. I hear the chimps calling outside. If I'm hand-rearing an infant gorilla or chimpanzee then it's the first thing I see, sprawled across my chest or in the crook of my arm. I splash water on my face, scrape my hair back and get dressed - though putting jeans on with a gorilla holding on to your leg is difficult. I make milk for the baby monkeys and walk to the village where the rest of the staff live. The gorillas in the trees look down at me and beat their chests; that gives me such a buzz in the morning.

I was about five when my mum first took me to the zoo, and there was a huge silverback gorilla behind a glass pane, just sitting there, staring. Even as a child, my heart stopped, I was so sad. Flying into Cameroon for the first time, I had this unbelievable feeling: I'm in the same country as wild gorillas. I was overwhelmed. It felt like coming home.

In Cameroon, gorilla and chimpanzee meat sells for anything from £15 a piece. The infants are too small to sell for meat, so, if they survive, the hunters tie them up and drag them through the forest and sell them into the pet trade. In town they get more than £100 each. In Cameroon you see chimpanzees on chains everywhere. In captivity they can live up to 50 years. But infant gorillas usually don't survive seeing their family slaughtered. They die of a broken heart.

When I get to the village, I'll have a cup of tea and half a stick of bread and Marmite and join the staff meeting. Around 11, I check with the head keeper that trees aren't overhanging the fences and the electric current is on. It's a constant battle between us and the chimps to keep them in. I look at the chimpanzee groups: how they work together, how they start an argument - they're exactly the same as us. The first time I heard a gorilla laugh I couldn't believe it. Lots of people believe that if you eat gorilla it gives you strength, and the meat is very sweet. But there is a 0.6% difference in DNA between us and them: we're eating our kin. As far as I'm concerned, it's cannibalism. More countries need to take Spain's example and propose human rights for primates.

Sometimes I'll come back to my room and have a cup of tea and a plate of rice and beans for lunch. Food is really basic - we haven't the money to buy luxuries.

I've eaten just about every type of leaf in this forest, just to show infants how to survive. Often infants come in with fractured legs and arms from gunshot wounds. When the mother's shot, they get the bullet too. We haven't got a vet in camp: we need one. If we're lucky we'll find a hospital willing for us to bring a chimp in to be x-rayed, but sometimes it's days before they are seen.

Years ago, locals would hunt gorillas and chimpanzees to feed their family. Now the bushmeat trade has gone commercial. It's huge. The timber companies have opened up the forest, putting roads in areas hunters could never have reached. We're just a plaster over the problem. The only way to stop this slaughter is to stop the people at the top. It's no good telling Cameroonians to stop killing chimpanzees and gorillas when you've got huge western companies raping the whole forest.

As the sun goes down at about six, I like to go outside and sit on my chair and think about my family. I miss them. I don't even consider having a relationship: this is 24 hours a day, seven days a week. But I'll make that sacrifice: I made a promise when I arrived that I wasn't going to let my babies down. But don't think of them as child substitutes, this is serious conservation. I've had malaria eight or nine times. It's horrendous but you carry on. Our director is a huge support. I never cry in front of the infants. Once I did, and this seven-month-old-gorilla looked into my face and wiped the tears away. You have to be the one to give them support so they get strong. It's humbling that humans have done this to them and they'll turn around and put trust in us again.

Normally at half seven I'll grab a packet of crackers and a banana and talk the head keeper through tomorrow's meeting. Sometimes I'm too tired to shower and just fall on my bed. I do the accounts and write my list of things to be done. I'll hear the chimps calling, or one of the monkeys having a shout at something. My eyes just close and that's it.

31 From the opening paragraph we can deduce that the writer

A. is slightly nervous of the wild gorillas.
B. often finds that baby gorillas or chimpanzees manage to break into her hut.
C. tends to keep infant gorillas or chimpanzees as pets.
D. has a natural empathy with the animals.

32 Why did the writer feel like she was 'coming home' in paragraph two?

A. Because it had been such a long time since she had last been there.
B. Because she was fulfilling a dream to live in the gorilla's natural habitat.
C. Because she had so many relatives there.
D. Because she'd never felt at home anywhere else.

33 According to the writer

A. eating gorilla meat can only be justified if the person needs it for medical reasons.
B. there is no difference between a gorilla and a human.
C. the Spanish are the only nation that have researched primate genetics properly.
D. it is as bad to eat gorilla meat as it is to eat human meat.

34 The writer's diet seems to be

A. the same as the diet of the infant gorillas and chimpanzees.
B. deliberately modest in order to stay fit and healthy.
C. dictated by what limited means are available to her at any time.
D. very unhealthy and making her ill.

35 What does the writer mean when she says they are 'just a plaster over the problem'?

A. What they are doing is pointless.
B. In the future they will be able to do a lot more than they can now.
C. They can't dramatically improve the situation.
D. They are eliminating the worst problems but they could do more.

36 The story of the infant gorilla that wiped away her tears reflects the writer's

A. determination not to get too involved with the animals.
B. belief that the animals have human-like feelings.
C. desire for revenge on the people who kill the animals.
D. depression that has been brought on by doing such a difficult job.

Part 6

You are going to read four reviews of a classical music performance. For questions 37-40, choose from reviews A-D. The reviews may be chosen more than once.

Riccardo Muti
Four critics comment on the concert

A

At one moment during the Chicago Symphony Orchestra's performance of the Verdi Requiem on Thursday evening, conducted by Riccardo Muti and streamed live from Orchestra Hall in Chicago, viewers could see the rosin glistening on a bow during close-up shots of the violinists. The performance, which had had a relatively low-key build-up, considering it was to be held in honour of the bicentennial of Verdi's birth, was the first concert the orchestra has streamed live on its Website. It was also viewable on Facebook and other sites and beamed to an outdoor screen at the Pritzker Pavilion in Millennium Park. Mr. Muti, widely admired as a Verdi interpreter, made his debut as the orchestra's music director designate in 2009, with the Requiem. He has also impressed with his brilliant, incisive conducting of Verdi operas.

B

With all the hype and media attention over Thursday's concert of Verdi's *Requiem*, by Riccardo Muti and the Chicago Symphony Orchestra, on the composer's 200th birthday, one wondered if there was any conceivable way the actual performance could transcend all the relentless build-up. Riccardo Muti is not a musician to fail to deliver on high expectations, especially where music of his compatriot, Giuseppe Verdi, is concerned. The concert, which was streamed live and free on the Internet to an international audience, provided a terrific exemplar to the world of the remarkable partnership of Muti and the Chicago musicians, with this riveting and combustible performance of Verdi's *Requiem* mass. Muti's skill and deep sympathy and understanding of this music, has been a constant throughout his career. He has recorded the *Requiem* three times, most recently the acclaimed Grammy-winning Chicago Symphony Orchestra recording; that preceded his music directorship in 2009.

C

Riccardo Muti often has deplored stage directors who run roughshod over the intentions of operatic composers, such as his beloved Giuseppe Verdi. There was no danger of that occurring at Saturday's long-awaited performance of Verdi's *Macbeth*, by the maestro and his Chicago Symphony Orchestra, because there wasn't a stage director within miles to distract attention from the music. And the musical glories of *Macbeth*, one of Verdi's early masterpieces, came across vividly in this first of four concert performances the music director is conducting at Symphony Centre to honour the composer's bicentennial. Today's foremost Verdi interpreter commanded an impressive international cast of singers, such as any major opera company would envy, most of them younger artists he has worked with in Rome and Salzburg, Austria, and trusts to realise his musical specifications.

D

Who needs sets or costumes? The much anticipated Chicago Symphony Orchestra concert performance of Verdi's *Macbeth* took place and, remarkably, exceeded even the high expectations for this event. Magnificently sung and played, and directed by Riccardo Muti, whose lifetime of Verdi experience and scholarship shone through every bar, this riveting *Macbeth* was one of the musical highlights of the year, and one of the great, memorable Chicago Verdi nights, even in a city with a long and rich history of Italian opera performances.
It was also a testament to the crackling partnership between Riccardo Muti and the orchestra. The hair-trigger responsiveness, whipcrack climaxes, lyric delicacy, and sheer vitality of the playing were technically faultless and, often, astounding. This roiling, powerful *Macbeth* marks the finest achievement yet from Muti and the Chicago Symphony Orchestra, even surpassing the *Othello* performances of two years ago.

Which reviewer

compares this Muti performance with a previous one with the Chicago Symphony Orchestra? **37** ___

implies that the performance exceeded expectations, like reviewer D? **38** ___

disagrees with the other three reviewers, saying that the performance was not as hotly anticipated as might be expected? **39** ___

highlights the technology used to broadcast the performance, like reviewer A? **40** ___

Part 7

You are going to read an extract from a wildlife book. Six paragraphs have been removed from the extract. Choose from the paragraphs **A-G** the one which fits each gap (41-46). There is one extra paragraph which you do not need to use.

The Big Game of Africa

We all know, in an academic sense, that man as a species has existed for a very long time and that we have only emerged with our present dominance in the comparatively recent past. The game country of Kenya puts this piece of knowledge into context and enables us to experience it at the deep, intuitive level where all knowledge is felt as well as known. When something is learnt in this deep sense the knowledge becomes part of ourselves and enriches our lives.

41 ______

Today this area is a network of roads and tracks and is almost entirely under cultivation. True, it contains the remnants of the Nandi and Kakamega forests but even these are rapidly being turned into charcoal and paper. I have driven over many roads in the area and walked the Nandi Hills without seeing any game. There are a few giraffe left on the high land between Kitale and Eldoret; the remaining antelope are rare and shy; the rhino and the lion have definitely gone. It is the same over vast tracts of Kenya; where seventy years ago there was an abundance of animals, today you will find almost nothing. I was hoping to see elephants.

42 ______

A number of cases of elephants aiding an injured comrade have been recorded by hunters and mother elephants have been seen to carry a dead baby around for several days. It has been known for a hunter to track a wounded elephant only to come on the corpse minus the valuable tusks, these having been broken off and smashed by his companions. It is common knowledge that wild elephants coming upon a skeleton of one of their own kind will examine the bones, carry them away, and scatter them far and wide, although they will ignore the remnants of other animals.

43 ______

But now pressure on the elephants' land is increasing. New strains of maize now make it feasible to grow crops in areas where only five years ago there was virtually no human population. The Masai, who until now have grazed their cattle alongside the plains game are beginning to plough their lands for wheat and corn. Other threats are posed by the increased use of insecticides; the expansion of cities and towns; and most worrying of all, the increase in the human population. Things must change.

44 ______

Above all the pace at which we disturb the natural environment must slow down. Our startling success with the physical sciences has convinced us that we can solve problems quickly by pushing the right buttons. But in nature, problems are not solved quickly, although they can be created overnight. A disturbance of the established order is a wound, quickly inflicted but slow to heal, with the ever-present possibility that the wound may cause a fatal infection. Even a carefully thought-out and well-controlled change is still a form of surgery from which the environment must recover by adjusting its complex mechanisms and balances to the new situation.

45 ______

Now, we humans and our greed are out of control all over the world; and in the same sense that a city child must visit a farm to find that milk comes from cows, not bottles, so most of us need to visit Africa to find where mankind came from. Even here there is a danger of losing touch with the past. Today the parks and reserves are last-ditch defences for Kenya's wildlife. The long-term outcome is far from certain, but meanwhile it is our privilege that enough remains for us to glimpse the original glory first hand.

46 ______

Try to stay longer with each group of animals. They will reward you in their time not yours - remember they are making the decisions. There is so much to see one is tempted to rush; more than one hundred species of mammals in Kenya, ninety-five in the Masai Mara Reserve alone. But these animals are not postage stamps or locomotive numbers to be ticked off on a list. Each of them has an individual character and fits into its own place in this complex system.

A

The men who started Kenya's wildlife sanctuaries were men of vision. They worked against heavy odds often with inadequate resources. What is now needed is a sense of vision in society as a whole - values which accept that man is a lesser part of a greater whole - an unfashionable idea in our rushing, modern world. We now need measures designed to preserve wildlife for centuries, conceived and administered at the international level.

B

Since life began the environment has been adjusting to change; today it is the speed of change which is new and potentially disastrous. A century ago man himself was part of the established order. The elephant hunters did not threaten the survival of the elephant any more than lions. The men of the Lingula tribe - great elephant hunters who used strong bows - had a toughness and knowledge which gave them nobility, in strong contrast to the furtive moral squalor of the international racketeers involved in today's ivory trade.

C

There is something inexorable about a herd like this moving across country. No browsing, no pausing to pluck branches or bunches of grass, no moving this way and that. Instead a steady marching, the young ones trotting to keep up. Other animals do not deflect them; they stride majestically, as though conscious they are invulnerable, and all give way before them.

D

In Kenya's game country, man is not yet the dominant animal and hopefully he never will be. Here, one can come to grips with the fact that for around half a million centuries mammals have been the dominant form of life in Africa and that only in the last of these centuries has man become the dominant mammal. But things are changing. In 1905 an army captain marching from Kitale to Nandi Fort in western Kenya, counted 124 giraffes, 85 waterbucks, 4 rhinos, 62 zebras, 27 ostriches and 4 lions in around 10 miles.

E

The slender security of this privilege makes it doubly sad that many visitors bring their own pace with them when they visit Kenya's wildlife. Too much dashing from one Game Park to another does not allow the visitor to attune himself. The use of a vehicle is an advantage in that it can approach the animals without alarming them. However, if it imposes a 21st-century rhythm on your visit to an area which still has the slow pulse of pre-history, you have failed to make the best of your privilege.

F

As well as being the biggest and in some ways the most interesting of the animals, elephants are in a sense the most tragic. A century ago they were the masters of the land. They had the run of the continent and generally managed their own affairs. No other large animal has had such a wide range of habitat, from mountain forests through savannah and semi-desert to the coast.

G

Like me, many visitors and scientists find elephants the most interesting animals to observe. There is the constant feeling that the elephants, too, understand, make decisions, have feelings, have friends. Stories of elephants are legion. Modern hunters say elephants know the boundaries of the National Parks and will smartly step inside when hunters are around. If only the poachers knew the rules and stuck to them as carefully as their victims.

Part 8

You are going to read some book reviews about earth exploration. For questions 47 - 56, choose from the reviews (**A-F**). The reviews may be chosen more than once.

In which review is the following mentioned?

Someone who left almost no stone unturned around the world.	47
The surprising anonymity of someone.	48
Disappointment that flora and other fauna are not mentioned.	49
A book that is physically difficult to carry around with you.	50
Some details are inaccurate in this book.	51
Information written like an old-fashioned diary.	52
Text that adds something to the images.	53
A collaboration that produced great results.	54
A book that covers all of nature's seasons.	55
A wide variety of subject matter.	56

Book Reviews on Earth exploration

A. *A Complete Guide to Life in a Cold Climate* by Richard Sale

This book is packed with information and deserves to be the ultimate Arctic wildlife guide for a long time to come. It begins well, with an introduction to Arctic geology, climate and habitats, an overview of all the people living and working in the region. The bulk of the book is an extensive field guide to Arctic birds and mammals, with distribution maps and information on confusing species. Its scope is broad and generous, but I have a few niggles. It should really include Arctic plants, fish and invertebrates. This would have doubled the size of the book and made it unwieldy and impractical, but it's fair to say that the title is misleading. But I'm being picky here, and these minor shortcomings don't detract from the overall value of the book.

B. *Burton Holmes Travelogues*

Burton Holmes was the greatest traveller not just of his own time but perhaps of all time. A pretty big claim, but there's evidence to back it up. Over a 60-year period, Holmes visited nearly every country on the planet, photographed all he saw, and invented the term 'travelogue'. His pictures are stunning, both as social history and as art. Holmes photographed everything: the dead on battlefields; the running of bulls in Spain; a mule train in Death Valley. A sequence of Vesuvius erupting in 1906 includes a shot of a woman under an ash-strewn sky that is positively apocalyptic, but Holmes' work wasn't restricted to the large canvas - he was as capable of capturing an intimate portrait of a chicken vendor in a Bangkok market as he was revealing the vastness and intricacy of the construction of the Panama Canal.

C. *No More Beyond* by Simon Nasht

In Simon Nasht's brilliant biography of Sir Hubert Wilkins, he says that his subject isn't like other great explorers, primarily because most of us have never heard of him. He had no lust for fame, instead being driven by a thirst that led him to remote environments and places that cried out for exploration, rather than towards the popular challenges so desired by newspaper editors of the day. Nasht couldn't believe "a man could achieve so much and yet be so little remembered." In 1917 Wilkins was under the command of veteran polar explorer and photographer Frank Hurley in the Australian Flying Corps. Their mutual interests were vital to the development of aerial photography as an integral part of modern geography.

D. *Farmland Wildlife* by James McCallum

As a refuge for wildlife, British farmland has had a bad press in recent years. Fortunately, the artist's beautiful visual journey through the seasons presented in this book reveals that there is still an abundance of wildlife if you know where to look for it and what to look for. McCallum shuns detailed portraiture in favour of sketches capturing the spirit of his subjects - and hooray for that. If I need precise anatomical detail, I can look at a photograph. But if I want to grasp how a stoat rolls an egg, how a male whitethroat makes his fluttering display-flights or how long-tailed tits work together to build their nests, then I need something more - and McCallum is stunningly good at translating these complex movements and behaviours onto the page. His simple explanatory captions - taken from his field notebook - are a bonus.

E. *Troubled Waters* by Sarah Lazarus

Sometimes it seems as though the size of books on whales is led by the size of the subject matter. This, however, is a small, readable book. There are no detailed species accounts and the text is almost entirely devoted to the threats that whales and dolphins face, such as chemical and noise pollution, ship strikes and entanglement in fishing nets. A careful read reveals factual errors but, on the whole, these do not affect the thoughtful and concise discussion. It is notoriously difficult to get to the bottom of the whaling issue, and here Lazarus struggles a bit. The International Whaling Commission comes in for a lot of criticism, which would perhaps have been better directed at the three of its members who have chosen not to abide by the spirit of its conservation decisions.

F. *The High Lowlands* by Derek Ratcliffe

For some, the south of Scotland is the plainer and less charismatic sibling of the breathtaking Highlands and the rugged West Coast. But it's every bit as wild as those famed areas, but with a gentler appeal. This book describes an unexpected Eden, a place whose heart pulses to a different beat. This is an epic piece of writing, its subject matter covered in a manner more akin to the journals of a Victorian chronicler than a modern natural history book. Derek Ratcliffe's recordings of the natural goings-ons in this lonely land spanned 50 years. His intimacy is apparent on every page. Everything is catalogued and described in meticulous detail, and few questions are left unanswered. It's a great pity that Derek did not live to see his life's work in print. This is a book for everyone, but it's a huge volume that you couldn't take with you on holiday unless you've got a pretty hefty rucksack and a strong back.

WRITING - Part 1

You **must** answer this question. Write your answer in **220-260** words in an appropriate style.

1. You have listened to a debate about UK university tuition fees. Then, you have been asked to vote in favour of some of the options provided. You have made the notes below:

Should UK universities charge tuition fees?
- tuition fees should not be charged
- universities should charge very low tuition fees
- universities need to charge high fees to have a high standard

Some opinions during the talk:
"Universities are facing substantial cuts in direct government funding."
"Universities will face additional economic pressures as student numbers increase."
"We should ensure access to university is based on the ability to learn, not the ability to pay."

Write an essay discussing **two** of the options in your notes. You should explain **which option would be best**, **giving reasons** in support of your answer.

You may, if you wish, make use of the opinions expressed in the talk, but you should use your own words as far as possible.

WRITING - Part 2

Write an answer to **one** of the questions **2-4** in this part. Write your answer in **220-260** words in an appropriate style.

2. You work for the local council. You have been asked to write a proposal, suggesting ways in which your neighbourhood could develop and be improved in order for it to be in an appropriate and good state for the next generation. You should include ideas for:

- environmental issues
- leisure
- education
- housing

Write your **proposal**.

3. You have received a letter from a friend:

I'm really enjoying the variety in my new job, which often allows me to travel on business. Actually, with that in mind, I'm contacting you now, as I'll be in your town for a week next month. Could you tell me the best places to go and what I can do, so that I can make the most of my free time when I have the odd evening or weekend free?

Sheila

Write your **letter**.

4. You see the following announcement on a website:

Reviews wanted for Entertainment Site
Send us a review of your favourite restaurant and get published on our Web page.

You have a favourite Italian restaurant you like to go to with your friends and family, that you want to submit for consideration. In your review, write about the food, service, decor and any other elements you think would provide a clear picture of the establishment.

Write your **review**.

LISTENING - Part 1

You will hear three different extracts. For questions 1-6, choose the answer (**A**, **B** or **C**) which fits best according to what you hear. There are two questions for each extract.

Extract One

You will hear two people talking about the wildlife in the area in which they live.

1 What is the man's reaction to the majority of visiting birdwatchers?

A He thinks they drive too fast.
B He believes they are ignorant of one of nature's delights.
C He doesn't understand why so many of them come to the area he lives in.

2 The speakers seem to

A be knowledgeable about their local wildlife.
B work for a local wildlife conservation group.
C resent people admiring the local wildlife.

Extract Two

You will hear two people talking about a disturbance in the night.

3 The man and woman are

A flatmates.
B neighbours.
C married.

4 What probably caused the disturbance?

A a cat
B a criminal
C a wild animal

Extract Three

You will hear two people discussing a site where domestic rubbish is officially dumped.

5 According to the woman

A there are no obvious benefits to landfill sites.
B landfill sites cause disease among local people.
C landfill sites are the lesser of the two evils compared to incineration.

6 Plans to build a new landfill site

A have been temporarily stopped.
B will probably never come to fruition.
C have been stopped by protesters who are blocking research.

LISTENING - Part 2

You will hear a radio report about marine life in the UK. For questions **7-14**, complete the sentences.

British marine life in crisis

Pollution, coastal developments and **7** ______ are the conventional threats to marine life.

8 ______ is most in danger along with turtles, sharks and salmon.

9 ______ passed by the UK and EU protects some areas of UK waters.

10 ______ per cent of UK waters are currently fully protected.

WWF-UK is calling for a **11** ______ of protected marine reserves to be established.

The way that marine life has been protected up until now is **12** ______ .

If fisheries were **13** ______ into the planning process, it would be more successful.

A general **14** ______ is needed for better marine management.

LISTENING - Part 3

You will hear part of a radio interview about fox hunting. For questions **15-20**, choose the answer (**A, B, C** or **D**), which fits best according to what you hear.

15 What surprises the interviewer about the hunt?

A The dogs are no longer allowed to run free.
B Nothing seems to have changed after the new law on hunting.
C The hunters seem to have adopted a strange system of hunting.
D The dogs seemed to be losing their ability to find a fox.

16 According to Brian Hook,

A he enjoys the thrill of the hunt as much as ever.
B the hunters try to deceive the public.
C it's difficult to keep up with a hunt to see what is really happening.
D it is impossible for them to monitor all the hunts.

17 The new law

A forbids dogs to chase foxes.
B allows dogs to kill a fox as long as the kill is monitored.
C has proved to be difficult to enforce.
D forbids foxes to be shot.

18 What was done wrong in the case of Richard Black?

A He should not have used dogs to flush the fox out of the hole.
B He was slow to intervene when the fox was caught.
C He realised too late that his dogs had caught a fox.
D He shot the fox and then gave it to the dogs.

19 Hook believes that

A the countryside will be overrun with foxes.
B the law was intended to make the killing of foxes less cruel.
C the fox could become an endangered species.
D traditional hunting methods are the only way to control the fox population.

20 The interviewer seems to think that

A the issue is too emotive to be settled easily.
B the police aren't really interested in the hunting laws.
C animal rights activists need to take a stronger stand.
D hunters and animal rights activists need to debate the issue further.

LISTENING - Part 4

You will hear five short extracts in which people are talking about animals.
While you listen you must complete both tasks.

TASK ONE

For questions 21-25, choose from the list **A-H** the person who is speaking.

A	a poacher	Speaker 1	21
B	a holiday guide	Speaker 2	22
C	a vet	Speaker 3	23
D	a shopkeeper	Speaker 4	24
E	a farmer	Speaker 5	25
F	an animal shelter worker		
G	an animal rights activist		
H	a photographer		

TASK TWO

For questions 26-30, choose from the list **A-H** what each speaker is expressing [the statement which most accurately reflects what is said by the speaker].

A	It's not my responsibility to protect animals.	Speaker 1	26
B	Some people have a selfish attitude towards animal preservation.	Speaker 2	27
C	I've been injured by a wild animal many times.	Speaker 3	28
D	People only listen to extreme behaviour.	Speaker 4	29
E	I think people should refrain from violence whatever the situation.	Speaker 5	30
F	I am as interested in the animal's character as its appearance.		
G	I'm thinking of selling my business.		
H	I feel like I'm being exploited.		

Test 6

Part 1

For questions **1-8**, read the text below and decide which answer (**A,B,C** or **D**) best fits each gap. There is an example at the beginning **(0)**.

Example:

0 **A** former **B** final **C** aftermost **D** utmost

0	A	B	C	D
	▬	▭	▭	▭

The birth of the London Marathon

In 1979, hours after having run the New York Marathon, the **(0)** .... Olympic champion Chris Brasher wrote an article for The Observer newspaper which began: "To believe this story you must believe that the human race is one joyous, happy family, working together, laughing together, **(1)** .... the impossible. Last Sunday, in one of the most trouble-stricken cities in the world, 11,532 men and women from 40 countries in the world, assisted by over a million black, white and yellow people, laughed, cheered and suffered during the greatest folk festival the world has seen." Enchanted with the sight of people coming together for such an occasion, he concluded by questioning "... whether London could **(2)** .... such a festival?"

Within months the London Marathon was born, with Brasher making trips to America to study the race organisation and finance of big city marathons such as New York and Boston, the oldest in the world. He **(3)** .... a contract with Gillette worth £50,000, established the organisation's charitable **(4)** ...., and **(5)** .... down six main aims for the event, which he not only hoped would echo the scenes he had witnessed in New York, but also put Britain firmly on the **(6)** .... as a country capable of organising major events.

His vision was realised on March 29th 1981, with the **(7)**.............. London Marathon **(8)** .... to be an instant success. More than 20,000 people applied to run: 7,747 were accepted and 6,255 crossed the finish line on Constitution Hill as cheering crowds lined the route.

	A	B	C	D
1	**A** appointing	**B** transacting	**C** making	**D** achieving
2	**A** perform	**B** act	**C** rehearse	**D** stage
3	**A** fastened	**B** tied	**C** secured	**D** possessed
4	**A** grade	**B** rank	**C** status	**D** class
5	**A** let	**B** set	**C** took	**D** gave
6	**A** map	**B** border	**C** atlas	**D** territory
7	**A** penultimate	**B** former	**C** inaugural	**D** primitive
8	**A** succeeding	**B** checking	**C** resulting	**D** proving

Part 2

For questions **9-16**, read the text below and think of the word which best fits each gap. Use only one word in each gap. There is an example at the beginning **(0)**.
Write your answers in **CAPITAL LETTERS**.

Example:

0	BECOMING

Karaoke fever

Karaoke is fast **(0)** .... the nation's Number One party pastime. Public humiliation has **(9)** .... been so fashionable. It's 1 a.m. at an exclusive location in the heart of London. A major pop singer has taken the stage but rather than sing her latest hit, she treats the crowd to a Michael Jackson song. What was **(10)** .... the party habit of teenagers is now favoured by London's coolest crowd and everyone is having a **(11)** .... So why are so many of our young celebrities queueing up to make fools of **(12)** .... in clubs and bars across the country? Maybe it's because belting out a naff pop song to a public audience shows that even though you may be a celebrity, you don't **(13)** .... yourself too seriously. And if you are a big movie star, that's a good message to get across. Nobody gets away without being laughed **(14)** .... on a karaoke evening, no matter how famous they are.

(15) .... all, that's the whole point of the exercise. But for the musical experts among you, a word of warning: this isn't about proving to the world that you know all the lyrics to a serious song. It's about expressing your inner performer. Don't bother **(16)** .... up at a karaoke night if you aren't prepared to sing; you've got to put in the effort and prove that you are one of the 'in-crowd'. Break a leg!

Part 3

For questions 17-24, read the text below. Use the word given in capitals at the end of some of the lines to form a word that fits in the gap **in the same line.** There is an example at the beginning **(0)**.
Write your answers **IN CAPITAL LETTERS**.

Example:	0	REMARKABLE

A day out to Rosslyn Chapel

If you have a spare afternoon why not take the kids to visit the **(0)** .... Rosslyn Chapel?	**REMARK**
This must surely be one of Britain's most **(17)** .... buildings. If you were shown	**ORDINARY**
pictures of it without any clues to its **(18)** ...., you might guess it to be somewhere	**LOCATE**
like Moldavia or Transylvania. In fact, it is just outside Edinburgh. The chapel and the	
neighbouring village of Rosslyn are both quite stunning; in fact, the whole area	
is generally very **(19)** .... Nearly the entire surface of the chapel's stonework	**PICTURE**
is carved with flowers or stars and another **(20)** .... feature of the chapel is that	**IDIOSYNCRACY**
although most of the design of the chapel is Gothic, the aisles are similar to architecture	
found in Babylon or Egypt. The chapel's 15th-century builder, St Clair Prince of Orkney,	
believed that he was **(21)** .... buying his way into heaven by creating	**ESSENTIAL**
such an exquisite chapel. He was famous for his **(22)** .... but this in itself	**PERFECT**
created problems. Because everything had to be exactly as he dreamed it should be	
it was **(23)** .... of him to expect the work to be finished in his lifetime.	**REAL**
The chapel is now considered to be a local treasure and a charitable trust	
was set up in 1996 to oversee and fund its **(24)** .... restoration.	**GO**

Part 4

For questions 25-30, complete the second sentence so that it has a similar meaning to the first sentence, using the word given. **Do not change the word given**. You must use between **three** and **six** words, including the word given. Here is an example **(0)**.

Example: 0 George should have worked harder if he wanted to pass the exam. **succeeded**
Had George worked harder, ... passing the exam.

Write the missing words **IN CAPITAL LETTERS**.

0	HE WOULD HAVE SUCCEEDED IN

25 If I'm being honest, I have to say that the play wasn't as good as I'd expected. **short**
The play ...., to be honest with you.

26 Alan is a much better pianist than Jenny. **nowhere**
Jenny is .... the piano as Alan is.

27 Only the timely arrival of the police prevented the fight from escalating. **been**
Had it .... of the police, the fight would have escalated.

28 I didn't get the impression that he was at all upset. **strike**
He .... at all upset.

29 I don't care which days you work next week. **consequence**
It .... me which days you work next week.

30 One day she is going to lose her temper with him. **matter**
It is .... she loses her temper with him.

Part 5

You are going to read an article about girls and their attitude to sport. For questions 31-36, choose the answer **(A, B, C or D)** which you think fits best according to the text.

High hurdles for girls

My 10-year-old daughter's face was screwed up with determination recently, when she won a gold medal in a long-distance run against 100 others in her age group. She is just as enthusiastic about swimming, gymnastics, athletics and football, and I try hard not to be insulted when people ask, after one or other of her sporting triumphs, 'Where on earth does she get it from?' As I am not particularly overweight nor have an appalling posture I'm not quite sure why it is obvious that I have never been in the slightest bit athletic.

Going round a girls' secondary school with my daughter a few weeks ago I was reminded just how dire school sport was for me. Little seems to have changed in the past 25 years - girls in the same old, ill-fitting Airtex tops, horrible kilt-like games skirts and scratchy nylon socks. On our visit, a group of girls hung about the edges of the hockey pitch trying to hide their mottled, freezing legs while the more hearty ones whacked each other with hockey sticks. It all came back to me; the horrible cheesy smell of the changing rooms and the muddy winter horrors of traditional girls' team games, such as lacrosse, netball and hockey and, worst of all, the cross-country run through the suburban streets of Hendon. What a sight 60 of us must have made thundering down the pavements in our tiny, flapping skirts and mortadella sausage thighs.

Small wonder, then, that a study released last month about young people's behaviour in relation to health found that although many girls wanted to be fit and improve their appearance they were too embarrassed to exercise. Helen Haste, a professor of psychology at Bath University and the author of the report, based her research on 687 interviews with 11- to 21-year olds. The most active youngsters did team sports and at least one other form of exercise, but Professor Haste says that fewer than half exercised once a week: 49 percent of girls said they did not feel comfortable exercising in front of other people, while 34 percent didn't like the way they looked in exercise clothes.

Haste says, 'The study shows that appearance is important to both sexes, but in particular to girls under 16. We need to take this seriously. Girls feel self-conscious exercising in front of people, while boys don't feel this so much. There seems to be a real tension between teenagers wanting to be fitter to look good and worries about how they look when they are actually exercising,' says Haste. Appearance therefore, is both a driving force to exercise and a reason why girls don't actually want to do it. 'It is a real waste of an opportunity to have fun and get fit if school sports are making girls feel so ill at ease,' Haste adds. 'We need to think about ways of exercising within the school curriculum which make sure that girls feel comfortable.'

When I asked a group of 14-year-old girls at a mixed comprehensive school what they thought of the games on offer at their school, some were fairly enthusiastic. Cathy Dale is good at football, and enjoys its competitive spirit, but thinks it is hard to get sports teachers to give girls the training they need. 'They tend to concentrate on the boys' team even though I think that some of the girls are better than the boys. I think that they expect us to give up pretty soon, so there just isn't the interest. I'm not sure if it's the teachers' fault or the girls' fault.'

At the girls' school where we found the unenthusiastic hockey players, the headmistress gave a speech to the parents after the tour of the school and the school grounds. She was unapologetic about the lack of sporting facilities on offer: the message was that as the school was doing well academically it didn't really matter that the girls didn't get much of a chance to succeed at sport. My daughter sneered and whispered that she would never go to a school that didn't take sport seriously, and could we please leave right away? So now the search is on for a secondary school that will nurture her sporty side, although I'm not sure that one exists in my London neighbourhood.

31 How does the writer feel about the way people react to her daughter's successes?

A. She is jealous of her daughter.
B. She is put out that they don't credit her for her daughter's athleticism.
C. She is very proud of her.
D. She gets quite defensive with them.

32 How did the visit to the girls' school make the writer feel?

A. Nostalgic for her own schooldays.
B. Hopeful that her daughter would like the school.
C. It gave her unpleasant memories.
D. It made her want to take up a sport again.

33 According to Helen Haste,

A. most girls aren't interested in exercising.
B. there aren't the facilities for girls to get exercise.
C. girls tend to tease each other when they are exercising.
D. girls are very aware of being watched while they exercise.

34 Haste comes to the conclusion that

A. schools will never be able to make girls more comfortable with sport.
B. girls will never be able to compete with boys at sport.
C. teachers are mainly responsible for making girls feel uncomfortable in sports lessons.
D. the schools themselves need to change their attitudes to sport.

35 The headmistress of the school that the writer visited

A. regretted that she could not improve the school's sports facilities.
B. wanted the girls to excel academically and athletically.
C. didn't hold sport high in the school's priorities.
D. discouraged the girls from doing any sport at all.

36 The writer's daughter

A. was rude when she spoke to the headmistress.
B. felt little respect for what the headmistress said.
C. was not impressed with any aspect of the school.
D. was intimidated by the headmistress.

Part 6

You are going to read four reviews of a theatre performance. For questions 37-40, choose from reviews A-D. The reviews may be chosen more than once.

Hamlet
Four critics comment on the play

A

There can rarely have been such an angry young Dane. In Michael Grandage's fast and filleted production of *Hamlet*, Jude Law is alight with ire. Thickened with disgust, he becomes almost ugly. He plunges in at full tilt; he jabs with each verb and gesture. At times he becomes a parody of his own vehemence: even 'and' can sound like an insult in his mouth. Yet, against the odds, by the end of the play he has found another register. Law doesn't have the sardonic wit of David Tennant, or the philosophical fluency of Jamie Ballard in Jonathan Miller's recent Tobacco Factory production, but he makes a Hamlet who truly discovers himself. He delivers his anguished 'to be or not to be' in a literal blizzard of uncertainty, speaking amid a flurry of snowflakes, but when he comes to say 'the readiness is all', he is steady: he is not merely parroting a proverb; he makes the words sound like the anchor of the play.

B

This week we had the great *Hamlet* bout. Could Jude Law be as good in the role as David Tennant was in last year's Royal Shakespeare Company production?
And the news from the West End ringside, so far as I'm concerned, is that it's a squeaker - and that Mr Law is just ahead on points. That said, the Wyndham's production is not a patch on the RSC show in several other respects. The company has been strangely miscast. Its Claudius, Ophelia, Laertes, Horatio, Gertrude and ghost are all disappointing. Ron Cook's Polonius is an almost embarrassingly bad stab at the part. He is more like a subservient waiter than a fruity old courtier. Still, the Ron Cook fan club seemed to be in attendance at Wednesday's opening night. Polonius's jokes kept getting wild laughs from one section of the audience. At times in this patchy show it is as though director Michael Grandage has not wanted to intervene on the text - or perhaps been too busy to tell his actors what to do.

C

Actor Jude Law was recently quoted in a newspaper as saying *Hamlet* was 'a bit like a great song that's been covered by a load of different singers'. If so, judging by the cheers at the end of his *Hamlet* debut last night, Law has a hit on his hands, despite a few off-key notes (more notably, in the production, itself). So it was, then, that Law took to the stage as the Prince of Denmark in the last production in the Donmar's West End season, at Wyndham's Theatre. As the second high-profile star to play the Danish prince in under a year, the comparisons with *Doctor Who* star, David Tennant, are inevitable. Both played Hamlet at roughly the same age and both are better known for their roles on TV and film, but it's about there the comparisons end. While Tennant was a frenetic Hamlet for the Royal Shakespeare Company (RSC), switching seamlessly between sanity and feigned madness, Law was filled with ferocious anger, snarling and squaring up during the soliloquies, making more compelling viewing than Tennant, in the end.

D

'Who's there?' The most exciting opening scene in all drama begins thus, but the phrase was lost last night as Jude Law's Hamlet waited in the wings. At the Royal Shakespeare Company in Stratford last year, it was *Dr Who's* there, as David Tennant performed the role with scintillating astuteness. Jude's sexier, though the hair line's receding - at 37 years old and like Tennant, he's a bit early middle-aged for the eternal student aspect of the role - and his voice is perhaps too huskily monotonous for someone who speaks almost half a play and over three hundred speeches. But we have to give the contest on points, if not quite a knockout, to Tennant. And Michael Grandage's speedy production for the Donmar in the West End season - coming in at just over three hours with some clever cutting and hectic acceleration towards the end - is looking just a bit over repetitive in the Donmar style of black brick and musty lighting design, with portentous sound track to match.

Which reviewer

commends the performance of Jude Law but finds the rest of the cast lacking?	37
disagrees with the other three reviewers, by finding no flaws in the production?	38
like reviewer A, believes Law's *Hamlet* is not as good as Tennant's?	39
like reviewer B, suggests that Law has the edge on *Hamlet*?	40

Practice Test 6

Part 7

You are going to read an extract from a magazine article. Six paragraphs have been removed from the extract. Choose from the paragraphs **A-G** the one which fits each gap (**41-46**). There is one extra paragraph which you do not need to use.

Art In bloom

Anyone who's been to Monet's garden at Giverney, or Derek Jarman's garden at Dungeness, knows that artists make good gardeners. But do gardens make good art? That is the question Tate Britain poses in its summer exhibition, *Art of the Garden*.

41 ______

Perhaps it's because gardening - like fishing and DIY - is generally a private pursuit. It's not so much something you tend to do with other people. It's a contemplative activity that induces a state of relaxation, calm and general wellbeing. So, the Tate show may be the first exhibition to examine the relationship between gardens and British art, but where are the major artworks?

42 ______

Instead, Art of the Garden quietly opens a door into the private world of the British garden - in fact, the Secret Garden would have made just as good a title for the show. What's striking about these images is how little our attitudes towards the garden have changed in the last 200 years - from Samuel Palmer's *A Shoreham Garden* of 1829 to David Rayson's *Night Garden* of 2003, what we see is a quiet, dreamlike place.

43 ______

I guess it's not surprising that painters should make fine gardens: colour and composition after all, are at the heart of both painting and gardening. Monet may be the most famous example, but his garden at Giverney was created so long ago that what we see today may bear only a vague relation to the original - gardens being, oddly, far more ephemeral than a painting of the most fleeting atmospheric effect.

44 ______

But the current artistic icon of contemporary gardening is surely the late Derek Jarman, whose tiny garden on the vast pebble beach of Dungeness in Kent has become a modern place of pilgrimage. Jarman's garden is an inspiring example of how to create a sense of mystery and magic in apparently unpromising surroundings - in this case a bleak shingle bank dominated by a nuclear power station.

45 ______

But tourist attractions aside, it's the more personal, intimate images of gardens that say so much about the artist. Some painters focus on a section of their garden, maybe a splash of colour in one particular corner. Or the way a single flower can fill a whole canvas making a strong statement about form, colour or detail. Or perhaps a more impressionistic interpretation may be used where shape and form are loose and sketchy but different hues blend for an overall impact.

46 ______

But it is precisely this kind of inference about an artist's character that is so interesting in a piece of art. Art is after all, a vehicle of communication between two human beings and this too can be said about a garden. A garden is indeed a reflection of the people who own it and that is why 'garden art' is such a telling and yet natural phenomenon.

A What's intriguing is that unlike Monet's garden, Jarman's is, arguably, his greatest artistic creation. But then, unlike Giverney, Dungeness remains absolutely uncommercialised. Long may it remain that way! My enduring memory of Giverney is not of its lily ponds but of its electric, revolving toilet seats. Apparently they're popular with Japanese coach parties.

B Which makes perfect sense, when you come to think of it. For aren't gardens, for most of us, an escape from the rational world of work - somewhere for children to play, or for us to play at being children again? The British idea of gardens has an engaging innocence to it.

C The other extreme can be seen in the works of Sir Stanley Spencer. Full of intricate detail, almost like an illustration. Spencer would painstakingly include delicate brickwork and single petals. He must have been a man of order, discipline and precision. You can't imagine him living in a messy house with an untidy garden.

D Given our well-known obsession with gardens and gardening, what's curious is how few, rather than how many depictions of gardens there are in British art. You could, of course, say the same for some of our other national pastimes: how many iconic images of fishing can you think of or DIY and home improvements?

E The curator of the gallery has a strong opinion about this show. He believes that this important work needs to be seen by a wide audience and that it has the power to transform the work of the next generation of British artists. He refuses to give in to the political pressures that have been put on him.

F More recently, Ivon Hitchens and Reynolds Stone created semi-wild woodland gardens in Sussex and Dorset, while Patrick Heron made brilliant use of strong colours in both his paintings and his Cornish garden. In Scotland, Ian Hamilton Finlay has updated the garden at Little Sparta, juxtaposing texts and landscape in witty and often ironic ways.

G There are some favourite paintings - John Singer Sargeant's *Carnation, Lily, Rose* and David Inshaw's *The Badminton Game* - to be sure. However, I don't think anyone would claim either as masterpieces of European art. So the question is, why would a gallery of great prestige such as the Tate have a show that is apparently so low key? Where is the razzmatazz?

Practice Test 6

Part 8

You are going to read some reviews of art events. For questions 47 - 56, choose from the reviews (**A-F**). The reviews may be chosen more than once.

In which review is the following mentioned?

Institutions could suffer because of a thoughtless act.	47	
Many different styles offered by artists in Europe.	48	
A substantial amount of time needed to complete one piece of work.	49	
Land and sea treated very differently.	50	
Paintings about other paintings.	51	
Man's negative impact on the environment.	52	
Finding ways to pay off debts.	53	
A primitive style of interior decoration.	54	
Showing how something is set up for public viewing.	55	
Fantasy images based on a real environment.	56	

Reviews of art events

A Ben Cook and Phil Whiting

Landscape, such a dominant theme in Cornwall, has the chalk and cheese treatment from two artists showing in Penzance this month. At Cornwall Contemporary Gallery Ben Cook uses abstract vocabulary to make almost entirely conceptual references. His use of found objects and time spent surfing drew him to look at the processes involved in surfboard manufacture. Based on these, his constructions and paintings combine areas of high resist, high speed, water deflecting sheen with those tempered by wax to produce mottled, opaque, non-slip surfaces that smack of stone and solidity. Phil Whiting is a painter. His vigorous use of materials - acrylics in thick impasto inks, charcoal applied with a brush, knife and 'whatever' - recalls a terrain smarting from the brute force of man's misuse of it. This is not the celebrated, picturesque Cornwall we so often see but its dirty, rain-soaked underbelly, a landscape left bereft by voracious mining and haphazard industrial development.

B Shanti Panchal

It is almost thirty years since Shanti Panchal first came from India to study art in London, where he has lived ever since. This retrospective at Chelmsford Museum elucidates his distinctive, radical water-colourist's achievement. Growing up in a Gujarati village, he decorated local houses with images of birds and animals. As a Bombay art student, cave paintings and images from Jain temples inspired him, and as a student in Europe, he was drawn to medieval icons. It is erroneous to say that his work is characterised by poignant nostalgia for India. The paintings are not nostalgic. Rather they evoke with subtle clarity what it is like to be exiled and dispossessed while at the same time rooted inalienably in nature and the cosmos.

Every watercolour is multi-layered, giving a similar surface to Buddhist cave paintings. It can take days in order to face what is going to happen in a piece. Each picture takes weeks and sometimes months. Recent pictures include portraits and even a homage to Frida Kahlo, a painter that Shanti respects immensely.

C Iwan Gwyn Parry

Iwan Gwyn Parry's first solo exhibition at Martin Tinney Gallery in Cardiff is a significant event. Until now the artist has shown mostly in North Wales. Now there is an opportunity to experience, further south, a coherent and powerful assemblage of his latest work. It is clear the show will be something special. For these remarkable landscapes and seascapes appear to have emerged from deep within his psyche and are a highly imaginative response to a coastal terrain familiar to the artist. There is a strong sense of mysticism, the painting suffused with ethereal vapours and incandescent light; there are restless swathes of deep orange and yellow. The seascapes are haunting and elemental while the landscapes are more reflective studies in grey, black and white. His oil *The Irish Sea,* for example is on an awesome scale, its seething waters of churning paint intensely lit by a low sun. Definitely a show not to be missed.

D Art auctions

Of the top three Modern British sales last month, it was Christie's who kicked off the proceedings, but not without controversy. Bury district council, in their wisdom, auctioned a major painting by L.S. Lowry so as to cover a £10 million shortfall in their finances. The £1.2 million hammer price, less expenses, will not make all that much difference but the issue has raised the wrath of the Museums Association, who in future, could block lottery and National Arts Collection Fund resources in all aspects of museum and gallery development. Bury may well live to regret their foolhardy action as current and future donators will also not be encouraged to gift works of art which could be sold on a whim.

Bonhams followed ten days later with a good but not exceptional sale of which a solid 70% was sold and totalled £2.3 million.

It was then Sotheby's turn to shine which they succeeded in doing, with 80% of lots sold and an impressive total of £7.7 million, though some way behind their arch rival. Records were broken for works by Sir Winston Churchill, former British Prime Minister.

E Andrew Grassie

Andrew Grassie's exhibition at Maureen Paley Gallery is aptly entitled 'Installation', since it provides a look backstage at the rituals involved in hanging an exhibition before it officially opens to the public. To achieve this, Grassie devised and followed a pre-determined strategy, namely: "Install a series of paintings at the gallery depicting last year's previous exhibitions during their installation. Each painting should hang at the very spot from which the image was taken, enabling the viewer to compare views of the space." The result is five jewel-like paintings, each one painstakingly copied from a mid-installation photograph taken by Grassie before the opening of the previous year's shows. The paintings are executed with such detail that it is difficult at times to uncover the illusion that these are photographs rather than paintings.

F Story

Alexia Goethe has selected fourteen artists, including six resident in the UK and four from Leipzig, for her show 'Story'. She seeks to demonstrate that whatever technique is used - painting, text, video, photograph or concept - and regardless of style, the artist is telling a story. The tales being told made me come away feeling a sense of recovery. Tales of politics, war, social unrest, personal tragedy, to name just a few, are depicted here. Jin Meng who now resides in Europe, produces exquisitely framed views from the present onto China's past. Political statues, glimpsed from a deserted bedroom, evoke the vast changes sweeping his birthplace. Jean Tinguely's kinetic assemblages illustrate how the mechanical is subverted into the amusing and the desirable. This is an eclectic mix of treasures that can't fail to shock, amuse and move.

WRITING - Part 1

You **must** answer this question. Write your answer in **220-260** words in an appropriate style.

1. You have listened to a radio programme about which days should shops remain open in the European Union. You have made the notes below:

Which days should shops be open in the European Union?
- shops should be open 7 days a week and holidays
- shops should be closed on Sundays and all public holidays
- shop owners should have the right to open their shops whenever they want

Some opinions expressed during the talk:
"Allowing shops to be open seven days a week might be better for consumers, but at what price for workers."
"I am convinced that all citizens of the European Union should benefit from a work-free Sunday."
"Let shop owners and workers decide for themselves."

Write an essay discussing **two** of the points in your notes. You should **explain which option is the best** for consumers, shop owners and workers, **giving reasons** in support of your answer.

You may, if you wish, make use of the opinions expressed in the talk, but you should use your own words as far as possible.

WRITING - Part 2

Write an answer to one of the questions **2-4** in this part. Write your answer in **220-260** words in an appropriate style.

2. A friend of yours has written a letter to you telling you that they have started to suffer from asthma. You know that they started to smoke a few months ago and you are worried that they will become addicted. They are very enthusiastic about athletics and would like to win a scholarship to study sport technology at university.

   Write to your friend and tell them that you think that smoking could be the cause of their health problems and how it might affect their future. Suggest ways in which they might get help in giving up smoking.

   Write your **letter**. You do not need to include postal addresses.

3. You work for an advertising agency and a new junior management position has opened in your department. Your boss has asked you to make a proposal on what skills and qualities the ideal candidate should have. Read the ad below and make your own suggestions about the candidate's skills, giving reasons for your opinion.

   Junior Management position in Advertising Agency
   Candidate should be able to work in a team structure

   Write your **proposal**.

4. You are looking through your favourite technology magazine and see the following ad:

   Become a Technology Writer
   Submit reviews on your favourite gadgets and high-tech devices like the new iPod or iPhone to our web forum. We are looking for new voices with fresh perspectives on the latest tech advances!

   You just got a new smart phone that you are not very happy with. Write a review discussing the problems with the user experience, slow speed and other aspects that have left you disappointed.
   Write your **review**.

LISTENING - Part 1

You will hear three different extracts. For questions **1-6**, choose the answer **(A, B** or **C)** which fits best according to what you hear. There are two questions for each extract.

Extract One

You will hear two people talking about a lost Leonardo Da Vinci painting.

1 The interviewer implies that Seracini is

A fashion-conscious.
B conceited.
C modest.

2 Seracini believes that Vasari

A would have been jealous of Da Vinci.
B wouldn't have wanted to destroy Da Vinci's work.
C saw Da Vinci as a rival.

2

Extract Two

You will hear two people talking about the new Sylvester Stallone film.

3 What does the man think about the new Stallone film?

A It makes a refreshing change from his usual style.
B It doesn't break any new ground.
C He's offended by the violence.

3

4 What does the woman like about the film?

A the music
B the story
C the car chases

4

Extract Three

You will hear two people talking about sailing.

5 The woman thinks that yacht owners are

A obstinate.
B timid.
C courageous.

5

6 The man believes that

A sailing tends to be an exclusive hobby.
B sailing is an overrated pastime.
C only the strongest of swimmers should attempt to sail.

6

LISTENING - Part 2

You will hear a radio report about an art exhibition. For questions 7-14, complete the sentences.

History through portraiture

7 ______ are depicted in portraits of the 18th and 19th centuries.

The exhibition at the Royal Academy is called 8 ______ .

The new subject matter for portraits included 9 ______ , philosophers and naturalists.

Mary Anne Stevens is the 10 ______ at The Royal Academy.

Both Louis XVI and Marie Antoinette were 11 ______ during the French Revolution.

In the portrait of George Washington, he is holding 12 ______ .

Within just one year great 13 ______ can be seen by comparing the portraits of two women.

The scientist, James Hutton is depicted standing next to 14 ______ .

LISTENING - Part 3

You will hear an interview with a yoga teacher. For questions 15-20, choose the answer (**A**, **B**, **C** or **D**), which fits best according to what you hear.

15 **The interviewer**
- **A** tried yoga once but found it impossible to do.
- **B** is finding yoga hard to do but is improving with practice.
- **C** has only a vague idea about yoga.
- **D** has quite a good understanding of yoga.

16 **According to Sarah,**
- **A** yoga demands control of all aspects of being.
- **B** you need to be highly intelligent to practise yoga well.
- **C** you need to empty your mind completely when practising yoga.
- **D** meditation is like being hypnotised.

17 **Which of the following does Sarah not say is necessary in order to practise yoga?**
- **A** an empty stomach
- **B** comfortable, flexible clothing
- **C** a lot of confidence and a fit body
- **D** a place where you won't be disturbed

18 **The interviewer seems concerned about**
- **A** people paying a lot of money for public classes with unqualified teachers.
- **B** people getting stuck because the teacher is not supervising the class properly.
- **C** people buying too many yoga guides.
- **D** beginners practising yoga unsupervised.

19 **Sarah recommends that**
- **A** you take strenuous exercise to help you sleep at night.
- **B** you meditate to deal with insomnia.
- **C** you push your body to its limits even if it hurts at times.
- **D** you do no more than 15 minutes of yoga each day.

20 **Sarah sums up by saying that**
- **A** you need to learn more about your own character before attempting to do yoga.
- **B** yoga can solve any problem you have in life.
- **C** yoga is better than conventional medicine.
- **D** in order to fulfill your potential you need to have a positive outlook.

LISTENING - Part 4

You will hear five short extracts in which people are talking about extreme sports.
While you listen you must complete both tasks.

TASK ONE

For questions 21-25, choose from the list **A-H** the person who is speaking.

A a chef
B a teacher
C a police officer
D a taxi driver
E a shop assistant
F a postal worker
G a doctor
H a pilot

Speaker 1	21	
Speaker 2	22	
Speaker 3	23	
Speaker 4	24	
Speaker 5	25	

TASK TWO

For questions 26-30, choose from the list **A-H** what each speaker is expressing / talking about.

A the opportunity to experience a different reality
B the significant risk of fatality associated with a particular activity
C the need to understand the natural qualities of your equipment
D the necessity to give up an unhealthy habit
E the importance of choosing the right specialisation quickly
F the importance of posture to doing a particular activity
G the tendency for all beginners to get badly injured
H the abundance of choices that exist for what to go up next

Speaker 1	26	
Speaker 2	27	
Speaker 3	28	
Speaker 4	29	
Speaker 5	30	

Test 7

Part 1

For questions 1-8, read the text below and decide which answer (**A**,**B**,**C** or **D**) best fits each gap. There is an example at the beginning (0).

Example:

0 **A** general **B** typical **C** usual **D** norm

0	A	B	C	D (marked)

The British dental catastrophe

For most of us, going to the dentist every six months used to be the **(0)** .... True, we might not have relished the **(1)** ...., but at least it didn't mean taking out a second mortgage to pay for any possible treatment, or queueing overnight in the rain with hundreds of others just for the chance to register with an NHS dentist. But these days, fewer than half of us visit the dentist on a regular basis and it's not hard to see why. There simply aren't enough dentists to go round. Finding a dentist **(2)** .... to provide NHS treatment can be almost impossible in some areas. Official figures show that half the people in England have no **(3)** .... to an NHS dentist, while research shows that not going to the dentist regularly will not only **(4)** .... to bad teeth, but it could also put you at risk of serious health problems such as heart disease, stroke, diabetes and even mouth cancer.

Although it's difficult to make direct comparisons, a recent survey that compared access to NHS dentists in Britain with access to dentists in other European countries and the US, shows how serious the situation has become. The survey found on **(5)** .... there were fewer than four NHS dentists per 10,000 in England, compared with six dentists per 10,000 in the US. Things tend to be worse away from major cities so if you live in the country, your chances of seeing an NHS dentist are **(6)** ....

The situation has arisen because dentists, overwhelmed by the pressures of NHS dentistry, are increasingly moving into private work. Dentists say NHS fees mean that they can't offer patients a high-quality service. The current system makes only minimal **(7)** .... for preventative work, although dentists are trained to detect symptoms that could have implications for both your dental and general health, and should **(8)** .... out for suspicious signs at every check-up.

	A	B	C	D
1	**A** ideal	**B** prospect	**C** opinion	**D** view
2	**A** willing	**B** helpful	**C** beneficial	**D** accustomed
3	**A** access	**B** entrance	**C** allowance	**D** commencement
4	**A** move	**B** push	**C** lead	**D** submit
5	**A** mean	**B** common	**C** average	**D** broad
6	**A** slim	**B** skinny	**C** weak	**D** shallow
7	**A** permission	**B** limitation	**C** existence	**D** allowance
8	**A** search	**B** look	**C** scan	**D** anticipate

Part 2

For questions 9-16, read the text below and think of the word which best fits each gap. Use only one word in each gap. There is an example at the beginning (0).
Write your answers in **CAPITAL LETTERS**.

Example: | 0 | REMEMBER |

Memory lapse or dementia?

It's a horribly disconcerting experience - groping to **(0)** .... your best friend's name, forgetting an arrangement that you made only yesterday or realising that your pin number has vanished into a memory black hole. These 'senior moments' affect us all at times, but when do brief memory lapses or moments of confusion become something you **(9)** .... to worry about? The fear that you might, literally, be losing your mind, is one that can be very real, **(10)** .... if you've seen a parent or relative develop Alzheimer's. Dementia affects around 750,000 people in the UK, and although there are 100 different forms of it, Alzheimer's is the **(11)** .... common. This disease destroys brain cells and as the structure and chemistry of the brain become increasingly damaged, the person's ability to remember, understand and communicate gradually declines. It's a particularly cruel disease because it robs us of the memories that make us **(12)** .... we are, define our experience and provide us with the means to communicate with other people.

Although lots of us experience memory problems at some time, in most **(13)** .... these have **(14)** .... to do with dementia. It's important to put the risk into perspective. The reality is that, although it does happen, dementia is unusual under the age of 65. For the majority of people memory lapses will be nothing **(15)** .... than occasional blips. It is important to realise that your memory slows down a bit as you age, but this is a very gradual decline, quite different from the more dramatic deterioration that happens with Alzheimer's. The most common early sign of a problem is forgetting recently learned information.

(16) .... it's normal to forget appointments and telephone numbers occasionally, people with early dementia tend to forget more frequently and they also forget the same information again later.

Part 3

For questions 17-24, read the text below. Use the word given in capitals at the end of some of the lines to form a word that fits in the gap **in the same line.** There is an example at the beginning **(0)**.
Write your answers **IN CAPITAL LETTERS**.

Example:

0	CRAVINGS

Why you can't say no to certain foods

Are you a chocoholic or a fast food addict? Don't blame yourself - certain foods can trigger	
an eating binge, but there are ways to control the **(0)** .... Even if you're a fairly disciplined	**CRAVE**
eater, there are sure to be foods you'll have no **(17)** .... to. For some it's a bar of	**RESIST**
chocolate, for others a burger. You probably think there's no one to blame but your weak-willed self.	
But the reassuring truth is that when it comes to controlling your junk food intake,	
the odds are heavily stacked against you. High-fat, high-sugar foods can act like an **(18)**	**ADDICT**
drug, making us crave even more of the same. In the States, where **(19)** .... rates are	**OBESE**
reaching epidemic proportions, there's even a group called Junk Food Anonymous, which aims to help	
people recover from their **(20)** .... on synthetic or refined food. Fat is often added	**DEPEND**
to food to make it more palatable so it's a good way of making **(21)** ...., bland food	**EXPENSE**
seem tastier. Another reason certain foods are so **(22)** .... is that they have	**RESIST**
a very real effect on our mood, making us feel more relaxed.	
Our eating habits develop when we are young and as we move into adulthood the chocolate that	
we were rewarded with as a young child becomes a guilty **(23)**	**INDULGE**
We might feel we've earned the right to treat ourselves after a hard day at work, for example.	
Past **(24)** .... can reinforce bad eating habits that are difficult to break free from.	**ASSOCIATE**

Part 4

For questions 25-30, complete the second sentence so that it has a similar meaning to the first sentence, using the word given. **Do not change the word given**. You must use between **three** and **six** words, including the word given. Here is an example **(0)**.

Example: 0 George should have worked harder if he wanted to pass the exam. **succeeded**
Had George worked harder, ... passing the exam.

Write the missing words **IN CAPITAL LETTERS**.

0	HE WOULD HAVE SUCCEEDED IN

25 Did anything about his behaviour seem strange to you? **strike**
Did anything about his behaviour .... strange?

26 She takes photographs as a hobby rather than as a job. **much**
Taking photographs .... a job as a hobby for her.

27 Ben needs to clean his car. **high**
It's .... his car.

28 I didn't turn the TV on because I didn't want to wake the baby. **fear**
I didn't turn the TV on .... the baby.

29 I'm not surprised he looks tired if he only had three hours' sleep last night. **given**
It's not surprising that he looks so tired .... slept for three hours last night.

30 You'll need to practise every day if you want to be a professional musician. **do**
Only by .... you stand a chance of becoming a professional musician.

Practice Test 7

Part 5

You are going to read an article about encouraging teenagers to keep fit. For questions **31-36**, choose the answer **(A, B, C or D)** which you think fits best according to the text.

Get them going!

Welcome to the world of the 21st century teenager - where DVDs and computer games rule and trainers are something you wear to look cool rather than run in. As a result, at a time when they should be at their peak fitness, the UK's teenagers are lagging badly behind. A national survey recently found that many 16- to 20-year-olds had less aerobic capacity and muscle strength than healthy 60-year-olds. And not surprisingly this is giving cause for concern.

Roger Draper, chief executive of Sport England, agrees. 'If they want to give themselves a head start in staying healthy for life, teenagers need to get into the exercise habit now', he says. 'We want to see more teenagers channelling their natural energy into exercise in any shape or form.'

Many parents think that encouraging teenagers into sport is something schools should take responsibility for but Andrew Findley, a former PE teacher, points out that schools can only go so far. 'The majority of pupils only get two hours of PE a week so although it's better than nothing there's only so much teachers can do - parents have a major role to play too', he says. 'It always amazed me how many pupils would come with a note from home excusing them from PE without good reason. A lot of teenagers also feel it's not cool to do well at school and that goes for PE as much as other subjects.'

A recent survey of 11- to 14-year-olds revealed that sport is becoming a less popular way of spending leisure time while the number of children in that age range who say they love sport has dropped by 10 percent compared to previous years. Roger Draper puts this down to the number of other pursuits competing for teenagers' leisure hours, from playing on the computer to going out clubbing. 'That's why we're looking to support sports such as skateboarding and other street sports, which young people are increasingly interested in. We cannot just promote the old traditional sports of football, hockey and cricket - many teenagers still want to play these but many others don't and we need to broaden sport's appeal.'

Membership of sports clubs drops significantly in teenage years; 71 percent of 7- to 10-year-olds belong to a club compared to 43 percent of 15- to 19-year-olds. The danger is that those who have dropped out may not take up another activity to keep them fit and will enter adulthood with a sedentary lifestyle. While for teenagers who wouldn't even dream of joining a sports club in the first place, it's particularly important that they find alternative exercise they enjoy - or at least do regularly.

It's great if teenagers show an interest in competitive sport but if they don't, it's essential to realise that exercise and the health benefits it brings are more important than becoming brilliantly skilled in a particular discipline. It's all very well talking about the benefits of exercising but when you're faced with telling a sulky 16-year-old you're not driving them down the road because the walk will do them good, it's another matter. So is it really worth the effort? Bearing in mind the way a teenager's mind works can help parents to strike a balance between encouraging a more active lifestyle and what will be viewed as nagging. Dr Dawn Skelton points out that most teenagers find it hard to imagine themselves getting older and live for today not tomorrow, so the importance of keeping fit for the future may be lost on them.

'Parents need to focus on how a healthier lifestyle can help them now', she says. 'If they are studying for exams for instance, research shows that exercise can boost their concentration levels. Girls might be inspired by the fact that exercise can improve their looks in terms of their skin as well as their figures and teenage boys might like the idea of building up their muscle mass. Sport can also be useful social contact through which they can form relationships that last a lifetime.'

And of course, setting a good example helps too. It's no good telling your child to get up and be active if you are slouching in front of the TV. Family trips to the swimming pool, bowling alley or nearest country park will help you all to stay active - with family harmony as an extra bonus. If they try something they aren't keen on, encourage them to give it a good go but if they are still adamant it's not for them try and find an alternative rather than insisting they carry on or just give up. Many clubs provide taster sessions so you don't have to shell out for a whole course and risk your teenager dropping out after a few tries. Maybe the most important thing is to remember that whatever they choose to do, it can be challenging but it should be fun. That way they are more likely to stick at it and reap the rewards of a healthier lifestyle.

31 What is suggested in the opening paragraph?

A. Teenagers don't want to get their clothes dirty.
B. Teenagers are more interested in fashion than health.
C. Older people are much healthier than they used to be.
D. Teenagers won't take exercise if older people are around.

32 According to Andrew Findley

A. children write false notes to excuse them from PE at school.
B. parents need to be skillful at the sports that children like.
C. parents are unhappy with the sports facilities in schools.
D. parents sometimes aggravate the situation.

33 Roger Draper believes that the situation could be improved by

A. offering a wider choice of activities.
B. scrapping all traditional sports.
C. banning all team sports in schools.
D. introducing extreme sports to inspire teenagers.

34 One of the problems with pushing a teenager to be more active is they may

A. not appreciate the wider benefits of exercise.
B. become too tired to do their schoolwork.
C. insist on their parents taking up a sport too.
D. resent the fact that they can't do certain sports with their friends.

35 In order to inspire a teenager, you

A. should tell them about the sports you used to play when you were young.
B. should stress how lucky they are to have good sports facilities.
C. ought to practise what you preach.
D. should ban them from watching TV in the evening.

36 When a teenager is willing to try something new, parents

A. should never pay money upfront for them to take part in a sport.
B. shouldn't force the issue if things don't turn out as expected.
C. shouldn't risk them joining a club unless it has been recommended.
D. should be careful to avoid any sports that are expensive.

Part 6

You are going to read four reviews of a new restaurant. For questions 37-40, choose from reviews A-D. The reviews may be chosen more than once.

Union Street Cafe

Four critics comment on the restaurant

A

If any among you still doubt that David Beckham is an exceedingly smart cookie, members of the jury, allow me to submit the clinching evidence. A few weeks ago, the *Daily Mirror* recently reported, he withdrew as an investor in his chum Gordon Ramsay's Union Street Cafe, which opened in Southwark on Monday. The *Mirror* did not explain why, revealing only that the two men 'wanted different things'. We could speculate for hours about what that means, but let me posit this theory: Beckham wanted a really good restaurant and Ramsay wanted something else. This is not to suggest he wanted a really bad restaurant. Eccentric as his psycho shtick may make him appear, he is not clinically insane, and this newbie, his 10th in Britain, is far from atrocious. It would be more endearing, or at least more memorable, if it were. What makes it so irk-some is the so-what-ishness of this rather brand new restaurant.

B

Here's what I'm going to do: I'm going to close my eyes, stick my fingers in my ears and pretend I don't know that this big, new, shiny restaurant in Southwark has anything to do with Gordon Ramsay. Otherwise, it's impossible to approach without being blind-sided by the baggage trailed in his wake. He's the tallest of poppies, our Gordon; everybody lining up to give him a trampling. So let's make believe that Union Street Cafe is brought to us by nice, anonymous people intent on giving us fine food and a good time. You in? This is Big Sweary's first opening without his eminence grise pa-in-law, with whom he fell out in spectacular, Greek tragedian fashion. Sorry, I'll try again. It's all cheery bustle in this high-windowed and handsome room, more New York than London, in its studied mix of haute-industrial and luxury: ducting and concrete, framing well-spaced tables and designer leather chairs. The open kitchen is set on high, pulpit-style; inside is chef Davide Degiovanni, formerly of the Four Seasons. It's a telling piece of recruitment: despite the warehouse disguise, this is not about the grunge.

C

Union Street Cafe is not a cafe and isn't strictly in Union Street (see address below) but it's certainly the most talked-about and 'in' new restaurant for the autumn. This, you'll doubtless know, is because it was rumoured that its owner, Gordon Ramsay, the former footballer who once had a trial with Rangers, was going into partnership with David Beckham, the well-known foodie. Why this macho convergence would have made for an ideal restaurant, is hard to fathom. Have we got a picture in our heads of Victoria in a lace pinny, sulkily announcing the daily specials? No? Just me, then. But it doesn't matter now, because Beckham chose not to invest any dosh. So the USC is just a new Gordon Ramsay joint, in a funny part of town. Great Suffolk Street isn't hopelessly grotty, just a bit down-at-heel. It, and Union Street which it bisects, are in the heart of Southwark, the raffish heart of Olde South London that's now so trendy, bounded by Tate Modern, Borough Market, Guy's Hospital and the London Dungeon. I think it appealed to Gordon because it's London's version of Brooklyn; edgy, but without the West End's gleam and swagger. And there's a famous Union Street in Brooklyn.

D

David Beckham pulled out at the last minute, but that hasn't stopped a rush for tables at Gordon Ramsay's new venture; and the fact that Union Street Cafe is doing brisk trade, proves that Ramsay himself retains impressive pulling power. With its casual urban setting and emphasis on Italian cooking, this venue marks a welcome departure for the megastar chef, who has drafted in Davide Degiovanni to head up the kitchen. Expect small portions of accomplished, ingredients-led dishes, ranging from intensely flavoured tagliolini with rabbit and provolone, or lamb cutlets with baked fennel and onion, to Amaretto and chocolate budino, a deliriously rich, custardy dolce. Switched-on young staff in casual garb are a good fit for the restaurant's warehouse-chic theme and there are cocktails aplenty in the basement bar. 'I absolutely loved the whole package,' said one fan.

Which reviewer

makes inferences to New York in their review when discussing the restaurant's decor, like reviewer B?	37
like reviewer A, suggests that the public might lack sympathy with Ramsay's public persona?	38
disagrees with the other three reviewers, believing Ramsay's new restaurant to be not particularly fashionable?	39
like reviewer C, believes that having a famous owner, has helped the popularity of the restaurant?	40

Part 7

You are going to read an extract from a magazine article about following your little passions in life. Six paragraphs have been removed from the extract. Choose from the paragraphs **A-G** the one which fits each gap **(41-46)**. There is one extra paragraph which you do not need to use.

Make it happen

'One person with passion is better than forty people merely interested', the author E M Forster once said. Some people's passion may be about winning Olympic gold, discovering a cure for cancer or sailing across the Atlantic single-handed, but passion doesn't always have to involve amazing, earth-shattering feats or superhuman efforts.

41 ______

In 1959 Dr Robert White, an American personality psychologist, introduced the term 'effectance motivation', or the urge we all have to engage with our environment to make our influence felt, and to master tasks in a competent fashion. You can see this if you watch children when they're transfixed with mastering a game or task. Time flies and they have no sense of anything going on outside their 'concentration zone': that's a slice of pure passion and emotion in action!

42 ______

Sometimes passion can be ignited by things we don't want to happen as much as by those we do. Almost every campaign for public good, from the abolition of slavery through to women's right to vote and Live Aid for Africa, started with a spark of passionate rage that grew to a far-reaching flame. The last of these examples reflecting the growing trend for celebrities fighting for a good cause.

43 ______

The truth is that passion can ebb and flow and when we're tired, depressed or despondent it tends to be the first thing to disappear. But according to Christine Dunkley, a psychological therapist, we have a lot of control.

44 ______

This is important because being passionate may help us live longer. A study by Professor Thomas Glass examined the impact of activities we might feel passionate about on longevity. The findings were dramatic. 'Social engagement was stronger than things like blood pressure, cholesterol, or other measures of health.' So do something for your health. Ask yourself what you feel strongly about. What would you like to do, change, make, become?

45 ______

Every one of us has an interest in something, but it often gets sidelined with the demands of daily life. We may come to view it as an indulgence, or worry we will be judged for it, particularly if the thing we love isn't something we're particularly good at. But passion doesn't necessarily mean being great at something. And what if you don't know where your passion lies?

46 ______

Whatever you settle on, the main thing is to find something. Reawaken your passionate side and appreciate the passion in others. You'll find life becomes more fulfilling and colourful. We may not be able to live every minute of every day passionately - that would probably be exhausting! But with a bit of thought and imagination, passion is something we can enjoy experiencing at least a little of every day.

A

In fact, if you're not feeling passionate, there is evidence that acting as if you are can help! 'If you jump, throw a fist in the air and shout "Yes!", a feedback loop in your brain will interpret this behaviour as passionate and you'll get a surge of adrenaline,' she explains. 'People who are under-emotive can increase their pleasurable hormonal responses by behaving enthusiastically.'

B

If you are not sure exactly what you want to explore, try tasters in subjects you're interested in first. Get a book about it, talk to someone who's done it, find a one-day workshop. Perhaps your passion could simply be trying new things?

C

Passion can be as simple as teaching children to play football or getting up early in the morning to photograph a beautiful sunrise. It's not about doing something because you think you should or because it will make you money - it's about doing something you love as well as you can, purely for the love of it.

D

Whether this particular example of passion is misplaced or not is another matter. It's about people standing up for something they really believed in. It was their 'cause', even though few people agreed with their ideals. They were prepared to fight for what they wanted and risked everything in the process.

E

It's fairly easy to identify passionate people in the public eye - most people at the top of their profession have needed a hefty amount to get them there. But there's a difference between pure passion and cold, calculating ruthlessness. True passion usually involves a positive gain directed outside ourselves - towards other people or nature. But what if you're struggling to muster enthusiasm for daily life, let alone to feel passionate about anything?

F

Consider what you are doing when time seems to fly. What did you love as a child or teenager? Consider anything you've felt 'naturally' drawn towards. What activity never seems like work and always boosts your energy?

G

According to international coach Anthony Robbins we each need to find the emotional force that drives us. 'The most important decision we make in life', says Robbins, 'is to focus on something that will get us inspired, excited, something that will move us, something that will ignite a spark.'

Part 8

You are going to read some extracts from a health advice magazine. For questions 47 - 56, choose from the extracts **(A-F)**. The extracts may be chosen more than once.

In which extract is the following mentioned?

People may be unaware of something that is causing disease in their body.	47	
Cutting back too much can be harmful.	48	
If you feel self-conscious, this could be for you.	49	
A shocking hygiene confession is made.	50	
This could be a flexible way to monitor your activity and performance levels.	51	
A change in body reaction could be dangerous.	52	
Drastic measures may not achieve the expected results.	53	
You should reassess your lifestyle to see if it is causing a bad habit.	54	
People need to be aware of the dangers of something that seems safe.	55	
A high-profile health problem boosts manufacturers' turnover.	56	

Health advice magazine

A

'here are now five times as many cases of food poison-
ıg as there were 20 years ago. It's partly down to the
act that we eat out more often. Consider that one in
hree men and one in five women admit that they don't
vash their hands after going to the toilet or before
ɪreparing food; it's enough to put you off popping out for
quick bite on a Friday night. And before you reach for
ne of those mints sitting on the counter by the till, think
ow many non-hand-washers have dipped their fingers into
hat bowl. But the problem isn't restricted to grubby
ateries. More than half of food poisoning infections are
ontracted in the home. This may be because people are
ating more pre-prepared food and shopping less often, so
ood is stored for longer. But most food poisoning is pre-
'entable if you know what you're doing.

B

ext time you have a headache, don't automatically reach
or the painkillers. Using them too often could be more
angerous than you think. For a vulnerable minority, the
oute to addiction can be alarmingly fast. It's thought
hat overusing painkillers leads to changes in the way the
rain handles pain signals, so it becomes oversensitive to
timuli that wouldn't normally cause pain. As the pain
hreshold lowers, people seek out stronger medication
nd increase the dosage and soon they are hooked.
omewhere along the line we have become blase about
he dangers of these medicines which are available in
etrol stations, news agents and supermarkets. People
nust not assume that over the counter drugs are safe
ecause clearly this is not the case.

C

The basic premise of detox is that we need to clear the
oxic waste from our bodies every so often in order to
tay healthy. It sounds a reasonable idea, but nutrition
xperts are quick to point out that there's no evidence to
upport it. Detoxing is a concept that underestimates the
bilities of our liver and kidneys. Any toxins that do get
bsorbed are very efficiently dealt with and secreted by
ur bodies. The concept of detox diets is irrational and
ınscientific. Those promoting detox diets often claim that
n order to detoxify, we should avoid foods such as wheat
nd dairy products. The reality is that these foods pro-
ide us with important nutrients, and it is unnecessary
nd potentially harmful to exclude them from the diet.

D

There is a lot of publicity about the dangers of having 'high cholesterol' at the moment - mainly coming from companies that make special foods that claim to lower it for you. It is a widespread problem though: according to the British Heart Foundation around two thirds of British people have a blood cholesterol level above the suggested healthy target figure. And as there are no symptoms until it causes disease, many people with high cholesterol may not be aware that they have it. However we need some cholesterol because the body wouldn't function without it! It is a key part of cell membranes and it is also found in bile, which is important for digestion and absorption of fat.

E

Just like a real-time personal trainer (PT), an online coach discusses personal goals, tailors exercise schedules and offers advice to clients of all abilities. Instead of face-to-face guidance, however, the virtual trainer gives feedback via emails and texts - perfect for the self-concious exerciser! While critics say that it is impossible to effectively train clients without meeting them, online coaches offer a valuable compromise when it comes to training. First they are a cost-effective alternative. Second, they represent a more flexible option, especially if your work takes up much of your time or makes it difficult for you to commit to regular sessions. And just because your coach is in cyberspace, it doesn't mean he won't be keeping tabs on you. The mere thought of the next email should have you racing to put on your sports kit.

F

Most of us are unclear as to where social drinking stops and alcohol dependency starts. A heavy-drinking student is fairly normal, but a 40-year-old party animal? A sozzled 60-year-old? At what point do the questions demand a serious answer? Recommendations from the government are that men should consume no more than three to four units of alcohol a day and women only two to three units. Of course, committed social drinkers of all ages often ignore units, taking comfort from the fact that they are not reaching for the bottle before lunchtime, and their friends are drinking as much as they are so it must be alright. But you can even test yourself online by looking at Alcohol Concern's website to determine if alarm bells should be ringing. Most people can reduce their alcohol consumption without professional help but it's not just about cutting down, it's about editing your life to remove the reasons you are drinking too much.

WRITING - Part 1

You **must** answer this question. Write your answer in **220-260** words in an appropriate style.

1. You have listened to a radio discussion programme about which measures could be taken, by local authorities, to reduce traffic and pollution in big cities. You have made the notes below:

Which measures should be taken, by local authorities, to reduce traffic and pollution in big cities?

- provide exclusive lanes for public transport
- introduce a congestion charge for vehicles accessing the city centre
- ban all vehicles from the city centre during busy hours

Some opinions expressed in the discussion:

"Cars are the main factor contributing to pollution and should not be allowed to the city centre."
"The costs of imposing a congestion charge is much higher than the benefits."
"Public transport is the best solution."

Write an essay discussing **two** of the solutions in your notes. You should **explain which solution would be the most effective** in reducing the pollution and the traffic in big cities, **giving reasons** in support of your answer.

You may, if you wish, make use of the opinions expressed in the discussion, but you should use your own words as far as possible.

WRITING - Part 2

Write an answer to one of the questions **2-4** in this part. Write your answer in **220-260** words in an appropriate style.

2. You have just completed six months working as a volunteer for a global organisation helping to educate children in Africa. In preparation for a meeting with the person in charge of your area, you have been asked to write a report to him/her.

   Your report should explain what you feel you have achieved in this position so far, describe any problems you have had, and suggest any improvements you think are necessary.

   Write your **report**.

3. Your teacher wants you and your classmates to improve your critical-thinking skills. She asks you to write a review of your favourite novel.

   Discuss the plot of the book, the writer's style in telling the story, the development of the characters, and what you find interesting as well as lacking. Mention if and how you would change the story in any way.

   Write your **review**.

4. You have recently taken up a new hobby which you really enjoy. Write a letter to a friend telling them all about your new hobby.

   Mention any special equipment or training that you need. Say what attracted you to the hobby in the first place and why you find it so enjoyable. Say if you think they would enjoy it or not and why.

   Write your **letter**. You do not need to include postal addresses.

LISTENING - Part 1

You will hear three different extracts. For questions **1-6**, choose the answer (**A**, **B** or **C**) which fits best according to what you hear. There are two questions for each extract.

Extract One

You will hear two friends talking.

1 Why did Karen want to go riding with Annie?

A to improve her daughter's riding skills
B to strengthen her relationship with her daughter
C to spend time with her friend who is a riding instructor

1	

2 How did Karen feel when she rode her horse?

A inadequate compared to the other riders
B relieved that it had gone better than she'd expected
C concerned about accidents

2	

Extract Two

You will hear part of a radio interview with an actor, about how he tries to keep fit.

3 Bob goes to the gym because

A he isn't disciplined enough to go running.
B he enjoys the social aspect of it.
C he is trying to lose weight for a particular event.

3	

4 Bob believes that New Year's Resolutions

A can never have a worthwhile effect on people.
B do more harm than good.
C can inspire people to make a change.

4	

Extract Three

You will hear two people talking about a new activity they have taken up.

5 George decided to go ice skating

A because he'd always wanted to try it.
B because he'd bought his daughter a pair of ice skates.
C to find out if he was still good at it.

5	

6 Alison was surprised when she went line dancing because

A it was a better workout than she had expected it to be.
B the music during her first lesson was very contemporary.
C most people were wearing strange clothes.

6	

Practice Test 7

LISTENING - Part 2

You will hear a radio report about panic attacks. For questions 7-14, complete the sentences.

People tend to have a panic attack when their brain tells them they are in a **7** _______ .

The first sign of a panic attack is often an abnormal beating of **8** _______ .

It may be useful to keep a diary of any **9** _______ you have so that you can analyse them.

You should not **10** _______ from places that cause you to panic.

If you tense and relax all your **11** _______ your whole body will actively relax.

Holding a **12** _______ to your face can help you breathe during an attack.

13 _______ for 10 to 15 seconds will calm hyperventilation.

14 _______ such as herbs, camomile tea and aconite can relieve panic attacks.

LISTENING - Part 3

You will hear part of a radio interview with a psychologist, about friendship. For questions 15-20, choose the answer (**A**, **B**, **C** or **D**), which fits best according to what you hear.

15 According to the presenter

A we have to adjust our friendships as our lives change.
B new books are being written to teach people how to manage friendships.
C it's almost impossible to keep childhood friends for life.
D the most important friends are childhood friends.

16 Barbara warns that foul-weather friends

A never want you to be happy.
B engineer bad situations so that they can feel superior.
C have their life perfectly organised.
D can spoil the times when you are feeling good about life.

17 The danger of a trophy friend is that

A he or she will inhibit your social life.
B you may develop unrealistic expectations.
C he or she will push you to be a higher achiever.
D he or she will expect you to become more popular.

18 A sisterly friend

A can be relied on but may be too involved in your life.
B will resent other close friendships in your life.
C will be as close to your family as she is to you.
D will want to go out on dates with you and your new partner.

19 According to Barbara, a good friend

A probably needs to be someone that you see very often.
B tends to ask for your help slightly more than you would like but you tolerate it.
C doesn't expend too much of your time or energy.
D never puts you in a serious mood.

20 When making new friends

A try to be as funny as you can.
B don't mention serious issues before you have got to know them well.
C be sensitive to their need for space.
D spend as much time with them as you can.

LISTENING - Part 4

You will hear five short extracts in which people are talking about their weight.
While you listen you must complete both tasks.

TASK ONE

For questions 21-25, choose from the list **A-H** the person who is speaking.

A	a hair stylist	Speaker 1	21
B	a car park attendant	Speaker 2	22
C	a police officer	Speaker 3	23
D	a primary school teacher	Speaker 4	24
E	a shop assistant	Speaker 5	25
F	a receptionist		
G	a driving instructor		
H	a gardener		

TASK TWO

For questions 26-30, choose from the list **A-H** what each speaker is expressing [which statement most accurately reflects what the speaker says].

A	I enjoy the encouragement people give each other.	Speaker 1	26
B	Job satisfaction inspired my weight loss.	Speaker 2	27
C	We aren't meant to talk while we are working.	Speaker 3	28
D	I eat at work because I am bored.	Speaker 4	29
E	Special events encourage me to eat badly.	Speaker 5	30
F	Convenience food has made me fat.		
G	I didn't realise I could find help for my illness.		
H	My job involves working with food so I eat too much.		

Test 8

Part 1

For questions 1-8, read the text below and decide which answer (**A,B,C** or **D**) best fits each gap. There is an example at the beginning (0).

Example:

0 A make B take C do D have

0	A	B	C	D

"Scramjet" - the future of flight technology

A new **(0)** .... on high-speed flight has **(1)** .... with a jet aircraft smashing all records by reaching seven times the **(2)** .... of sound - fast enough to get from London to Sydney in two hours. The global race to create the world's first "scramjet" was won by the United States recently, with NASA comparing the moment with the Wright brothers' achievements of a century ago. The **(3)** .... flight - in which the jet reached 5,000 mph - lasted eleven seconds and ended with a splashdown of the X-43A into the Pacific Ocean, never to be seen again.

"To put this into perspective, a little over 100 years ago a couple of guys from Ohio flew for 120ft in the first controlled powered flight. Today we did something similar in the same amount of time." Lawrence Huebner, NASA's lead propulsion engineer, said, "but our vehicle under air-breathing power went over 15 miles." The significance of the **(4)** .... is underlined by the margin between the X-43A and the world's **(5)** .... fastest jet, Lockheed's Blackbird. That two-man reconnaissance aircraft, painted black to avoid radar detection, served the United States for 25 years until the Cold War **(6)** .... in 1990. Its fastest speed was 2,193 mph. The X-43A is unmanned but NASA predicted that the inaugural flight would inspire business, industry and the military to **(7)** .... in its "hypersonic" revolutionary propulsion system.

A scramjet would **(8)** .... an aircraft which had already reached supersonic speeds. The US military is considering using the technology to create a warplane that could bomb targets anywhere on the globe in a matter of hours.

	A	B	C	D
1	instigated	dawned	switched	flown
2	pace	ratio	scale	speed
3	period	ancient	historic	contemporary
4	breakthrough	breakout	breakdown	breakneck
5	premature	belated	prime	previous
6	frosted	froze	thawed	liquidised
7	devote	enclose	invest	consist
8	boost	promote	amplify	diminish

Part 2

For questions 9-16, read the text below and think of the word which best fits each gap. Use only one word in each gap. There is an example at the beginning (0).
Write your answers in **CAPITAL LETTERS**.

Example:

0	WHICH

The future at your fingertips

There is a scene in the film *Minority Report* in **(0)** .... Tom Cruise stands in front of a vast Perspex-like screen housed in the police department's Pre-Crime Unit. He gazes **(9)** .... earnest at the transparent surface, waving his hands across the tablet to swirl great chunks of text and moving images across the screen to form a storyboard of yet-to-be-committed crimes. With a simple twist of his finger or a flick of his wrist, pictures expand and enlarge, words scroll, and whole trains of thought come to tangible fruition **(10)** .... there on the board. The year is 2054.

Yet it seems the era of true touch-screen technology is already here. Indeed, when Apple boss Steve Jobs unveiled the iPhone in San Fransisco a few years ago, he grandly declared: "We're reinventing the cell phone."
(11) .... of the main reasons for Jobs' bold claim was the iPhone's futuristic user interface - "multi-touch". As demonstrated on stage by Jobs **(12)** ...., multi-touch was created to make the most of the iPhone's large screen. Unlike most existing smart phones, the iPhone has only one conventional button - all the rest of the controls appear on the screen, adapting and morphing around your fingertips as you use the device, almost **(13)** .... the giant tablet in *Minority Report*.

The demonstration iPhone handset certainly looked like re-invention, but multi-touch, while it was new for Apple, is **(14)** .... no means a new technology. The concept has been around for years, waiting for the hardware side of the equation to get small enough, smart enough and cheap enough to make it a reality. While it still remains something of a novelty now, there's a good chance that the **(15)** .... years will bring many more computers and consumer gadgets that depend wholly or **(16)** .... on multi-touch concepts.

Part 3

For questions 17-24, read the text below. Use the word given in capitals at the end of some of the lines to form a word that fits in the gap **in the same line.** There is an example at the beginning **(0)**.
Write your answers **IN CAPITAL LETTERS**.

Example:

0	CIVILISATION

Man's greatest invention

The wheel might seem to be the most simple invention, but it did not occur to every **(0)**	**CIVIL**
to invent one and it surely has to be the greatest invention. Look around - the wheel is everywhere in our	
modern world. It's **(17)** .... simple, aesthetically perfect and arguably	**SATISFY**
the most useful thing in the world. What great moment of **(18)** .... happened	**REVEAL**
to bring us this gift? It should really have been invented much earlier than it was.	
If you consider the **(19)** .... opportunities man had to witness fallen trees rolling	**END**
downhill, man was **(20)** .... slow at catching on to the potential of roundness and	**REMARK**
gravity. The Mayas, the Aztecs and the Incas all achieved great things without the wheel.	
They must have just run a lot and were undoubtedly all the healthier for it.	
Sledges, usually pulled by humans, **(21)** .... to the Stone Age, were quite enough	**TRACE**
for them. The wheel came later in human **(22)** .... than most of us think.	**DEVELOP**
Once it did arrive there were many **(23)** .... made to it as man realised that	**REFINE**
the possibilities of the wheel were vast and this **(24)** .... spurred him on to greater things.	**AWARE**

Part 4

For questions 25-30, complete the second sentence so that it has a similar meaning to the first sentence, using the word given. **Do not change the word given**. You must use between **three** and **six** words, including the word given. Here is an example **(0)**.

Example: 0 George should have worked harder if he wanted to pass the exam. **succeeded**
Had George worked harder, ... passing the exam.

Write the missing words **IN CAPITAL LETTERS**.

0	HE WOULD HAVE SUCCEEDED IN

25 After what you've been through, it's only right that they help you out. **least**
The .... help you after all you've been through.

26 The accident resulted in the serious injury of many of the passengers. **left**
The accident .... injured.

27 John is unlikely to get the job that he applied for. **prospect**
There .... the job that he applied for.

28 Icy road conditions are thought to have caused the accident. **brought**
The accident seems to .... the icy road conditions.

29 I don't intend to reply to his rude letter. **no**
I have .... to his rude letter.

30 Andrew has been thinking about it all day, but he hasn't made a decision yet. **mind**
It's .... all day, but he hasn't made a decision yet.

Part 5

You are going to read a newspaper article about exam technology. For questions 31-36, choose the answer **(A, B, C or D)** which you think fits best according to the text.

The Future of Exams

Like it or not, technology is already an established part of the exam process and the only argument still to be fought at this year's e-assessment conference and exhibition, taking place in London this week, is just how much further in that direction we should go.

At one end, little has changed. Students still, by and large, take exams in much the same way as they always have. They walk into a room full of desks with an invigilator on hand to tell them when to start and stop and to make sure no one is texting anyone else, and everyone is ticking the right boxes, or writing out the answer in longhand if required. It's once the ink has dried that the real change in the system kicks in. Instead of divvying up the scripts between the thousands of markers, they are now scanned into a central computer and the markers then access them online.

The benefits are obvious. It's quicker, cheaper and more efficient. The really dull components, such as multiple choice or simple questions such as "name four things that contribute to global warming", can be marked automatically or by less experienced markers, whereas questions requiring a more nuanced, longer answer can be left to the old hands. Your best markers don't have to be wasted on the straightforward stuff.

Students can also benefit. "Markers can now give much more precise feedback", says Kathleen Tattersall, who chairs the Institute of Educational Assessors. "We can tell someone almost exactly what he or she needs to do to improve a grade because we can show them what they got right and wrong. This is particularly useful for anyone looking to resit a January exam in the summer, because teachers can tailor individual revision plans for all their students."

For all its advantages, no one reckons that this assessment model is the finished article. "There are difficulties that need to be ironed out", says Martin Walker, a former English teacher and a principal examiner for one of the main boards. "Because markers are now often only given a few questions from each paper, it's hard to get an accurate feel of exactly what a student does and doesn't know. When you had an entire exam script in front of you, you could build up a picture of the candidate's range of knowledge, so when there was room for doubt in an answer you could make a judgement call based on previous responses. It's much harder to do that now."

"There are also limits to what you can easily read on screen", he adds. "In my experience, most examiners end up printing out the long essays and working from a hard copy, which is both time-consuming and slightly self-defeating." The danger, as Tattersall concedes, is that schools end up teaching only what technology is capable of assessing. "Rather, we have to look at how IT is used in the classroom to improve teaching and learning and base our exams on that model", she says.

It is certain that we are only halfway through the electronic revolution. In the coming years, more and more exams will be completed - as well as marked - online, and the government and the Qualifications and Curriculum Authority will have to think hard about ways of maintaining standards.

By far the easiest form of online testing to implement is multiple choice. A student can take the test online and it can be automatically marked instantaneously; this system is almost foolproof. The downside is that most people associate multiple choice with dumbing down, on the grounds that anything that can be reduced to a yes or no, right or wrong answer is bound to be over-simplified.

"Not true", says Stevie Pattison-Dick, head of communications for Edexcel. "Some multiple-choice exams may be quite straightforward, but if they are, they only reflect the level of knowledge a student is expected to attain. There's nothing inherently simple about multiple choice. We've become very sophisticated in our question setting and are able to cross-reference the answers, so an examiner can now tell whether someone just got lucky by ticking the right box or actually understood the process on which he or she was being assessed." One of the final exams a medical student has to pass before qualifying as a doctor is multiple choice, so this method of assessment has to be extremely rigorous.

31 The writer believes that

A. nothing of significance has changed in the exam system.
B. a revolution in exam taking may soon be initiated.
C. many students cheat by using their mobile phones.
D. technology doesn't greatly affect students when they sit exams.

32 What does the writer mean by 'old hands' in paragraph 3?

A. retired examiners
B. experienced examiners
C. examiners who have reached a certain age
D. mature students

33 Which of the following is **not** mentioned as a benefit of computer marking?

A. better utilisation of examiners
B. more interesting questions can be set
C. many set questions do not need human markers at all
D. financial advantages

34 What is stated to be a disadvantage of the current system?

A. Many examiners complain that the work is boring now.
B. Examiners no longer have enough work.
C. Examiners have a limited impression of the candidate.
D. Examiners aren't as skillful as they used to be.

35 What is implied about the general perception of multiple-choice testing?

A. It is easy for a student to cheat.
B. It reduces the student's writing skills.
C. It lowers the standard of the exam.
D. It's impossible for a computer error to be made.

36 According to Stevie Patterson-Dick, multiple-choice exams

A. do have a large element of chance in them.
B. are not always the best way to test medical students.
C. are by far the best way to test students on particular subjects.
D. can be composed in a way that makes students reaffirm their knowledge.

Part 6

You are going to read four reviews of a rock concert. For questions 37-40, choose from reviews A-D. The reviews may be chosen more than once.

Radiohead
Four critics comment on a live show

A

"IT'S RADIOHEAD NIGHT!" shouts the menu poster outside the bar'n'grill just inside the O2 Arena's doors. At first you just roll your eyes at the crater-sized disconnect between knee-jerk corporate food marketing and the ethos of the band whose name is being taken in vain, in block caps. Even when Radiohead were a conventional outfit, singing grunge-pop ditties such as Creep, their image was that of haughty refuseniks, not shirtless Lotharios lairily gnawing buffalo wings. Thom Yorke had publicly aligned his band with the aesthetically disaffected, the creeps and the weirdos. Twenty years on, Radiohead remain one of the biggest bands in the world, one uncommonly in control of their own destiny. They are label-less and immune to corporate pressure. The last laugh is very much theirs. There is no little heroism in the fact that the Oxfordshire five-piece can come to giant sheds like these and sell them out with their jazz-tinged electronic rock, sung in falsetto by a nervy mendicant type sporting a beard and a top-knot.

B

It's a decade and a half since *OK Computer* catapulted Radiohead to global superstardom. They've now been one of the biggest bands in the world for so long that it's easy to forget how curious and unique their situation is: in a world where rock and pop is not much given to overestimating its audience, here is a band whose music long ago abandoned any pretensions to commerciality capable of filling out the kind of venues where Rihanna or Coldplay normally ply their trade. Anyone requiring a reminder of the incongruity of Radiohead's position, needs only to step inside the O2 arena. Jauntily yellow-jacketed stewards are flogging soft toys, emblazoned with the words VAMPIRES SUCK MY BLOOD in gothic script. In one of the O2's numerous chain restaurants, menus announce that it's Radiohead Night; quite how the dread-filled, agitated sound found on their last album, *King Of Limbs*, squares with bourbon-glazed baby back ribs and the Cajun spiced chicken sandwich, remains open to question, but you can't blame them for trying.

C

"Hello. My name's Lady Gaga." Thom Yorke's introduction to Radiohead's first British audience in four years, was happily and tellingly unpredictable. Saturday's sell-out show at O2 Arena, one of only three UK dates following a more substantial swing across the US, served as delayed support for another creative left turn in the form of 2011's *The King of Limbs*. That album dispensed with the more conventional textures of its predecessor, *In Rainbows*. In came a new fascination with samples and programming, leading to a hyper-physical kind of electronica that Yorke likened to the wildness of nature. He certainly had a point. There's a tendency to over-rationalise the music of Radiohead, but this gig proved that the Oxford five-piece band are more than capable of delivering on a gut level. *Separator*, for example, was an impressionistic space ballad given real heft by punishing dance beats, while the riot of grooves that shunted Feral out into drill'n'bass territory, was symptomatic of their entire approach.

D

By rights, Radiohead should have been here to relive the good old days. 1998 was the height of the British art-rock outfit's third album, *OK Computer*, making them a very big deal indeed. Their heyday alas is now long gone. However, that magnum opus, OK Computer, still casts a long and glorious shadow over their career and in fan memories - as was witnessed to the response to two of its tracks, *Airbag*, up early, and the symphonic *Paranoid Android*, last song in the first encore, by the sold-out O2 arena crowd. But this wasn't a greatest hits show. It wasn't even pushing their recent offering, 2011's *King of Limbs*, too much, with maybe half a dozen tracks in the two-hour two-encore show. Which might have left many present a bit non-plussed at no dusting off of breakthrough hit *Creep*, or anything off second big-chorus anthemic album *The Bends*.

Which reviewer

uses the food vendors at the O2 arena, like reviewer A, to illustrate a point about the band's attitude towards money?	37
conveys the idea that people may over-analyse the music of Radiohead?	38
disagrees with the other three reviewers, in believing that Radiohead have had their day?	39
like reviewer A, suggests that Radiohead avoid being a mainstream pop band?	40

Part 7

You are going to read an article about robotics. Choose from the paragraphs **A-G** the one which fits each gap (41-46). There is one extra paragraph which you do not need to use.

Robots to the rescue

In the war on terror, University of South Florida engineering Professor Robin Murphy finds herself a pioneer on the front line with a new kind of soldier: the search-and-rescue robot. Strewn about are piles of broken concrete blocks and pipes, metal and dirt. Amid the rubble, a small black object looking like some futuristic toy tank rolls into view. It surveys the damage, edges forward, climbs over a mound of debris, then stops. Suddenly, the rubber treads shift from horizontal to vertical, raising the lens into a better vantage point to transmit images. The robot has done its job.

41 __________

She looks like an emergency worker ready for action: work boots, navy-blue trousers, white hardhat over her short brown hair. One moment, she's answering questions from scientists. The next, she's racing to another robot demonstration, always keeping the program moving. In a larger sense, that's what Murphy does best - she keeps the relatively new field of robotics and rescue moving forward. January's "Discover" magazine honoured Murphy in its "Top 100 Science Stories of 2002" edition.

42 __________

Murphy, at 46, is in demand these days. When she's not teaching at USF, she's travelling the country giving presentations, serving as a co-chair on various committees, or coordinating with the Department of Defence. Murphy is hardly the stiff scientist one might expect from a robotologist. She is disarmingly casual in conversation. Yet she is also intense, pushing herself and the people around her. What separates Murphy from her colleagues is that many of them don't get out into the field. But that's where she thrives, and where she gets the knowledge to make her robots successful.

43 __________

"Imagine the scenario where something green is hanging over the city and you don't know what it is and or where it's coming from", she says. "These guys can roll in, and throw a robot off the back of a truck to carry all the gas meters and detectors. Then, the rescuers are able to figure out what safety precautions to take. The robots will help the rescuers make the right decisions."

44 __________

"Later, her work began to gain attention when she was a professor at the Colorado School of Mines, where she taught before going to USF six years ago. There, her ideas impressed Rita Virginia Rodriguez of the National Science Foundation. Rodriguez began funding Murphy's work in Colorado, and continues to do so at USF. "Robin is one of the most important people in this movement," says Rodriguez. "She's one of the engineers who is very good, very forward-thinking. What we've seen today is the first workshop of its kind and it is all her initiative."

45 __________

The birth of robot-assisted search and rescue began with one of the nation's worst disasters: the 1995 bombing in Oklahoma City. One of Murphy's graduate students, was appalled at the large, clumsy robots that sat unused in a car park. Blitch soon helped create a Defence Department programme to build small, mobile robots for battlefield applications. At the same time, Murphy and her students began focusing on software: how to control robots, how to integrate them with a computer. When 9/11 occurred, Murphy was there immediately. Yet her team was not accepted right away.

46 __________

The work never ends. Murphy says, "I just want to be of use. Look at what the guys in fire and rescue service have to do. The technology is there to help them, and it's up to scientists to provide the right technology to fit to the right people at the right time."

A

Her father was a mechanical engineer, so it was in the family. As a child she immersed herself in science fiction: "I never really identified with the heroes" she says. "I always thought the scientists who built things for these guys were far more interesting." She earned her Master's degree in computer science at Georgia Tech., won a fellowship and worked for a professor with expertise in artificial intelligence and within two months, she was on her way to her Ph.D.

B

At first, the USF contingent had trouble getting through the police lines. "The fire and rescue teams were a bit suspicious, because when they think of robots, they think of big explosive ordnance devices," she says. But eventually they were able to get close enough to help, and the smaller robots proved remarkably effective. Murphy has moved at an intense pace ever since, working to become even more effective in the event of another terrorist attack.

C

Applause fills the breezy morning air. Some 50 scientists are impressed by the brief demonstration of the VGTV, Variable Geometry Tracked Vehicle. They have come from universities, industry, the military and countries as far away as Japan, Sweden, Italy and England. They have left their classrooms, computers and academic theory behind to get their hands a little dirty: to see an array of search-and-rescue robots perform in simulated conditions. And they are all here because of Professor Robin Murphy.

D

Murphy and her students don't actually build the robots. What they do, in essence, is take models made by companies and create the software programmes to adapt them to search and rescue. The little VGTV that performed so effectively in the rubble of the twin towers collapse had been built to explore air-conditioning ducts. They gave it a new brain and figured out ways to transport it in a backpack and deploy it at a moment's notice.

E

However, there are still many problems with the whole project. Funding is the main one. Murphy often struggles to gain funding from the usual channels due to her lack of an academic background which tends to put off a lot of potential sponsors. They seem to ignore the fact that her achievements have more than made up for any official qualifications that she may be missing. It remains to be seen if this will, in the end, be the cause of the demise of her work.

F

The workshop is full of innovations. Nearby, a team from the University of Minnesota displays its robot named Scout - a tiny tube with two wheels and an antenna. One of the inventors picks Scout up and tosses it on the pavement. No problem. It keeps rolling. "People are starting to see what robots can do", Murphy says. "One thing we're trying to do is help rescue workers learn what's possible."

G

She was featured for her advances with rescue robots, in particular the work she and several graduate students performed at the World Trade Centre. With a cadre of robots packed in the back of her husband's van, they arrived on September 12 2001 and stayed for eleven days. A handful of the small VGTV robots squeezed deep into the collapse, helped identify five victims, and transmitted many detailed videos and photos. "But", she says, "we weren't in Discover just because we were at the World Trade Centre. It's what we've done since."

Part 8

You are going to read some reviews for different novels. For questions 47 - 56, choose from the reviews (**A-F**). The reviews may be chosen more than once.

In which review is the following mentioned?

It is easily forgotten once it has been read.	47	
People join together to fight a common enemy.	48	
A bad start but a good ending.	49	
Anti-government rebels are used as guinea pigs.	50	
A human transmitter.	51	
A predictable but enjoyable ending.	52	
The story of someone growing up.	53	
This book has been written perfectly for its target reader.	54	
Someone keeps remembering things in his/her past.	55	
Two eras existing at the same time.	56	

Book reviews

A *Gifts* - Ursula Le Guin

Gifts is a coming-of-age story, intended, at a guess, as a book for young teenagers, and as such has to be written with scrupulous care. In this respect it is exemplary. Tightly-plotted, there isn't a word out of place. Quintessential Le Guin, in fact.

This book is set on a world which might be Earth but could just as easily not be, in what is almost a default fantasy land, with a scrape-an-agricultural-living uplands, and towns sufficiently far off that they barely impinge on the main narrative.

The book is not quite a *Wizard of Earthsea* but it gets very close and as is usual with Le Guin's work, *Gifts*, despite its quota of disputes, conflict and death, is a life-affirming experience, well worth reading by adults of all ages.

B *Soul Purpose* - Nick Marsh

It shouldn't happen to a vet. Alan Reece, human wreck, is called out one night in late December to tend to a pregnant cow, but the calf is born transparent. This is but the first in a global outbreak of transparent births, and Alan finds himself at the centre of the oncoming apocalypse. Actually this book reminds me not a little of that book about exploding sheep from a few years ago. It's not a very bad book, it's just not a brilliant book either. The prologue is terrible; the epilogue is surprisingly good; in between it averages out.

This isn't the first metaphysical comedy adventure book I've read this year, so possibly it's arrived at the right time to take advantage of a trend of some sort. However, "memorable" and "original" are two words I can't, in all sincerity, use to describe it.

C *The Space Eater* - D. Langford

Wormhole travel is possible but only up to a diameter of 1.9cm. Through one such spyhole, the government discovers that a distant colony world is developing weaponry based on Anomalous Physics which could endanger whole star systems. Send in the marines! Oh no, wait, they don't make 1.9cm tall Marines. Enter Ken Jacklin, one of a team of soldiers trained to charge headlong into death and be grown back in regeneration tanks, even when blown to a pulp. Accompanying him is Rossa Corman, a woman who can send messages coded in pain back to Earth by jabbing herself in the arm.

The premise that someone can be remade - body and mind - from jam hours after their death is a little hard to swallow, but in general it's very hard to fault this novel. The characters are rounded and engaging, the story is lively and well told with intrigue aplenty, and the science, however out there it may be, is explained in accessible and thought-provoking terms. A very rewarding read.

D *Babylon* - Richard Calder

Babylon has a lush feel to it. Calder writes erudite and richly detailed prose which situates the characters first in the Victorian London of Jack the Ripper and later in the crumbling metropolis of a modern Babylon existing in a parallel dimension. The book is strong on atmosphere and there are some marvellously melodramatic set pieces in which major plot shifts are played out. I get the impression that Calder knows his material and wants the reader to be able to visualise his world clearly but this enthusiasm for detail is also one of the novel's drawbacks. The pages are cluttered with facts and at one point I began to feel some sympathy with the character who shouts out that she doesn't know anything.

Whilst the book jacket promises blood and gore and there are intimations of ravishment scattered throughout the first part of the novel, the second and third parts deliver little of either and the melodramatic quality of the set pieces seems increasingly at odds with the cerebral working out of the novel's conclusion.

E *Against Gravity* - Gary Gibson

In 2088, following a terrorist nuclear strike on Los Angeles, America's political dissidents are rounded up and sent to the Maze, a top secret research facility, to provide experimental hosts for military nanotech. This is a densely packed Science Fiction thriller, and for all the twists and action the pace felt quite sedate to me. I think it might be all the flashbacks - Gallon is the only viewpoint character, and his story is intercut with lengthy scenes of his time in the Maze, which he has escaped from. This material is well depicted, particularly the gruesome failed experiments and the survival-of-the-fittest tests.

Against Gravity is a good futuristic action novel, but the tagline "Live long enough and this could be your future" on the front cover tells me Gibson intends this novel first and foremost as a comment on the world we live in today.

F *The New World Order* - B. Jeapes

In Ben Jeapes' latest novel invaders arrive on Earth to find the locals already at war; with their superior technology, the invaders hammer both sides indiscriminately but end up uniting the humans against them. Except that these invaders not only come armed with machine guns and airships but also with witchcraft, their special wise cadre tapping the Earth's lay energy. This is a lively and intelligent novel from Ben Jeapes. A section at the end caps the story with historical notes and a revelation that you may guess before, but which you should still find entertaining.

WRITING - Part 1

You **must** answer this question. Write your answer in **220-260** words in an appropriate style.

1. You have listened to a debate about which new school facilities should receive money from local authorities. You have made the notes below:

Which school facilities should receive money from local authorities?
- library
- catering facilities
- swimming pool

Some opinions expressed in the discussion:
"New catering facilities are needed! It is important that children get a good meal at lunchtime."
"Students need a new well-equipped library."
"Swimming is the best way to exercise."

Write an essay discussing **two** of the facilities in your notes. You should **explain which facility is more important** for local authorities to give money to, **giving reasons** in support of your answer.

You may, if you wish, make use of the opinions expressed in the discussion, but you should use your own words as far as possible.

WRITING - Part 2

Write an answer to one of the questions **2-4** in this part. Write your answer in **220-260** words in an appropriate style.

2. You serve on your local town council. You have been asked to write a set of recommendations for the board and citizens to consider in order to improve the living conditions in your area.
Include in your proposal ideas for education, transportation, public services, tourism and entertainment.
Write your **proposal**.

3. A friend of yours has just bought a new computer and has high-speed Internet connection for the first time. Write them a letter telling them about the advantages of having the Internet.
Tell them about interesting websites that you have visited. You should also warn them of any security dangers and disadvantages of the Internet.

Write your **letter**. You do not need to include postal addresses.

4. An online tourism publication has asked you to write a review of a local scuba diving school in your area.

Discuss in your review:
- the quality of the instruction
- the size of the classes
- the costs
- hours of operation
- the availability of equipment, among other features.

Write your **review**.

LISTENING - Part 1

You will hear three different extracts. For questions **1-6**, choose the answer (**A**, **B** or **C**) which fits best according to what you hear. There are two questions for each extract.

Extract One

You will hear two people who are waiting for a friend.

1 The man seems to think that Pam is

A organised.
B inconsiderate.
C neurotic.

1

2 What does the woman think?

A They should have a coffee while they wait for Pam.
B They should prioritise their tasks for the afternoon.
C They probably won't have time to go to the cinema.

2

Extract Two

You will hear two people talking about forensic technology.

3 The woman believes that forensic technology

A has reached its peak.
B has a long way to go before it can be really useful.
C has the potential to produce evidence that we can't yet find.

3

4 The man worries that

A a false conviction is still possible.
B many police officers aren't trained well enough to use DNA as evidence.
C criminals can get access to personal information on police computers.

4

Extract Three

You will hear two people talking about their son.

5 What worries the man?

A The people that his son talks to on the Internet.
B The amount of time his son spends on the Internet.
C The cost of his phone bills because his son is using the Internet.

5

6 The woman accuses the man of being

A out of touch with his son.
B mean with his money.
C ignorant of what the Internet is used for.

6

LISTENING - Part 2

You will hear a radio report about a new security body scanner. For questions 7-14, complete the sentences.

Laying bare the traveller's secrets

The body scanner will be able to tell if someone has **7** ______ a weapon on their body.

The scanner will be able to **8** ______ private parts of the body.

The technology was first invented to help pilots flying in **9** ______ .

The scanner will show if someone has a **10** ______ fitted in their heart.

Operators of the machines will be carefully checked to ensure they are not being **11** ______ .

Air passengers will no longer need to be physically checked by **12** ______ .

The scanner can see through all **13** ______ .

The scanner has enabled officials to see **14** ______ that have been hidden in lorries at ports.

LISTENING - Part 3

You will hear part of a radio interview with a literary critic about Huxley's novel, *Brave New World.* For questions 15-20, choose the answer (**A**, **B**, **C** or **D**), which fits best according to what you hear.

15 Professor Protheroe believes that people enjoy science fiction because

A they want to do all that they can to protect their ancestors.
B they wish they could be immortal.
C they are naturally curious about the future.
D they dream about escaping from their own tedious life.

16 In the 1930s, Huxley

A was trying to launch his career as a writer.
B was known for his observations on social behaviour.
C could not settle happily in any country.
D could not decide what kind of writer he wanted to be.

17 In writing *Brave New World*, Huxley was

A trying to outdo Wells.
B tackling a dangerous topic.
C stealing Wells' ideas and pretending they were his own.
D going against the grain in literary trends.

18 When Huxley went to the United States he

A felt too nervous to stay there.
B found people to be very unfriendly.
C was offended by American art.
D disliked what he saw.

19 To Huxley, America was

A a warning of what might happen.
B violent.
C a place to make his fortune.
D an exciting symbol of the future.

20 Huxley seems to have been

A a man who embraced great change.
B biased against all nations other than his own.
C something of a puritan.
D arrogant when comparing himself to other writers.

LISTENING - Part 4

You will hear five short extracts in which people are talking about inventions.
While you listen you must complete both tasks.

TASK ONE

For questions 21-25, choose from the list **A-H** the person who is speaking.

A	an actor	Speaker 1	21
B	a pensioner		
C	a social worker	Speaker 2	22
D	an unemployed person	Speaker 3	23
E	an artist		
F	a postal worker	Speaker 4	24
G	a gardener	Speaker 5	25
H	a farmer		

TASK TWO

For questions 26-30, choose from the list **A-H** what each speaker is expressing [which statement most accurately reflects what the speaker says].

A	Someone was ahead of his time.		
B	I used to be a bit of a vandal.	Speaker 1	26
C	This invention breaks down prejudices of social status.	Speaker 2	27
D	I'm really tired of my job.	Speaker 3	28
E	You can fool yourself that something is true.	Speaker 4	29
F	There don't seem to be any inventors these days.	Speaker 5	30
G	I have to read between the lines in my job.		
H	My conscience is clear despite what people say.		

Test 9

Part 1

For questions **1-8**, read the text below and decide which answer (**A**,**B**,**C** or **D**) best fits each gap. There is an example at the beginning **(0)**.

Example:

0 **A meanings** **B senses** **C themes** **D points**

0	A	B	C	D
		▬		

Paper

Banana fibre is used in the production of banana paper. Banana paper is used in two different **(0)** ....: to **(1)** .... to a paper made from the bark of the banana tree, mainly used for artistic purposes, or paper made from banana's fibre, **(2)** .... from an industrialised process, from the stem and the non utilisable fruits. This paper can be either hand-made or made by machine. The volume of raw **(3)** .... for making banana paper around the world on plantations is vast and largely unutilised. The market for banana paper is seen as a growth industry. Since 1988, in Costa Rica, companies like EcoPaper.com and Costa Rica Natural Paper have been producing 100% industrialised fine environmental and ecological papers **(4)** .... from natural banana fibres, for the writing and stationery market.

In only 15 countries, the banana agro-industry processes each year 42 million tons of bananas with 2 million hectares planted. This industry **(5)** .... numerous waste products such as: the plastic that wraps the bananas, plastic cords to tie the wrapping, damaged bananas and the pinzote (stems). An alarming quantity of over 10 million metric tons of pinzote is thrown in landfills or even worse in local rivers. The pinzote is **(6)** .... of 92% of water, 3% of resins and 2% glucose; the rest is vegetal fibre. This **(7)** .... composition makes it decompose without the solid component being destroyed. This causes a severe impact on the **(8)** .... ecosystems - much to the detriment of rivers and underground waters.

	A	B	C	D
1	**A** refer	**B** concern	**C** name	**D** direct
2	**A** received	**B** obtained	**C** accepted	**D** gained
3	**A** materials	**B** tools	**C** cloth	**D** fabric
4	**A** pulled	**B** derived	**C** eliminated	**D** displaced
5	**A** develops	**B** causes	**C** generates	**D** makes
6	**A** created	**B** constructed	**C** collected	**D** composed
7	**A** particular	**B** prevalent	**C** private	**D** premature
8	**A** circling	**B** surrounding	**C** nearing	**D** rounding

Part 2

For questions **9-16**, read the text below and think of the word which best fits each gap. Use only one word in each gap. There is an example at the beginning **(0)**.
Write your answers in **CAPITAL LETTERS**.

Example: | 0 | OF |

The limits of magic in Harry Potter

Before publishing the first "Harry Potter" novel, J.K. Rowling spent five years establishing the limitations **(0)** .... magic; determining what it could and could **(9)** .... do. "The most important thing to decide when you're creating a fantasy world," she said in 2000, "is what the characters CAN'T do." **(10)** .... instance, while it is possible to conjure things out **(11)** .... thin air, it is far more tricky to create something that fits an exact specification **(12)** .... than a general one; moreover, any objects so conjured tend not to last.

It is also impossible to resurrect the dead. Dead bodies can be enchanted to **(13)** .... a living wizard's bidding, but these bodies remain mere puppets and have no souls. It is also possible via the rare Priori Incantatem effect to converse with ghost-like "shadows" of magically murdered people. The Resurrection Stone also allows one to talk to the dead, but those brought back by the Stone are not corporeal, **(14)** .... do they wish to be disturbed from their peaceful rest.

Likewise, it is impossible to make oneself immortal unless one makes **(15)** .... of a mystical object of great power to sustain life. If one were to possess the three Deathly Hallows, it is fabled that they would possess the tools to become the "master of death". However, **(16)** .... a true "master of death" is to be willing to accept that death is inevitable.

Part 3

For questions 17-24, read the text below. Use the word given in capitals at the end of some of the lines to form a word that fits in the gap **in the same line.** There is an example at the beginning **(0)**.
Write your answers **IN CAPITAL LETTERS**.

Example: | 0 | ACTIVISM |

Two broad themes run in bicycle **(0)** .... : one more overtly political with roots in the **(17)** .... movement; the other drawing on the traditions of the established bicycle lobby. Such groups promote the bicycle as a **(18)** .... mode of transport and emphasize the potential for energy and resource conservation and health benefits gained from cycling versus automobile use. Due to **(19)** .... interest in cycling, many cities also have community bicycle programs that promote cycling, **(20)** .... as a means of inner-city transport.

ACTIVE
ENVIRONMENT
REAL
PRECEDE
PARTICULAR

Controversially, some bicycle activists seek the construction of segregated cycle facilities for journeys of all lengths. Other activists, **(21)** .... those from the more established tradition, view the safety, **(22)** ...., and intent of many segregated cycle facilities with suspicion. In some cases this **(23)** .... has a more ideological basis: some members of the Vehicular Cycling movement oppose segregated public facilities, such as on-street bike lanes, on principle. Some groups offer training courses to help cyclists integrate themselves with other traffic. This is part of the **(24)** .... cycle path debate.

SPECIAL
PRACTICAL
OPPOSE
GO

Part 4

For questions 25-30, complete the second sentence so that it has a similar meaning to the first sentence, using the word given. **Do not change the word given**. You must use between **three** and **six** words, including the word given. Here is an example **(0)**.

Example: 0 George should have worked harder if he wanted to pass the exam. **succeeded**
Had George worked harder, ... passing the exam.

Write the missing words **IN CAPITAL LETTERS**.

| 0 | HE WOULD HAVE SUCCEEDED IN |

25 I didn't find it hard to answer their questions. **difficulty**
I .... their questions.

26 I wish he would stop criticising my work . **fault**
I wish he would stop .... my work.

27 The factory may be forced to close if demand doesn't increase. **facing**
The factory may .... if demand doesn't increase.

28 It doesn't make a difference to me what you decide to do. **matter**
Your .... to me.

29 You definitely will not win the lottery. **chance**
You have got .... the lottery.

30 It's impossible to say who will win the match. **telling**
There's .... who will win the match.

Part 5

You are going to read a newspaper article. For questions 31-36, choose the answer **(A, B, C or D)** which you think fits best according to the text.

Parking hell: The parking industry investigated

Local authorities in England and Wales now make more than £1 billion from the parking business. Yet there are growing accusations of sharp practice, and all over the country motorists are gearing up for battle.

Wednesday, 3.20pm: David Nicknam, a North London parking attendant until last May, shuffles nervously down Hampstead High Street explaining the "tricks" he says he was taught here for issuing what he nonchalantly calls "dodgy tickets".

"I was told to give tickets no matter how legally a car was parked," Nicknam says with a disapproving frown, his greying ponytail and wispy beard incongruous among the impeccably groomed ladies strolling up the hill. "If a driver's got a disabled badge, you write that there's no badge. If there's a visitor's permit, sometimes you ignore it - it's a question of 'Who's going to believe the driver?' And if you ask me if you can park for five minutes to collect someone, I'd be expected to say OK - and then ticket you once you've gone. He doesn't have your name, the thinking goes, so what's he going to do?"

Nicknam, 39, was taking home £226.79 for a 42-hour week when he says he was sacked after three months' probation. The reason, he says, is that he found grounds to ticket only five or six cars "legally" in a typical day, rather than the ten or more he says his superiors expected. "If I wanted to survive, to get a permanent job, I was told I'd have to bring in at least ten tickets no matter how," he says with ill-disguised contempt. The scams, he says, ranged from falsely claiming that bays had been suspended to hand-issuing deliberately mistimed tickets after claiming his computer was down. "I told them, I can't do that. I said I believed in God. I asked my supervisors, 'How do you sleep? Do you lie there dreaming about ticketing cars all night'?"

Camden council rejects his allegations, and, as a clearly disaffected former employee of the council's parking contractor, Nicknam is by no means neutral. He readily accepts that he bears grudges against NCP, whose management, he says, refused to hear his complaints and promoted supervisors who openly broke the rules. Yet his claims - of attendants falsifying observation times, issuing "ghost" tickets when cars were not present, dishonestly claiming tyres were outside parking bays - have all been made by other London parking attendants (PAs) in recent months. At stake is public confidence in the entire system of parking enforcement.

"You have to ask why drivers hate the PAs," Nicknam reflects as he crosses into Prince Arthur Road, a favourite spot, he explains, for colleagues to hide before pouncing on cars left for three minutes at school pick-up time. "How many people have spoken out before me? You have to ask why the council doesn't want PAs to help the drivers. You might call it cheating, but I call it stealing." He shakes his head and whispers disapprovingly. "It's money, isn't it? Money talks."

Council coffers are swelling not simply through parking tickets and bus-lane fines, but also from meter feeds and the sale of permits. Yet by any standards, the business of ticketing, clamping and removing cars is booming as never before.

The London boroughs issued almost seven million penalty charge notices in last year, up from 5.4 million in three years ago. Outside London, English and Welsh councils handed out almost three million more. By law, local authorities must regulate parking not primarily to raise money, but "to secure the expeditious, convenient and safe movement of vehicular and other traffic". Yet as the surpluses have risen over the years, so have public suspicions about the councils' true agenda. As Brian King, director of the RAC Foundation, sees it, local authorities now see parking as "a convenient and easy way to raise money, rather than as a policy issue".

Public tolerance is being tested with every television investigation alleging corruption, and with each outraged report of target-fixated attendants ticketing buses, fire engines, even a rabbit-hutch whose owner, delivering to a Manchester pet shop, moved his van before a warden could pounce.

"It's the biggest fraud that goes on," claims Jim Carlson, a Pimlico accountant who runs Appeal.com, one of a growing number of websites campaigning against what they see as unjust use of parking regulations to make money. Carlson has heard it all: PAs falsifying information in their notebooks to "prove" that correctly parked cars were elsewhere; motorists illegally ticketed long after they had driven off. He makes an annual award to the victim of what he considers the most absurd abuse of a PA's powers. Its latest winner was Nadhim Zahawi, who was, handed a penalty charge notice in central London as he lay in the road with a broken leg after coming off his scooter.

"The councils are very happy to allow a poor system to continue, because they get the revenue," Carlson says wearily. "Nobody now has faith in the system. I certainly don't."

31 It is claimed in the article that 'dodgy tickets' are
A. given to disabled drivers.
B. unfairly given to legally parked cars.
C. given in excess to illegally parked cars.
D. still being issued by Nicknam.

32 Nicknam was fired
A. with no warning.
B. for giving out illegal tickets.
C. for not giving out enough tickets.
D. because he didn't want a permanent job.

33 Nicknam's reasons for disobeying his employer are
A. moral.
B. corrupt.
C. deceitful.
D. profitable.

34 Multiple claims of dishonest ticketing are
A. not being taken seriously by too many.
B. making people distrustful of the parking system.
C. posing no threat to the parking system.
D. getting a lot of employees fired.

35 The business of ticketing, clamping and removing cars is
A. becoming increasingly illegal.
B. under inspection by the RAC.
C. making more money than in the past.
D. becoming an important policy issue.

36 The conclusion of the article is
A. hopeful.
B. pessimistic.
C. neutral.
D. passionate.

Part 6

You are going to read four reviews of a musical. For questions 37-40, choose from reviews A-D. The reviews may be chosen more than once.

Billy Elliot
Four critics comment on the musical theatre production

A

This is not a time to beat about the bush. *Billy Elliot* strikes me as the greatest British musical I have ever seen and I have not forgotten Lionel Bart's *Oliver*! or Andrew Lloyd Webber's *Phantom of the Opera*. There is a rawness, a warm humour and a sheer humanity here that are worlds removed from the soulless slickness of most musicals. Yes, there are rough edges that would give Cameron Mackintosh a fit of the vapours, yes, there are occasional scenes that are not as powerfully played as those in the film. But there is so much more that is big and bold, imaginative and great-hearted. Once upon a time, they used to make films out of stage musicals, but these days the traffic is all the other way. Following *The Producers*, *Mary Poppins* and *Spamalot*, comes this stage version of Stephen Daldry's beautiful and moving Brit flick about an 11-year-old boy from a coal-mining village in County Durham, who is determined to become a ballet dancer.

B

Turning small-scale movies into big musicals is a treacherous business. It failed with *The Full Monty*, which lost all of its gritty truth when musicalised. But *Billy Elliot* succeeds brilliantly because Elton John's music and, especially, Peter Darling's choreography enhance Lee Hall's cinematic concept. The musical, even more than the film, counterpoints Billy's personal triumph with the community's decline. Eleven-year-old Billy is an Easington miner's son who overcomes family bigotry and financial hardship to make it to the Royal Ballet School. But a show that begins with grainy newsreel footage celebrating the nationalisation of the coal industry ends with the collapse of the 1984 miners' strike. Billy's aspirations have been realised, but a local community faces ruin. It is the tension between those two facts that gives the musical its drive. But, even more significantly, dance is used to express narrative in a way that evokes *West Side Story*. You see this early on in an extraordinary sequence where the choreographed conflict between the miners and police invades Mrs Wilkinson's dance academy, filled with little girls in tutus. The effect is both comic and tragic, in that it suggests no aspect of Easington life is untouched by a savage industrial dispute.

C

Not since *Blood Brothers* first opened in 1983, has there been a new British musical to combine social commentary with a heartfelt story of adolescence, as powerfully and melodically as *Billy Elliot*. Adapted for the stage from the hit film of 2000 by its original director Stephen Daldry, screenwriter Lee Hall and choreographer Peter Darling, who are newly joined by composer Elton John, the material has been deepened and given a vibrant immediacy that can only come from the dynamics of live performance. And the rites-of-passage journey the show charts - of an 11-year-old boy transcending his working class background to gain admittance to the Royal Ballet School - is played out against the background of the 1984 Miners' Strike, implying the fierceness of Billy's own struggle.

D

Together, Stephen Daldry and Lee Hall have concocted a piece that's tougher, bolder and, as my tear-ducts can attest, no matter how hard I tried to disguise it, more moving than its admittedly admirable celluloid precursor. With its rags-to-riches, or rather poverty-to-pirouette, story, the piece invites sentimentality. But that's almost entirely missing in the Geordie pit village where young Billy discovers he has a gift for dance. Billy not only has to struggle against a society that could not understand a young boy wanting to enter the world of ballet, but he also, to a certain extent, is forced to turn his back on the traditional job of mining that his father and grandfather before him had endured. Not only is his physical strength pushed to the limits with the demanding training and practice sessions that ballet requires, he also has to harden himself to a path that is without doubt going to be a very lonely one. Against all odds he reaches for the stars and eventually manages to fly.

Which reviewer

unlike the other three, does not compare the musical to previous musicals in the West End?	37
highlights the importance of the economic backdrop from which the musical is set, like reviewer C?	38
like reviewer B, refers to a historical event that serves to accentuate Billy's success?	39
disagrees with the other three reviewers, in finding certain aspects of the film better than the musical?	40

Part 7

You are going to read an extract from a novel. Choose from the paragraphs **A-G** the one which fits each gap (41-46). There is one extra paragraph which you do not need to use.

Death in Malta
Rosanne Dingli

Gregory had the old doctor at his heels, and could hear a slight wheezing coming from the man's chest. He looked sprightly this morning, with hair well slicked back as usual and sharp creases in his trousers.

41 ______

'Like this,' the doctor interrupted. 'Like we did the first time.' He was already wrestling the knife back and forth forcibly, trying to edge it underneath the wax seal. The effort gave no result. The wax seemed to have hardened, fused into the porous clay surface of the jar neck. 'Like this!' the older man repeated, words coming out in a grunt through clenched teeth.
Gregory gently took the knife from his hand when he looked up, sweat standing out in beads on his forehead. Gregory tried himself, levering the blade at a different angle, cautiously forcing it with both hands.

42 ______

It was the doctor. He brushed past Gregory to grab the mallet abruptly. His audible breathing filled the cellar, his arm waving, gesturing with the mallet. Almost immediately, Gregory was by his side, but it was already too late. With one massive lunge, he swung the mallet round sideways at waist level, bringing its impact to the broadest curve on the bomblu's side.

43 ______

Patricia stood immobile, the expression on her face frozen. 'What on earth did you do that for?' she muttered. Gregory watched the doctor squeeze his head between his hands, then turn, looking for something. He looked at the broken pieces of clay at his feet, appearing startled to see them and the vinegar that pooled on the ground and drenched his trouser legs and shoes. 'It's blood,' he said, seemingly unaware of anyone else around him. Then he took off in a lop-sided run, out of the cellar door, up the stone steps and away from where the others stood.

44 ______

'We all waited a week for this,' Patricia gestured, indicating the wreckage about their feet.' He seemed to check there was nothing there, on the floor, before he left,' she continued, baffled. 'He said blood. Why did he say that?'
'Oh - I don't know,' answered Gregory, resigned to the mystery. 'All our eyes were on the jar. We were all looking to see if there was anything there. Well there isn't. All there is is vinegar. Just vinegar.' Patricia started to flick ineffectually at her jeans.

45 ______

He had fully expected to see a sodden bundle of clothes and flesh, a little parcel; the remnants of a life, virtually pickled in rancid wine. He had laid awake at night picturing what they would see inside the emptied bomblu; grey fabric in colourless tatters preserved by the wine; grey skin angled over bone; the skull rounded and turned forward, over a small caved-in chest. He was surprised it was not there.

46 ______

How could she possibly know? He turned to look at her, perplexed, a touch annoyed. He was still not completely accustomed to the way she would never chastise him for having feelings or imaginings, for pre-empting things, for having a totally separate world in his head. He was silent for a long time, allowing her the closeness. 'But there's nothing there,' he said finally.
'Nothing there,' she repeated.

A

'Blood?' Patricia looked at Gregory. 'Why did he say that? Why did he smash the jar?' Her face was a picture of incredulity.
'I don't know. What a mess,' said Gregory blankly. 'It was as if he couldn't bear to wait any longer.'

B

Patricia was calm, almost purring like a cat in the sun. Her eyes were bright and she anticipated the work in the cellar with cheery eagerness.
The three entered the large room, intent on getting the bomblu open.
Patricia handed a knife to the doctor. 'I wonder whether this clay jar is full of oil or wine.'
'Or water,' answered the old doctor. He turned a bit pale, the heat making his top lip glisten only seconds after he returned his handkerchief to his pocket.
'Now,' started Gregory, 'If we ...'

C

'You had imagined it...' Patricia did not finish. She looked at his eyes.
Gregory raised a hand and shielded his eyes from her. She knew him too well, too soon. His feet had still not moved from the puddle of dark vinegar. 'I - yes,' he said finally, accepting the scrutiny. 'I imagined more than just the words, you see,' he said softly. She came round to him and touched his arm. 'I know.'

D

Gregory couldn't tell whether she was disappointed or glad they had not discovered anything more gruesome than several litres of acetic wine. He realised he did not initially register surprise at finding nothing in the liquid. But he was surprised.

E

The jar smashed, a cry from Patricia accompanying the crashing sound made by the fragments of earthenware and the sudden copious flow of vinegar that splashed out, soaking the three of them from the knees down. As if in slow motion, the Doctor wheeled around on his heels, raising his hands to his head, the mallet falling with hardly a sound to the ground. His face was ashen, his teeth gritted underneath stretched lips.

F

Patricia looked at the doctor with a childish glee. The contents that had spilled so tumultuously out onto the floor was everything they had been hoping for. Yet, it was also everything the writer had dreaded. Gregory looked at the other two with a desperate suspicion.
'Why?' Patricia and the Doctor looked at each other for an answer that would appease their friend.

G

'Shall I try the other side, opposite to you, with another knife?' asked Patricia. She sensed the doctor's impatience, and was now full of it herself.
But Gregory had managed to insert the point of his knife under the wax rim. It was going to require precise movements. Patricia looked as if she was thinking of some other method to remove the wax plug from the jar mouth. Gregory looked at her as she gripped the earthenware rim thoughtfully. Then out of the corner of his eye, a sudden movement made him straighten.

Part 8

You are going to read an article containing film reviews. For questions 47 - 56, choose from the reviews (**A-F**). The reviews may be chosen more than once.

In which film review is the following mentioned?

An actor didn't win despite performing well.	47
A character plans to kill the leader of a country.	48
Is full of feeling but not successful as a film or DVD.	49
The plot spans over many years.	50
The director of the movie was born in a foreign country.	51
The writers were trying not to dully depict history.	52
The director sees elements of their own life in the film.	53
It is only ideal for a specific group of people.	54
The prospect of violence was exciting.	55
A lot of people die in the film.	56

Film Reviews

A Keira Knightley gives "her best performance yet" in Joe Wright's adaptation of the Jane Austen classic *"Pride & Prejudice"*. It snagged her Golden Globe and Oscar nominations for Best Actress although she was eventually beaten to the globe by Reese Witherspoon for *Walk The Line*. Nonetheless this period romance went down well on both sides of the pond. While Austen's work derives much of its tension from the buttoned-down customs of 18th century society, Matthew Macfadyen, who plays Mr Darcy, finds it all "quite releasing". Naturally the cast offer their interpretations although these tend towards the obvious; "Elizabeth is very human," says Keira. She hits closer to the mark in a separate tribute to the novelist, saying, "She puts across this absolutely gorgeous fairy tale in a rather realistic way."

B After endless TV runs of *"Mr Bean"*, Rowan Atkinson has proved that he's an inspired physical comedian. His second big screen outing as the tweed-donning doofus was generally better received than the first Bean flick, trading on slapstick shtick rather than fart gags as he travels all over France. The film also did brisk business at home and abroad, raising sacks of cash for Comic Relief.
Cameras follow Bean and company on location across the sun-drenched South of France in *"French Beans"*. Director Steve Bendelack confesses he's having a lot of "fun", while poor old Atkinson works up a sweat madly cycling after a chicken in a complex chase sequence. While critics talk about Atkinson's "effortless" ability to make people laugh,the man himself doesn't see it that way, saying that having to carry a film with so much physicality is "quite stressful." Obviously this DVD is very much a love it or hate it proposition, but for fans of the TV series, it's the perfect escape on a wet afternoon.

C Three years after *"Super Size Me"*, director Richard Linklater put the burger business through the mincer again. It's just a shame that *"Fast Food Nation"* is slathered in self-importance as it takes the point-of-view of various people affected by the contamination of meat at a Texan processing plant. After opening to mixed reviews, the box office numbers were as flat as a cheap beef patty.
He admits that, going into the project, he knew very little about the politics of fast food and even dares to confess, "I eat meat." Oh, and by the way, the meat is also a metaphor for the plight of illegal immigrants. Referring to the character played by Catalina Sandino Moreno, he says, "It's about her being turned into a piece of meat." Bet you didn't see that coming, eh?
Without question this film is full of heart, unfortunately the mishmash of storylines and speechifying doesn't go down any easier on the small screen.

D Yes, there is a high body count and a lot of stuff gets blown up but *"Shooter"* was not an entirely mindless film. In it, a world-weary ex-Marine sniper gets drawn into a plot to assassinate the US president. Maybe it was this hackneyed premise that meant it fell slightly below target at the box office.
Stephen Hunter, who wrote the novel on which the film is based, talks about the inspiration for the story in Survival Of The Fittest. He calls his leading character Bob Lee Swagger "a Faustian intellectual of war," which might be slightly overstating it. Co-star Micheal Pepa was apparently thrilled at the chance to shoot people. "It's really hard not to get into it," he says, later adding, "The explosions were really neat." Somehow we don't think he quite understood Hunter's intentions...

E *"Monsoon Wedding"* director Mira Nair drew on her own experiences for this poignant family saga *"The Namesake"*. Adapted from Jhumpa Lahiri's Pulitzer prize-winning novel about the pains of immigration, it stars Bollywood actress Tabu and erstwhile movie stoner Kal 'Kumar' Penn. Although the film didn't break any box office records, glowing reviews helped to put bums on seats in all corners of the globe. Throughout the film, Nair picks on scenes that resonate with her own experiences of coming to America and raising children there, but she is also very instructive on the technical aspects of filmmaking. She explains why she chooses a close-up over a wide-angle shot and how that decision feeds the underlying emotion of a scene. Aspiring filmmakers will glean lots of practical advice, and for the average film fan, you'll be transported across continents from the comfort of your own sofa.

F A period political drama is never an easy sell at the box office. Take the example of *"Amazing Grace"*, starring Ioan Gruffudd as bewigged human rights activist William Wilberforce. For director Michael Apted the challenge was in trying to show "how heroic politics can be", while trying to avoid a dry historical re-enactment of Wilberforce's life, and instead put the focus on the battle between young revolutionaries and a fusty establishment.
About his preparations for the role Gurffudd says that, as well as reading up on British/African history, there was the matter of how to age convincingly on screen. The young actor light-heartedly assures us that lots of makeup was involved because making him look old is "very hard to do...".
Despite the weighty themes it deals with, the surprise is that, overall, this DVD isn't as heavy as you'd think.

WRITING - Part 1

You **must** answer this question. Write your answer in **220-260** words in an appropriate style.

1. You have listened to and watched a Youtube video about the best methods of producing healthy food in a cost-effective way. You have made the notes below:

Which are the best methods of producing healthy food in a cost-effective way?

- genetically engineered food
- use new technological methods and new pesticides
- produce food using traditional old-fashioned methods with no pesticides

Some opinions expressed during the talk:

"Genetically-engineered food can provide an increased supply of food with reduced cost."

"Organic food produced with no pesticides is the best for us!"

"Without the introduction of new technological methods people will starve."

Write an essay discussing **two** of the methods in your notes. You should **explain which method of producing healthy food in a cost-effective way,** is the best, **giving reasons** in support of your answer.

You may, if you wish, make use of the opinions expressed in the discussion, but you should use your own words as far as possible.

WRITING - Part 2

Write an answer to one of the questions **2-4** in this part. Write your answer in **220-260** words in an appropriate style.

2. You have a younger sister who is struggling in her classes at school because of poor organisation and work habits. Your school director asks you to come up with a plan to help improve her grades.

   Write a proposal including strategies for studying, time management and organisation to improve your sister's grades.

   Write your **proposal**.

3. A new online publication is looking for new writers to review car models. The e-magazine asks that you write about the current car that you drive or ones that you have driven in the past.

   Discuss in your review how the car runs, features, safety record and petrol mileage, among other attributes

   Write your **review**.

4. You have just come back from seeing a play at the West End with a classmate and want to tell your sibling about it so they go to see the play/performance before it leaves to tour in the United States.

   - Tell your sibling in a letter about the play including the characters, story, direction, stage props and audience reaction, among other aspects.
   - Mention anything you would have changed or done differently, if applicable.

   Write your **letter**. You do not need to include postal addresses.

LISTENING - Part 1

You will hear three different extracts. For questions **1-6**, choose the answer (**A**, **B** or **C**) which fits best according to what you hear. There are two questions for each extract.

Extract One

You will hear a discussion in which a woman talks to her good friend about his career choice.

1 Why did David's career plans change?

A He didn't get into graduate school.
B He realised he disliked research.
C He enjoys his current lifestyle.

2 What lesson did David learn?

A Don't sacrifice happiness out of obligation.
B Aim high and follow your dreams.
C Experience makes you better.

2

Extract Two

You will hear a conversation where two friends discuss the concert they just attended.

3 What was Joan's main complaint?

A She didn't hear enough of the featured artist.
B The other fans were screaming too loud.
C The weather was miserable.

3

4 What did Joan think of the opening acts?
A They weren't very talented.
B They didn't sing enough songs.
C They were better than Luda.

4

Extract Three

You will hear a conversation in which two friends talk about what they can do to change their way of life.

5 Alexandra thinks

A that she should probably follow George's lead.
B George's actions are a little drastic.
C George should do something more enjoyable.

5

6 George is running in the marathon

A only because his doctor told him to.
B for the feeling of achievement.
C in order to lose weight.

6

LISTENING - Part 2

You will hear a woman talk about an adventurous bike ride she recently took. For questions 7-14, complete the sentences.

The ride Molly chose was not too **7** ______ for someone her age.

Molly stopped at the top of the hill to have some **8** ______ and look around.

Molly wanted to move the calf **9** ______ near the gate.

When riding in cow pastures you should be careful not to get your tires sucked into **10** ______.

Being thrown over the handlebars will end with a **11** ______ landing.

Molly didn't want to lose **12** ______ of the calf as it ran away.

In chasing the calf for the second time, Molly now had to ride her bike **13** ______, as they were going in the opposite direction than before.

To illustrate her frustration with the creature, Molly calls it a **14** ______, instead of a calf.

LISTENING - Part 3

You will hear part of a radio interview in which a Japanese astronaut, Dr. Takao Doi, talks about his work. For questions 15-20, choose the answer (A, B, C or D), which fits best according to what you hea

15 What happened to Dr. Doi in 1983?

A He first decided he wanted to be an astronaut.
B He started having success in his career.
C There was a setback in his career.
D He founded the National Space Development Agency.

16 How did Dr. Doi feel emotionally after the Challenger incident?

A hopeful for the future
B frustrated with himself for not training harder
C discouraged about the fate of the space programme
D scared to go into space after such a tragedy

17 What advice does Dr. Doi give about one's psychological health?

A Be true to your instincts.
B Don't let anything surprise you.
C Exercise while on board.
D Follow orders diligently.

18 What did Dr. Doi do while taking off to space?

A panic
B reassure Leonid Kadenyuk
C reflect
D question his sanity

19 What did Dr. Doi do in 1971?

A He looked at sunspots.
B He got a telescope.
C He looked at a planet.
D He decided to become an astronaut.

20 What is the next thing Dr. Doi wants to do

A walk on the moon
B study stars
C retire
D go on another space mission

LISTENING - Part 4

You will hear five short extracts in which people are talking about their position in a company.
While you listen you must complete both tasks.

TASK ONE

For questions 21-25, choose from the list **A-H** the person who is speaking.

A a boss [senior manager]
B an accountant
C an assistant manager
D a receptionist
E a sales person
F a human resources manager
G a corporate director
H a business client

Speaker 1	21	
Speaker 2	22	
Speaker 3	23	
Speaker 4	24	
Speaker 5	25	

TASK TWO

For questions 26-30, choose from the list **A-H** what each speaker is expressing.

A an extreme dislike for their job
B low aspirations
C the acceptance of something ending
D resentment towards their superiors
E an inexplicable esteem for their job
F a willingness to exceed the minimum required
G an ability they are not proud of
H frustration with failure

Speaker 1	26	
Speaker 2	27	
Speaker 3	28	
Speaker 4	29	
Speaker 5	30	

Test 10

Part 1

For questions 1-8, read the text below and decide which answer (**A**,**B**,**C** or **D**) best fits each gap. There is an example at the beginning (0).

Example:

0 **A falls** **B dates** **C lays** **D leans**

0	A	B	C	D
		▬		

Whale watching

Whale watching as an organised activity **(0)** .... back to 1950 when the Cabrillo National Monument in San Diego was **(1)** .... a public spot for the observation of Gray Whales. In 1955 the first water-based whale watching commenced in the same area, and customers were charged $1 per trip to view the whales at closer quarters. The spectacle **(2)** .... popular, attracting 10,000 visitors in its first year and many more in subsequent years. The industry spread throughout the western coast of the United States over the following decade.

In the late 1970s the industry mushroomed in size **(3)** .... to operations in New England. By 1985 more visitors watched whales from New England than California. The rapid growth in this area has been **(4)** .... to the relatively dense population of Humpback Whales, whose acrobatic behaviour, such as breaching (jumping out of the water) and tail-slapping, was an obvious crowd-pleaser, and the close proximity of whale populations to the large cities on the east **(5)** .... of the US.

Throughout the 1980s and 1990s whale watching spread throughout the world. In 1998 Erich Hoyt **(6)** .... out the largest systematic study of whale watching yet undertaken and concluded that whale watching trips were available in 87 countries around the world, with over 9 million participants generating a(n) **(7)** .... to whale watcher operators and supporting infrastructure of over one billion dollars. His estimate for 2020 was for 11.3m participants spending $1.475bn, representing a five-fold increase over the decades. Whale watching is of particular importance to developing countries as coastal communities start to profit directly from the whales' presence, significantly **(8)** .... to popular support for the full protection of these animals from any resumption of commercial whaling.

1	**A** dedicated	**B** destined	**C** declared	**D** denied
2	**A** showed	**B** proved	**C** assured	**D** demonstrated
3	**A** gratitude	**B** thanks	**C** resulting	**D** through
4	**A** assigned	**B** assuaged	**C** anticipated	**D** attributed
5	**A** coast	**B** frontier	**C** boundary	**D** beach
6	**A** made	**B** left	**C** carried	**D** went
7	**A** receipt	**B** income	**C** means	**D** bill
8	**A** supplying	**B** participating	**C** adding	**D** gaining

Part 2

For questions 9-16, read the text below and think of the word which best fits each gap. Use only one word in each gap. There is an example at the beginning (0).
Write your answers in **CAPITAL LETTERS**.

Example:

0	ITS

Oberon

The name Oberon got **(0)** .... literary start in the first half of the 13th century from the fairy dwarf Oberon **(9)** .... helps the hero in the chanson de geste, titled "Les Prouesses et faitz du noble Huon de Bordeaux". When Huon, son of Seguin count of Bordeaux, passed **(10)** .... the forest where he (Oberon) lives, he was warned against Oberon by a hermit, but his sense of courtesy had him answer Oberon's greetings, and **(11)** .... gain Oberon's aid in his quest: **(12)** .... killed Charlot, the Emperor's son, in self-defense, Huon must visit the court of the amir of Babylon and perform various feats to win a pardon, and only with Oberon's aid **(13)** .... he succeed.

The real Seguin was Count of Bordeaux under Louis the Pious in 839, and died fighting against the Normans in 845. Charles l'Enfant, a son of Charles the Bald, died in 866 **(14)** .... wounds inflicted by a certain Aubouin in the circumstances of an ambush similar to that carried out by Charlot in the story. Thus Oberon appears in a 13th century French courtly fantasy that is based **(15)** .... a shred of 9th century fact. He is given some Celtic trappings, **(16)** .... as a magical cup that is ever-full for the virtuous: "The magic cup supplied their evening meal; for such was its virtue that it afforded not only wine, but more solid fare when desired".

Part 3

For questions 17-24, read the text below. Use the word given in capitals at the end of some of the lines to form a word that fits in the gap **in the same line.** There is an example at the beginning **(0)**.
Write your answers **IN CAPITAL LETTERS**.

Example:

0	PROTECTION

Smoking bans

The major rationale cited for smoking bans is the **(0)** .... of workers, in particular, from the harmful effects of second-hand smoke, which include an increased risk of heart disease, cancer, emphysema and other chronic and acute diseases. Laws implementing bans on indoor smoking have been introduced by many countries in **(17)** .... forms over the years, with legislators citing scientific evidence that shows tobacco smoking is often **(18)** .... to the smokers themselves and to those inhaling second-hand smoke.

PROTECT
VARY
HARM

Such laws may reduce health care costs in the short term but do not account for the increased health care cost of an ever ageing population. However, consequent improvements in worker productivity and lower overall labour costs make the "smoke-free" community more**(19)** .... for bringing new jobs into the area and keeping current jobs and employers there. In Indiana, USA, for example, the state's economic development agency wrote into its plan for **(20)** .... of economic growth that it encourages cities and towns to adopt local smoke-free workplace laws as a means of promoting job growth in communities. **(21)** .... rationales for smoking restrictions include: reduced risk of fire in areas with **(22)** .... hazards or where **(23)** .... materials are handled and cleanliness in places where food or pharmaceuticals, semiconductors or precision instruments and machinery are produced. Also, the cancellation of many previously **24)** .... events due to rising insurance costs.

ATTRACT
ACCELERATE
ADD
EXPLODE/FLAME
ENJOY

Part 4

For questions 25-30, complete the second sentence so that it has a similar meaning to the first sentence, using the word given. **Do not change the word given**. You must use between **three** and **six** words, including the word given. Here is an example **(0)**.

Example: 0 George should have worked harder if he wanted to pass the exam. **succeeded**
Had George worked harder, ... passing the exam.

Write the missing words **IN CAPITAL LETTERS.**

0	HE WOULD HAVE SUCCEEDED IN

25 More than fifty guests came to the party. **showed**
More than fifty guests .... the party.

26 I'd help you, but I have very little free time on my hands. **hardly**
I'd help you, but I .... free time on my hands.

27 He's still planning on attending as far as I know. **knowledge**
To .... , he is still planning on attending.

28 It's no use trying to convince her to go. **point**
There's .... to convince her to go.

29 Women outnumber men by two to one on the art course. **twice**
There .... men on the art course.

30 I can't promise that you will get the job. **guarantee**
There .... will get the job.

Part 5

You are going to read a magazine article. For questions 31-36, choose the answer **(A, B, C or D)** which you think fits best according to the text.

What makes us different?

You don't have to be a biologist or an anthropologist to see how closely the great apes - gorillas, chimpanzees, bonobos and orangutans - resemble us. Even a child can see that their bodies are pretty much the same as ours, apart from some exaggerated proportions and extra body hair. Apes have dexterous hands much like ours but unlike those of any other creature. And, most striking of all, their faces are uncannily expressive, showing a range of emotions that are eerily familiar. That's why we delight in seeing chimps wearing tuxedos, playing the drums or riding bicycles. It's why a potbellied gorilla scratching itself in the zoo reminds us of Uncle Ralph or Cousin Vinnie; and why, in a more unsettled reaction, Queen Victoria, on seeing an orangutan named Jenny at the London Zoo in 1842, declared the beast "frightful and painfully and disagreeably human."

It isn't just a superficial resemblance. Chimps, especially, not only look like us, they also share with us some human-like behaviours. They make and use tools and teach those skills to their offspring. They prey on other animals and occasionally murder each other. They have complex social hierarchies and some aspects of what anthropologists consider culture. They can't form words, but they can learn to communicate via sign language and symbols and to perform complex cognitive tasks. Scientists figured out decades ago that chimps are our nearest evolutionary cousins, roughly 98% to 99% identical to humans at the genetic level. When it comes to DNA, a human is closer to a chimp than a mouse is to a rat.

Yet tiny differences, sprinkled throughout the genome, have made all the difference. Agriculture, language, art, music, technology and philosophy - all the achievements that make us profoundly different from chimpanzees and make a chimp in a business suit seem so deeply ridiculous - are somehow encoded within minute fractions of our genetic code. Nobody yet knows precisely where they are or how they work, but somewhere in the nuclei of our cells are handfuls of amino acids, arranged in a specific order, that endow us with the brainpower to outthink and outdo our closest relatives on the tree of life. They give us the ability to speak and write and read, to compose symphonies, paint masterpieces and delve into the molecular biology that makes us what we are.

Until recently, there was no way to unravel these crucial differences. Exactly what gives us advantages like complex brains and the ability to walk upright, and certain disadvantages, including susceptibility to a particular type of malaria, AIDS and Alzheimer's, diseases that don't seem to afflict chimps, remained a mystery.

But that's rapidly changing. Just a year ago, geneticists announced that they had sequenced a rough draft of the chimpanzee genome, allowing the first side-by-side comparisons of human and chimpanzee DNA. Already, that research has led to important discoveries about the development of the human brain over the past few million years and possibly about our ancestors' mating behaviour as well.

And sometime in the next few weeks, a team led by molecular geneticist Svante Pobo of the Max Planck Institute for Evolutionary Anthropology, in Leipzig, Germany, will announce an even more stunning achievement: the sequencing of a significant fraction of the genome of Neanderthals - the human-like species we picture when we hear the word caveman - who are far closer to us genetically than chimps are. And though Neanderthals became extinct tens of thousands of years ago, Pobo is convinced he's on the way to reconstructing the entire genome of that long-lost relative, using DNA extracted, against all odds, from a 38,000-year-old bone.

Laid side by side, these three sets of genetic blueprints - plus the genomes of gorillas and other primates, which are already well on the way to being completely sequenced - will not only begin to explain precisely what makes us human but could lead to a better understanding of human diseases and how to treat them.

31 What is something apes do NOT do that humans do?

A. communicate
B. kill their own kind
C. walk on two limbs
D. have a social order

32 A mouse and a rat are mentioned

A. because they are also similar to humans genetically.
B. in order to demonstrate the variety of species that exist.
C. to highlight the difference between our genetic code and theirs.
D. to help readers understand how similar humans and apes are.

33 Scientists

A. still have no clue what makes us so similar to apes.
B. know approximately what makes humans different from apes.
C. think the differences can be traced to more than just genetics.
D. have completed sequencing the chimpanzee's genome.

34 Compared to apes, human behaviour is more

A. sophisticated.
B. expressive.
C. problematic.
D. basic.

35 Neanderthals

A. are what we used to call humans.
B. were thought to be extinct, but evidence has been found that they are not.
C. have had part of their genome sequenced.
D. have the same genome sequence as apes.

36 The purpose of this research

A. is solely to understand what makes us human.
B. is unclear.
C. is multi-faceted.
D. is to sequence the human genome.

Part 6

You are going to read four reviews of a ballet. For questions 37-40, choose from reviews A-D. The reviews may be chosen more than once.

Romeo and Juliet
Four critics comment on the ballet production

A

Returning to the stage after a long injury, Natalya Osipova is back in peak condition. She takes real risks in the giddy, swooning steps, swooping right off balance and trusting her Romeo, Carlos Acosta, to catch her. Yet this revival just falls short of passion. There's plenty of care in the storytelling, but the ballet's star-crossed lovers need headlong ardour and despair. It's been a long wait for Osipova to come back. She had surgery on her foot more than a year ago, with several return performances announced and cancelled. She's a sleek dancer, tall and dark, prompting extra attention. This performance shows new thought in her acting. Juliet is dancing with Paris, her approved fiance, when she first sees Romeo. She can't take her eyes off him, even when she tries to remember Paris.

B

As one of the jewels in the Royal Ballet's crown, this rendition of *Romeo and Juliet* offers a rare opportunity for dancer and spectator to forge a close relationship. Familiar as the story is, we can focus our entire attention on the interpretation without having to wonder what's coming next. In spite of Nicholas Georgiadis' monumental sets, this latest production is characterised by its extraordinary intimacy. It takes a while to warm up as Carlos Acosta's Romeo doesn't appear to be unduly upset by his failed courtship of Rosaline and only really takes flight with the arrival of the three firecracker harlots (Laura Morera, Romany Pajdak and Laura McCulloch) who blast through the townspeople with exuberant naughtiness. As a prelude to the street fight between the Capulets and the Montagues, it is a terrific sequence, full of dazzle and spark. The key sequence that unlocks the production, is the grand ball with Prokoviev's magnificently doom-laden, *Dance of the Knights*, thundering out of the pit before the first encounter between the two lovers.

C

Not quite what one might have hoped. Natalya Osipova's debut as Juliet with the Royal Ballet was eagerly anticipated: here is an artist prodigious in technique, vivid in dramatic sensibilities, who has illuminated every role that I have seen her dance. And yet on Thursday night, she seemed isolated at moments from the staging. This was, I sense, in part owed to an unlikely relationship with Carlos Acosta's Romeo. Osipova's pairing with Acosta brings her a secure partner, but also a dancer whose account of his role is now underpowered in both means and manner: I did not for a moment believe in him as a youth ardently in love. But what I once saw with Lynn Seymour, and saw with Natalya Makarova, and then ravishingly saw again last week with Yevgenia Obraztsova in the arms of Steven McRae was the traditional interpretation of the role. Unfortunately, Osipova, in trying to make the role her own, decides to show a knowing Juliet.

D

The slim shoulders of the Russian ballerina Natalia Osipova were carrying a twin weight as she made her debut with London's Royal Ballet. Would this international shooting star be able to add lustre to a company that is depleted of ballerinas of her class? The answers to those questions varied from moment to moment during the course of the evening. Rarely has a performance flickered so rapidly between the astonishing and the disappointing. Having said that, the overall impression was satisfying, as one would expect from a dance company that has such a high profile leading lady. It will be interesting to see how she continues to settle in with future productions with the Royal Ballet.

Which reviewer

like reviewer A, remains unconvinced of the dancers' portrayal of the passion between Romeo and Juliet? | 37 |

like reviewer C, had eagerly anticipated Osipova's performance, only to be disappointed in some way? | 38 |

disagrees with the other three reviewers, in finding Osipova's performance faultless? | 39 |

compares and contrasts this rendering with past performances of Romeo and Juliet? | 40 |

Part 7

You are going to read an extract from a novel. Choose from the paragraphs **A-G** the one which fits each gap (41-46). There is one extra paragraph which you do not need to use.

Excursion vehicle 15

Ten years old, he moved with his father across the curved polished floor of the freight bay, their booted feet squeaking on the high-gloss surface; the two of them suspended above their own dark reflections; a man and a boy forever walking up what looked to the eye like an ever steepening hill, but which always felt perfectly level.

"We're going outside, aren't we," Sky said.

Titus looked down at his son. "Why do you assume that?"

"You wouldn't have brought me here otherwise."

41 ______

After what seemed like days, the adults had made the main lights come on again. He noticed the air-circulators began to work again. All that time, his father told him later, they had been breathing unrecirculated air; slowly turning staler and staler as the hundred and fifty waking humans dumped more and more carbon dioxide back into their atmosphere. It soon would have started causing serious problems, but the air became fresher and the ship slowly warmed back up until it was possible to move along the corridors without shivering. The food improved, but Sky had hardly noticed that they had been eating emergency rations during the black-out.

42 ______

Now however - in a mood of eager forgiveness - he pushed such thoughts from his mind; awed by the sheer size of the freight bay and the prospect of what lay ahead. What made the place seem all the larger was the fact that the two of them were quite alone. The rest of the chamber was suggested rather than clearly seen; its dimensions only hinted at by the dark.

43 ______

Titus halted near one of the small shuttles. "Yes," he said, "we're going outside. I think it's time you saw things the way they really are."

"What things?"

But by way of answer Titus only elevated the cuff of his uniform and spoke quietly into his bracelet. "Enable excursion vehicle 15."

44 ______

Sky hopped into the spacecraft, feeling the floor vibrating beneath his feet. The taxi was considerably more cramped inside than it had appeared it would be - the hull thickly plated and armoured - and he had to duck to reach his seat, brushing his head against a gristle-like tangle of internal pipework. He fiddled with the blue-steel buckle until he had it tight across his chest. In front of him was a cool turquoise green display -- constantly changing numbers and intricate diagrams.

45 ______

"Word of advice, Sky. Never trust these damned things to tell you that they're safe. Make sure for yourself."

"You don't trust machines to tell you?"

46 ______

"What happened to change your mind?"

"You'll see, shortly."

A

Parked here and there were various spacecraft. The taxis could enter the atmosphere in an emergency, but they were not designed to make the return trip to space. The delta-winged landers which would make multiple journeys down to the surface of Journey's End were too large to store inside the Santiago; they were attached instead to the outside of the ship and there was almost no way to see them unless you worked on one of the external work crews, as his mother had done before her death.

B

There was no hesitation; no questioning his authority. The taxi answered him instantly, lights flicking on; cockpit door craning open. Steam was beginning to vent from ports spaced along the vehicle's side, and Sky could hear the growing whine of turbines somewhere inside the machine's angular hull. He hesitated at the door, until his father beckoned that he lead. "After you, Sky. Go and take the seat on the right of the instrument column. Don't touch anything while you're about it."

C

Titus said nothing, but the point could not be denied. Sky had never been in the freight bay before; not even during one of the illicit trips with Constanza. Sky remembered the time she had taken him to see the dolphins, and the punishment that had ensued, and how that punishment had been eclipsed by the ordeal that had followed; the flash of light and the period he had spent trapped alone and cold in the utter darkness of the nursery. It seemed so long ago now, but there were still things that he did not fully understand. No one would speak of that day when the whole ship had turned dark and cold, yet to Sky the events were still clearly fixed in his memory.

D

His father settled into the seat next to him. The door had closed on them now, and suddenly it was quieter, save for the continuous rasp of the taxi's air-circulation. His father touched the green display with his finger, making it change, studying the results with narrow-eyed concentration.

E

"I used to, once." His father eased the joystick forward now and the taxi commenced gliding along its departure track, sliding past the parked ranks of other vehicles. "But machines aren't infallible. We used to kid ourselves that they were because it was the only way to stay sane in a place like this, where we depend on them for our every breath. Unfortunately it was never true."

F

The spacecraft had some technical difficulty upon it's take-off. Titus and Sky jolted precariously as their taxi struggled to break through the atmosphere. Sky could feel his body begin to tremble with fear, but focused all his energy preventing that from happening. He did not dare let his father see him being anything but brave.

G

Eventually, when something like normal shipboard life had returned, Sky managed to sneak back into the nursery. The room was lit, but everything else looked more or less as he had left it; Clown frozen in that distorted shape he had assumed after the flash. Sky had crept closer to examine his friend. Clown had been a kind of moving picture that only made sense when seen from precisely Sky's point of view. Clown had seemed to be physically present in the room - not just painted on the wall . For three years, Sky had never doubted that Clown was in some sense real. Yet his parents had given up responsibility to an illusion.

Part 8

You are going to read some articles written by different football players. For questions 47 - 56, choose from the articles (**A-E**). The articles may be chosen more than once.

Which footballer

started playing the sport only because his/her parents insisted?	47	
didn't surprise people with his/her talent?	48	
got injured frequently?	49	
was involved in many activities?	50	
is grateful for the attention?	51	
didn't enjoy a major victory?	52	
decided against fame and glory?	53	
demonstrated leadership off the field?	54	
doesn't deny a lack of talent?	55	
was a member of a brand new team?	56	

Football players

A I started playing football seriously at a very young age. I played on teams all year long. But even that wasn't enough. When my dad would get home from work, we'd pass the ball back and forth until supper. As I got older, I'd invite my three best friends to come over to my house. They didn't really like football, but we had an agreement; I'd give them a snack, we'd watch a little TV, then we would play. One against three, and if I won, they had to play me again. During university I had a chance to try-out for a professional team in Germany and I thought, 'this is my chance to really make my dreams come true.' Yet, when I arrived in Germany, I couldn't shake the feeling that I had made a huge mistake. To make a long story short, I made the team, but turned them down and returned home. I had realised that my dream wasn't all I had built it up to be. I had imagined the glory of that life, but what I failed to consider was the fact that I would be doing it all alone, without my family and friends. So, I came home, finished university, and began coaching football. I love my job, and I still get to play football. It's more fun now than it's ever been.

B I come from a family of footballers. My dad played in competitive leagues all his life and my mum was on the national team. Needless to say, I began playing football at about the same time I began to walk. I played on the top teams since the age of thirteen. I was always the best on my team by far but, considering my background, that was expected. My parents were very committed to my football career and on some level I am very grateful. However, at times, their zeal was a little overwhelming. It was always in my head that I was playing football mostly to please my parents, which really stripped the joy of the game from me. I still remember when my team won the biggest youth tournament in the nation. All my teammates were crying with joy and were so proud; I was just happy the tournament was over so I could go home and be with my friends. That's when I realised that while I may have the talent for the game, I didn't have the passion for it. So at age 16 I told my parents I didn't want to play anymore. I couldn't believe how supportive they were. I guess I put most of the pressure on myself.

C Football was always just one of my extra-curricular activities. I was president of my class at school, a member of the school orchestra, on the debate team, and in the autumn, I played football. I was a decent player, but definitely not the best. Tactics weren't my strength, but I was tough! It was always a joke that I chose to go through other players, rather than around them. Of course, that aggressiveness didn't come without consequences. I left many games covered in bruises and blood, but the worst came the summer before my final year in high school when I was seriously injured and had to have knee surgery. I was devastated because I was supposed to be team captain that year and I was afraid they were going to take the title away from me. Luckily, I still got to be captain and I really loved my role from the sideline. I worked hard at my therapy and was able to play in the last game of the season, which was great, but I had learned that my talents are best used on the sideline. I've been coaching youth teams for five years now.

D My parents were tired of me doing nothing but play video games so one day they said I was starting football practice. I protested a bit, but I knew my efforts would be worthless. My parents are unmovable. I have always hated exercise. I admit it. I am lazy. I went to practice prepared with multiple excuses to sit on the sidelines. I was getting the flu, I twisted my ankle, I was asthmatic. Yet, when I got there, I could tell by the look of the coach that he wasn't the kind of man who put up with excuses. There was something in his presence that told me he meant business. So I played the whole practice. And I really was the most awkward one out there. I never learned to love that game, but being on a team had some perks; at the end of every game some parent brought snacks. The snacks were undoubtedly the best part. I stuck with football until high school then became involved with the school newspaper, which really suits me better, considering I am not the world's best athlete.

E I've been a professional footballer for fifteen years now. That may seem like a lot considering my age, but older generations of women did not have the opportunity to play as youths. So when England decided to start its first women's national team, they had to recruit from a younger age group. The first five years were quite difficult. The team had basically no money. We stayed in cheap motel rooms or set up mats on gymnasium floors when we travelled. For a long time, despite our success, we had no fans, no news coverage, nothing. It was definitely frustrating, but I also believe it is a huge testament to our love of the game. We didn't play for the glory or the fame. We played because we loved it. This is not to say we are not enjoying the recent attention being focused on our team; it is sure nice to finally be recognised, praised and admired for our hard work and talent. We have been through so much together, I feel like my teammates are my family. I work hard mainly because I know I owe it to them. And we support each other and encourage each other when one of us has made a mistake or is having a tough time getting through training. I'm a better player and person because of my teammates.

WRITING - Part 1

You **must** answer this question. Write your answer in **220-260** words in an appropriate style.

1. You have listened to the radio programme about what kind of facilities should receive planning permission to be built on the seafront of a seaside town. You have made the notes below:

What kind of facilities should be allowed to be built on the seafront of a seaside town?
- a hotel
- beach volley facilities and a park
- coffee shops and restaurants

Some opinions expressed in the discussion:
"More open space is needed and not big hotels."
"Sports facilities are always welcome."
"New hotels can provide jobs to local people."

Write an essay discussing **two** of the facilities in your notes. You should **explain which facility should receive planning permission to be built** on the seafront, **giving reasons** in support of your answer.

You may, if you wish, make use of the opinions expressed in the discussion, but you should use your own words as far as possible.

WRITING - Part 2

Write an answer to one of the questions **2-4** in this part. Write your answer in **220-260** words in an appropriate style.

2. You are reading a local newspaper editorial where the publication argues that the citizens of the city should pay higher taxes to help fund the building of new facilities to host the Olympic Games. You disagree with this idea and write a letter to the editor explaining your reasons.

   You argue that the hard economic times have made it difficult for people to live and more taxes now would only increase their burden. You don't see the value after the Olympic Games are over, and, moreover, you are against all the traffic and noise that will result from the new construction.

   Write your **letter**. You do not need to include postal addresses.

3. You see the following announcement on a TV series reviews website:

   TV Reviews Wanted
   Send us a review of your favourite TV series. In your review try to explore the characters, the plot, and the setting. Also explain why you found it interesting to watch and what you think is its best feature.

   Write your **review**.

4. For a political science class you are taking, the professor asks you to conduct a small survey of students to learn more about their voting habits in elections of local officials.

   The professor asks that you create a report organising the data you collect on:
   - if and why people vote
   - do they vote based on single issues
   - political party affiliation
   - what do they read or consult to inform themselves about the issues and political leaders and candidates of the day

   Include other factors or ideas in your report as you see fit.

   Write your **report**.

LISTENING - Part 1

You will hear three different extracts. For questions 1-6, choose the answer (**A**, **B** or **C**) which fits best according to what you hear. There are two questions for each extract.

Extract One

You will hear a discussion in which a man talks to his good friend about her upcoming trip.

1 Leaving for Australia

A was a last minute decision.
B was John's suggestion.
C was considered for a few months.

1

2 The purpose of Michelle's holiday

A is to take a break from the stress of work.
B is to give her a change of pace.
C is to spend time with her family.

2

Extract Two

You will hear a conversation where two friends discuss the restaurant they just left.

3 Tate thinks Julie raves about the restaurant because

A she liked the elaborate environment.
B she has bad taste in food.
C she was so hungry she would have eaten anything.

4 Julie doesn't want to get a burger because

A they just ate and are not hungry.
B it would make them late for the show.
C their clothes would make them noticeable.

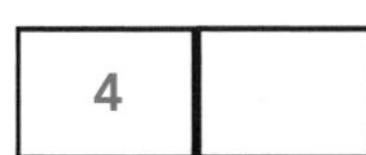

Extract Three

You will hear part of an interview with a medical student.

5 According to Gus, his career choice

A was forced on him.
B was made using the same criteria most people use.
C was a poor one, but it's too late to change now.

5

6 Being an ophthalmologist

A does not give good financial reward.
B involves frequent night shifts.
C has a family-friendly schedule.

6

LISTENING - Part 2

You will hear a freelancing Graphic Designer called Alec Zaki talking about how he came into his career. For questions 7-14, complete the sentences.

Although Alec has worked for other companies, he likes being **7** ______________.

In order to maximise his possibility of success, Alec became an expert in a variety of **8** ______________

There have been some corporate jobs that Alec has done **9** ______________ for.

Alec created 3D virtual sets for a show that featured **10** ______________ computer game releases.

The TV show took place on **11** ______________ that resembled a game controller.

Unlike **12** ______________ Alec entered the field by way of television.

Alec wanted to stand out in college because he was **13** ______________ than the other students.

Alec is now a freelancer because of **14** ______________.

LISTENING - Part 3

You will hear part of a radio interview in which professional golfer, Amy Hartman, is being interviewed. For questions 15-20, choose the answer (**A**, **B**, **C** or **D**), which fits best according to what you hear.

15 Why did Amy ultimately decide on golf as her sport choice?

A She had the most talent for golf.
B She realised she could play golf for longer.
C She had no success in the other sports.
D It was her favourite sport.

16 How often does Amy eat cheeseburgers?

A never
B fairly often
C rarely
D she ate them often as a child, but does not anymore

17 To what does Amy attribute her eating habits?

A her coaches
B her dedication to her sport
C superstitions
D her upbringing

18 Why does Amy think she appears to be pathetic?

A She never has any free time.
B She spends a lot of time with her pet.
C She's always watching DVDs.
D She never gets bored.

19 Why does Amy apologise for possibly disappointing (the interviewer)?

A She doesn't depend on anything for luck.
B She didn't know the answer to a question.
C She didn't win a tournament she was expected to win.
D She hasn't updated her profile.

20 Based on her age and her experience, we can assume Amy

A is one of the youngest golfers in the sport.
B will have a long career.
C started golfing later in life than the other girls.
D will make it to the LPGA Tour.

LISTENING - Part 4

You will hear five short extracts in which people are talking about their job in transport.
While you listen you must complete both tasks.

TASK ONE

For questions 21-25, choose from the list **A-H** the form of transport that the speaker is talking about.

A a cargo aeroplane
B a limousine
C a private jet
D a carriage
E a train
F a school bus
G a city trolley
H a taxi

Speaker 1	21	
Speaker 2	22	
Speaker 3	23	
Speaker 4	24	
Speaker 5	25	

TASK TWO

For questions 26-30, choose from the list **A-H** what each speaker is expressing.

A envy of another lifestyle
B a disrespect for people's wishes
C awe at someone's ability to keep order
D regret about what they do for a living
E a fascination for people's reactions
F a fear of the people they transport
G a sense of humour in a foul situation
H a sense of authority

Speaker 1	26	
Speaker 2	27	
Speaker 3	28	
Speaker 4	29	
Speaker 5	30